setting captives free

NEW WINE

A Biblical Approach to Substance Abuse

Mike Cleveland & Jeff Perry

Table of Contents

Table of Contents

Introduction

Setting Captives Free: New Wine is a 60-Day interactive course that will help you drink deeply of the "New Wine" that satisfies the heart, and thereby find freedom from drinking and drugs. It is possible, and you can do it.

"You were like a burning stick snatched from the fire." Amos 4:11

The **New Wine** course may be studied individually or in a small group setting.

Small Group Setting:

There should be an appointed leader/teacher to head the group, which will meet weekly. The first meeting of the group should be for the purpose of becoming acquainted. The leader will make introductions and explain the method for completing the study. Each group member will work individually through one lesson each day, recording their answers to discuss with the class the following week. At the close of this first meeting, the leader will explain from Hebrews 3:13 the importance of daily accountability, and he/she will pair up the students as each reports daily to the other of their freedom from sin. The brief reports may be given on the phone, fax, email, or in person, but they should be given daily. At the second meeting, the discussion leader will take time to review/expound upon the previous week's material, soliciting the members to share their answers for the material they have studied. The leader will also ask if the members have been providing daily accountability reports to their assigned partner.

Individual Study

When using this course individually, it is highly recommended that you find a trusted Christian friend with whom you may discuss what you are learning from the course material, and who will also be available to you for accountability. This accountability partner should be someone of the same sex who is walking in victory over habitual sin. Possible options include your pastor, an elder in your church, or a fellow Christian. You may also use your spouse for your accountability partner if he or she is willing. Students need to initiate daily reports to their accountability partner, providing the status of his/her purity.

The genesis of the **New Wine** course began on the Internet website, www.settingcaptivesfree.com and the ministry continues to operate successfully. Should you desire to work with an available mentor in the ministry, you may contact us at feedback@settingcaptivesfree.com.

To the extent that their schedules allow, Mike Cleveland and Jeff Perry are available for conferences and speaking engagements.
You may contact Mike via postal mail at the following address:
Setting Captives Free
P O Box 1527
Medina, OH 44258-1527

You may reach Jeff Perry at this email address:
Jeff.Perry@om.org

DAY 1 - MOTIVATION

My name is Mike Cleveland and I, along with Pastor Jeff Perry, am the author of this course. We will be walking you through the next 60 days as you seek to be free from alcohol and drug addiction. Jeff has firsthand experience dealing with and overcoming both of these addictions through the power of Jesus Christ. Throughout the course Jeff is going to share his story with you, so before we explain how the course works, I've asked him to begin to tell us of his journey.

Jeff writes, "My struggle with alcohol and drugs began when I was 13. It began as a way of fitting in with others and I soon found that I could escape the problems I faced for a while when I was intoxicated. It didn't take long to discover that this 'escape' was very short-lived, and the same problems were still there when I would sober up. The problems actually seemed to get worse and my life began a downward spiral that led a seemingly well-adjusted teenager to become an out-of-control young man.

I quit college soon after high school to follow the dream of being a rock musician. For the next 12 years I lived in a nightmarish world of bars and parties that destroyed my first marriage, my relationship with my family, and even led to severe, suicidal depression. I tried self-help groups, psychiatric counseling and treatment for the depression. Nothing helped or even made a dent in the pain I felt—I was totally out of control. I tried over and over to quit, but never had any success as the alcohol, pills, and cocaine held me tightly in a death grip. I remember standing at the graveside of a friend who had died in an alcohol related car crash. I stood there thinking that I was heading for the same, horrible end and I knew that I could do nothing to stop it.

I will share more of my story with you as we go through the course, but I would like to give you this bit of hope as we start—there is freedom from both of these addictions! I say this because I have been set free by the power of Jesus Christ since September, 1999. That is what this course is about—freedom through Christ—and if you will apply the principles set forth here, there is freedom for you as you drink deeply of life with Jesus Christ! He has the power to set anyone free from bondage to alcohol and drugs."

Now, let's begin!

Right from the start, we must understand some fundamentals or we will not be successful in obtaining freedom from any addiction. The truth is that in order to be successful in carrying out a battle plan against alcohol and drug addiction, two things must be accepted. First and foremost, we must have a personal relationship with Jesus Christ so that the power of His Holy Spirit is available to us. Secondly, we must also be making the decision to change for the right reasons.

One of the most important questions to ask a person desiring freedom from addiction is often a question that doesn't get asked at all. It is, "Why do you want freedom from alcohol and drugs?" The motives behind our decision to seek help are very important. Unless our motives are the right ones, chances are the healing we desire will elude us.

Questions

Question 1. Why do you want freedom from alcohol and drug addiction?

> **Course Member Teresa writes,** "I have turned to alcohol instead of Christ to meet my needs. When I don't want to deal with something, I numb myself rather than ask Christ to help me. I have lived as a hypocrite saying one thing and doing another. My family has been hurt also."

So what is the proper motive, the one that will lead to freedom? The proper biblical motive for any kind of life change must be the glory of God.

> Therefore, whether you eat or drink, or whatever you do, do all to the glory of God (1 Corinthians 10:31).

When I have talked with married men, I've learned that their motivation is a desire to keep or regain their wife and family. While this is a noble motive, it is not a bedrock kind of motive, the kind that will withstand the trials and tribulations that inevitably come our way. Suppose the wife leaves anyway? Is the journey out of alcoholism still worthwhile? Probably not in the mind of the person who's prime motivation is to keep the family intact. If the family's presence in our lives is the only thing keeping us on track, where are we if they should suddenly not be there? Friend, do you see the importance of having our motive be the unchanging rock of Jesus Christ?

Question 2. Analyze your reasons listed above. Did they come from a desire to please God? If not are you willing to set aside any personal agenda and make pleasing God your primary objective?

> **Chris wrote,** "When I read what I wrote above, I realized that I do not necessarily or wholly want to get clean for God. I really want to get clean so that I can be the best father I can be, and I thought that would lead and allow me to become a better Christian, as well. Perhaps I have it reversed? I can see where it could be difficult, but I am willing to try setting aside my personal agenda and make pleasing God my primary objective."

Friend, if we set out on this course for any reason other than to glorify God we cannot expect God's assistance. Since God is the greatest good, He sets out to work all things for His own glory, and if we seek freedom from alcohol and drugs for reasons other than His glory we are at cross purposes with God. He will not share His glory with another (Isaiah 48:11).

This concept is very important to understand, so let's look at an illustration of this in Judges 7:2.

> And the LORD said to Gideon, "The people who are with you are too many for Me to give the Midianites into their hands, lest Israel claim glory for itself against Me, saying, 'My own hand has saved me.'"

Do you see it? God had to REDUCE the size of Gideon's army so that when they won the battle Israel would not claim glory for themselves. God desires His glory to be great in our salvation (Psalm 21:5). God works for His own glory! And this is why we must settle this issue of motivation right here in the beginning. Is our motive in overcoming alcohol addiction to honor Him or ourselves? Are we working with Him, or are we at cross purposes with Him?

Now that we understand our purpose here, let me tell you that there is great hope in having the glory of God as our motivation! If we have a purpose in our hearts to glorify God then we are working in concert with Him, and He will enable us to do what we seek to do. Please don't miss this. Proper motive will ensure our success, as God Himself comes to our aid so that He will be glorified. Do you see it?

> Therefore, whether you eat or drink, or whatever you do, do all to the glory of God (1 Corinthians 10:31).

There is a connection that must be made here. Controlling what we put into our bodies and acting like the man or woman God created us to be is honoring the Lord. He is glorified in the daily choices we make to take care of our bodies. He is also glorified in our acting in a manner not controlled by intoxicating influences. This is not to say that sobriety guarantees that we are glorifying God. There are many people who have never tasted alcohol that live their lives daily for their own glory. The motivation for the Christian must be to honor the Lord in everything. Our goal is not to be like everyone else, it is to be as God wants us to be. Seek God in everything we do!

I finally realized that I wanted to be free from alcohol and drugs to stop the pain and to keep from losing everything I had, including my life. I wasn't concerned about "holiness" in this; I just wanted to find peace in my life. I wanted to continue to pursue my desires and to be able to drink like other people, not live like a drunk. I couldn't control my drinking and I felt like there was something terribly wrong with me. I wanted to be able to smoke a little or take drugs with my friends for "fun," but not be controlled by them. I just wanted to be like everybody else. God had other plans for me. His timing is perfect and He led me to the point that my motivation was for the right reason. He gave me that peace and freedom from the pain of what I had become. He also gave me so much more—a family, friends, even a purpose. Look at Matthew 6:33 with me:

> But seek ye first the Kingdom of God, and His righteousness; and all these things shall be added unto you.

Friend, do you want freedom from alcohol and drug addiction even though it may have plagued you for years? Do you long to be the man or woman God would have you be? Take that verse to heart. Seek FIRST the kingdom of God and His righteousness!

We should be able to say with the Psalmist in Psalm 115:1:

> Not unto us, O LORD, not unto us,
> But to Your name give glory,
> Because of Your mercy,
> Because of Your truth.

Question 3. Friend, would you like to pray right now for God to give you the desire to serve Him? To make His Glory the goal of your journey, not only out of alcoholism but of life? Yes, these types of prayers can be personal, just between you and God, but if you'd like to write yours here; it will remind you to pray for new motives and new desires.

There is real hope for obtaining freedom from alcoholism and drug abuse when our motive is the glory of God. If we begin to focus on the glory of God we will inevitably change. Let's look at the Scriptures below:

> [16]Nevertheless when one turns to the Lord, the veil is taken away. [17]Now the Lord is the Spirit; and where the Spirit of the Lord is, there is liberty. [18]But we all, with unveiled face, beholding as in a mirror the glory of the Lord, are being transformed into the same image from glory to glory, just as by the Spirit of the Lord (2 Corinthians 3:16-18).

Question 4. According to verse 18 above, what is it that enables us to be transformed?

Questions

This is starting to get good isn't it? Look at the HOPE we should have for real change as we focus on the glory of God. According to the above passage, as we behold the glory of the Lord we are being transformed into the same image; that is, into Christ-likeness. As our motives become the glory of God, and we begin to focus on the glory of God, we become transformed!

Question 5. If you have tried to obtain freedom in the past and failed, according to the teaching so far, why did you fail?

Course Member Teresa writes, "I was doing it on my own through my 'willpower' instead of looking to Christ. I was still trying to maintain my reputation rather than expose the deeds I was committing in the dark. I wanted to make my family happy."

Question 6. Are you now sensing a hope that you can truly change? If so, upon what is that hope based?

Finally, let us notice what the glory of God really is. The glory of God is multi-faceted and difficult to reduce to words. I feel inadequate to even try. And yet, God has not left us in the dark as to what His glory is. Notice this passage of Scripture:

> [1]God, who at various times and in various ways spoke in time past to the fathers by the prophets, [2]has in these last days spoken to us by His Son, whom He has appointed heir of all things, through whom also He made the worlds; [3]who being the brightness of His glory and the express image of His person, and upholding all things by the word of His power, when He had by Himself purged our sins, sat down at the right hand of the Majesty on high, [4]having become so much better than the angels, as He has by inheritance obtained a more excellent name than they (Hebrews 1:1-4).

Notice that verse 3 above calls "the Son" who is Jesus Christ, "the brightness of His glory." This is important. When the above Scriptures direct us to focusing on the glory of the Lord, what they are really saying is to see this glory in Jesus Christ, God's Son. So let us make the connection here. If we desire to be transformed we must focus on God's glory, and God's glory is wrapped up in the Person of Jesus Christ. **New Wine** seeks to focus our attention on Christ, to have us contemplate His glory, so that in fixing our eyes on Him we will become transformed into His image.

Question 7. Where is the glory of God seen most clearly?

In closing, we must have proper motives to live our lives correctly. This course will test our motives as we are confronted with Scriptural truth, and we will seek to focus our attention on Jesus Christ, for in doing so we will inevitably become transformed. And this is what we are after, isn't it?

Question 8. Please summarize the teaching of this first day. Include what you have learned, any changes being made in you and how you will apply what you have studied today.

Steve wrote, "I have tried to live life without centering my motivation on glorifying God, but rather on the satisfaction of my own flesh. My attention is constantly focused on me. I must turn my attention toward God, and focus on His glory that I might be transformed into his image by the working of His power. So ... I will turn the eyes of my heart towards Jesus, His words, and the stories of Him from the Scriptures."

Jesus said "Here I am! I stand at the door and knock. If anyone hears my voice and opens the door, I will come in and eat with him, and he with me" (Revelation 3:20). This picture is so powerful as the King of glory stands outside the door—wanting to come and wrap His arms of love around His own. Won't you drink of the **New Wine** that He offers?

Note: Any addiction can have serious withdrawal effects that may require medical consultation. This happens in only a small percentage of the cases, but the chemical dependency is not being overlooked. We do not attempt to give medical advice and cannot take the place of a physician in these cases. If you have any questions or concerns, contact your doctor.

Now take a second and think about these next questions. You will be asked them every day and you will probably get sick of answering them, if they don't mean something to you. But, we want you to answer them truthfully. We are dealing with reality throughout this whole course, so we want you to give us your answers based on reality, not just how you think you should answer. Just be real, okay?

4

Questions

To clarify what the first accountability question means, we have included the following explanation.

What does "feasting" mean?

"Feasting" is more than just reading the Bible; it is a term to express the nourishing of our souls in Jesus Christ. It means that we are sitting at the feet of Jesus, hearing His Word and believing it, for the purpose of implementing the truths into our lives. It means we are receiving spiritual nourishment and we are delighting our souls in His grace and truth. This may be done in reading our Bibles, hearing God's Word preached, interacting with others in the Scriptures, and studying through this course, etc. This definition is at least a start; further explanation is included in the lessons.

Question 9. At this point in your life, what has "feasting" meant to you?

Scripture to Consider

You will make known to me the path of life. In Your presence is fullness of joy. In Your right hand there are pleasures forever (Psalm 16:11).

Did you feast on God's Word in the last 24 hours?

> Yes   No

If so, how did you feast? In other words, circle the ways you enjoyed God today. Reading? Prayer? Worship? Fellowship? Witnessing?

Were you free from drug and alcohol abuse since you did the last lesson?

> Yes   No

Did you spend personal time with the Lord since you did the last lesson?

> Yes   No

If you answered "no" to any of the above questions, describe what led to your fall.

If you answered "yes" to the above questions, you may use this area for additional comments.

We are very glad that you are interested in taking this **New Wine** course. We are excited to help you enjoy the Lord and enjoy the abundance of life that we chose to forego in the past by choosing to be addicted to drugs and alcohol. It will be a challenge even after this course is finished, but rising to the challenge, and claiming victory will be indescribable in its rewards and benefits.

DAY 2 – LIVING WATER

In Lesson One, Jeff Perry shared some of how he became a slave to alcohol and drugs. Here is more of his story:

Jeff writes, "I realized that I was headed down a path to destruction, so I began a painful and very unsuccessful string of attempts to rid my life of alcohol and other substances. On one side, I hated what I had become—out of control and defeated. On the other hand, I felt that I could not live without it. It hurt to be without it, so I kept coming back for more, always hoping that my life would take a turn for the better and the pain would go away. There were so many near-misses with jail, injury, and even death. I woke up in places that I didn't remember going. Everything I held dear seemed to crumble in my hands and I felt like I was alone. I vividly remember one 'close call' as a friend and I, both very intoxicated, climbed to the top of a very tall water tower in a lightning storm. As I stood on top and thunder crashed around me, it was like I was daring God to end it all right then. He did not, of course, as He had other plans.

I met my wife in 1996 and after several months we married. I was still drinking very heavily, but had become so dissatisfied with my life that even this joy could not ease the pain inside. We soon were expecting our first child and both decided to 'give church a try' as we were not happy with our lives. We attended a church close to us. Our attendance was off and on for quite a while, but eventually we began going regularly and something amazing happened—God began changing me. As I listened to the messages, and then eventually began reading the Bible myself, it was like God reached deep inside me and flipped a switch. One day in September, 1999, I literally realized that I didn't drink anymore. I did not plan this and I certainly did not suddenly develop a super-strong willpower. Rather, God changed me from within as I began to fill myself with Him. A whole new life was beginning!"

Please read through the following story from Scripture and answer the study questions below. (You are about to learn how to be free from enslavement to alcohol, prescription meds, cocaine, amphetamines, heroin, etc.)

> When a Samaritan woman came to draw water, Jesus said to her, "Will you give me a drink?" (His disciples had gone into the town to buy food.) The Samaritan woman said to him, "You are a Jew and I am a Samaritan woman. How can you ask me for a drink?" (For Jews do not associate with Samaritans.) Jesus answered her, "If you knew the gift of God and who it is that asks you for a drink, you would have asked him and he would have given you living water." "Sir," the woman said, "you have nothing to draw with and the well is deep. Where can you get this living water? Are you greater than our father Jacob, who gave us the well and drank from it himself, as did also his sons and his flocks and herds?"

> Jesus answered, "Everyone who drinks this water will be thirsty again, but whoever drinks the water I give him will never thirst. Indeed, the water I give him will become in him a spring of water welling up to eternal life." The woman said to him, "Sir, give me this water so that I won't get thirsty and have to keep coming here to draw water." He told her, "Go, call your husband and come back." "I have no husband," she replied.

> Jesus said to her, "You are right when you say you have no husband. The fact is, you have had five husbands, and the man you now have is not your husband. What you have just said is quite true." "Sir," the woman said, "I can see that you are a prophet. Our fathers worshiped on this mountain, but you Jews claim that the place where we must worship is in Jerusalem."

> Jesus declared, "Believe me, woman, a time is coming when you will worship the Father neither on this mountain nor in Jerusalem. You Samaritans worship what you do not know; we worship what we do know, for salvation is from the Jews. Yet a time is coming and has now come when the true worshipers will worship the Father in spirit and truth, for they are the kind of worshipers the Father seeks. God is spirit, and his worshipers must worship in spirit and in truth."

> The woman said, "I know that Messiah (called Christ) is coming. When he comes, he will explain everything to us." Then Jesus declared, "I who speak to you am he."

> Just then his disciples returned and were surprised to find him talking with a woman. But no one asked, "What do you want?" or "Why are you talking with her?" Then, leaving her water jar, the woman went back to the town and said to the people, "Come, see a man who told me everything I ever did. Could this be the Christ?" They came out of the town and made their way toward him (John 4:7 - 30).

Observation: In the above story, Jesus Christ spoke to a woman about two kinds of water:

1. **"This water,"** which would not satisfy and would not quench thirst. The woman would have to keep coming back again and again to get more of "this water."

2. **"The water I give,"** which would quench thirst eternally.

Then Jesus brought up the fact that the woman had had multiple relationships (5 husbands and a current live-in, 6 total). Obviously, she was not finding permanent satisfaction in these relationships so she had to keep going back to find a new love, each time hoping that this time would be the last. In bringing up her "unquenchable thirst" for different relationships, Jesus revealed to her that she would never be truly satisfied until she began "drinking" from the water He would give her.

Questions

Question 1. List the "water" from which you have been drinking and how it has left you "thirsty."

> **Chuck wrote,** "The water I have been drinking from is addictions and things of every kind—everything from religion, alcohol, poppers, and immoral encounters—looking for satisfaction. Trying desperately to believe at times that I may finally have what I am looking for, or at least some semblance of that. Quickly, I am empty again, numbing myself so that I don't have to face my life for what it really is."
>
> **Chris wrote,** "I have found that I have a thirst for pleasure and desire in the form of chemicals such as heroin, oxycontin, marijuana, and other substances. Every time I use, I am merely left wanting more. Even when I don't necessarily want these drugs, when I have become weary of them, I am still compelled to use them."
>
> **Jackie wrote,** "I have been living from the 'water' of prescription pain meds. It leaves me 'thirsty,' in that it only satisfies for a short time, whereas Jesus' 'living water' will quench my thirst forever."

Question 2. How many relationships did Jesus say that the woman at the well had?

Question 3. To what did Jesus compare these multiple relationships? (Circle one)

    a.   Eating fruit from a rotten tree

    b.   Drinking water from a well that does not satisfy

Question 4. What did Jesus mean when He said, "Everyone who drinks this water will be thirsty again?" (Circle one)

    a.   The water in that well contained a high amount of salt.

    b.   Ongoing relationships (or substances) will not ultimately satisfy, and will have to be repeated over and over.

Question 5. What kind of water did Jesus offer the woman at the well?

Question 6: What did Jesus say was the difference between the water she had been drinking and the living water He offered her?

Question 7: What did Jesus say the effects of drinking this water would be?

Note: Jesus offered this woman living water. He said that if she drank it she would not be thirsty anymore; in other words, she would be satisfied and not desire one relationship after another. Here is hope for you and me! Here is the **New Wine** of which we have been speaking—freedom from alcohol, drugs, or any addiction. If you discover how to receive this "living water" and how to drink it, you will not be thirsty anymore; in other words, you will be free from the craving of and slavery to alcohol or drugs. The remainder of this **New Wine** course is designed to help you receive and drink.

Question 8: Please describe how this teaching is giving you hope. How is drinking this water going to satisfy you and change the way you live? Be specific.

By admitting that alcohol or drugs does not permanently satisfy you, that you have to "drink" of it again and again, you are ready to discover what will satisfy—permanently.

Question 9: Have you attempted to stop drinking alcohol and/or using drugs in the past, but failed?

Question 10: According to the teaching that you've learned today, why did you fail last time and what will be different now?

> **Course Member Teresa writes,** "I tried on my own by employing my 'willpower' in addition to keeping what I had been doing as a secret. It was like a safety net. I knew that if I didn't tell anyone and started drinking again there would be no accountability. Plus I was arrogant enough to think that I would come to a point of only drinking occasionally."

Questions

Friend, as you contemplate continuing on in this course there is something that must be done, and without doing this there is no hope of real freedom. You must rid yourself of any and all sources of alcohol or drugs. We have become so accustomed to drinking alcoholic beverages to try and fill ourselves that unless we cut off access then we will, out of habit, return to it. Pour out the bottles, smash them in the trash can, poke holes in the cans—have fun with it and enjoy this process. Pour it all down the sink and laugh as it disappears. This is the first step to freedom!

> And I said to them, "Each of you, get rid of the vile images you have set your eyes on, and do not defile yourselves with the idols of Egypt. I am the LORD your God" (Ezekiel 20:7).

Carol writes, "A lot of what I was doing to stop was basically for my own benefit and for my family. Yesterday I realized that it isn't about me at all. It is about Jesus. If I partake of the Word and feast on it, then I will be filled with the living water and will not thirst after the waters of this world."

Vickie wrote, "I was drawing from my own broken place instead of from a complete relationship with Christ. I kept coming back for more of the same thing, and I have gotten more of the same rejection, fear, loneliness, sorrow, and defeat. I am now ready to recognize the wrong ways I have been trying to satisfy my flesh. I am ready to face the future completely stripped of myself and ask Jesus to clothe me with Himself. I desire that more than anything else."

Chuck wrote, "I am grateful that I do not have an overwhelming desire to drink tonight. I poured the last two beers down the drain last night, have poured the poppers and over-the-counter sleeping pills down the drain tonight. There may be more somewhere, but I will wash those down the drain, too, if I come across them. Someone told me at work this morning that I looked really alert or something like that. No one has told me that in a long time. I had a restless night, but I know that if I look to Christ, He will fill me. Thank you for your e-mail, and sharing how God has delivered you from things also. I appreciate your encouragement."

Question 11. Will you trash all access to alcohol or drugs right now?

Question 12. Please take a moment and record how you are doing today:

Scripture to Consider

Nothing in all creation is hidden from God's sight. Everything is uncovered and laid bare before the eyes of him to whom we must give account (Hebrews 4:13).

Jesus said: "The Spirit of the Lord is on me, because he has anointed me to preach good news to the poor. He has sent me to proclaim freedom for the prisoners and recovery of sight for the blind, to release the oppressed, to proclaim the year of the Lord's favor" (Luke 4:18 - 19).

Did you feast on God's Word in the last 24 hours?

Yes   No

If so, how did you feast? In other words, circle the ways you enjoyed God today. Reading? Prayer? Worship? Fellowship? Witnessing?

Were you free from drug and alcohol abuse since you did the last lesson?

Yes   No

Did you spend personal time with the Lord since you did the last lesson?

Yes   No

If you answered "no" to any of the above questions, describe what led to your fall.

If you answered "yes" to the above questions, you may use this area for additional comments.

DAY 3 – MORE LIVING WATER

¹Come, all you who are thirsty,
come to the waters;
and you who have no money,
come, buy and eat!
Come, buy wine and milk
without money and without cost
²Why spend money on what is not bread,
and your labor on what does not satisfy?
Listen, listen to me, and eat what is good,
and your soul will delight in the richest of fare
³Give ear and come to me;
hear me, that your soul may live
I will make an everlasting covenant with you,
my faithful love promised to David (Isaiah 55:1-3).

The "wine" in the above verse is the **New Wine** of which this course speaks. We know that physical things and pleasures will not satisfy—they all fall short eventually. This **New Wine** is the living water of Jesus Christ that we began to study yesterday! Let's take a deeper look at this **New Wine**. Are you thirsty, my friend?

Wine, in its essential allurement, promises to quench our thirst. In other words, it promises satisfaction. And honestly, it does satisfy—but only for a time. Pretty soon we discover that we are "thirsty" again, and as the years go by we find that we are really never genuinely satisfied, right? That is because sin never purely satisfies! It depletes us, not fulfills us.

Jeff writes, "I can remember drinking a couple of beers with friends and having 'the time of our lives.' But soon it became more and more—hard liquor and bigger quantities. There were hangovers and eventually blackouts where I couldn't even remember what I had done. There was no fun in that and I became moody and depressed. In short, I was a miserable wreck." This is the nature of sin. It takes us further and further and though it promises to satisfy, it never does satisfy eternally. This is why we keep coming back to it over and over again.

Questions

Question 1. Verse 2 of Isaiah 55 above asks an important question: "Why spend money on what does not satisfy?" Have you done this? How does this relate to our involvement with alcohol or any drug addiction? Write your answer here:

Questions

Course Member Teresa writes, "I drank to comfort myself. I drank to numb the guilt and sorrows of my soul instead of turning to Christ. I felt as thought I was too dirty and disobedient to be forgiven. The guilt drove me further and further into finding an escape route. Yet, it took more and more alcohol to find that numb state. It didn't satisfy so I would consume more and more. I knew that it would not satisfy yet I was drawn more and more to the alcohol."

Chuck wrote, "Yes, I have spent what has been for me a large amount of money on alcohol, and many things that have not satisfied me. As Teresa said, it satisfied for a short time, gave me an ego burst, and took away my conscience at times, but always left me wanting more. I think about that now, as I have already had thoughts about going after my addictions in one way or another. It is an appropriate question for me even now. 'Why spend money on what will not satisfy me?' Afterwards, and sometimes even while it is going on, I know in my heart that I will regret it, and will only wake up to have to face my life again as it really is, empty, without God. I have been so numb and foggy for so long that I have not been able to think clearly."

The verses above in Isaiah 55 are an invitation to the thirsty. Play along with me as we question the author of these verses. He says, "Come, all you who are thirsty."

"Alright, I am thirsty, I will come. But where do I come to quench my thirst?"

"Come to the waters."

"Yes, that makes sense; if I am thirsty I should come to the waters, but where are the waters?"

Ah, excellent question. "Listen, listen to me, and eat what is good, and your soul will delight in the richest of fare. Give ear and come to me; hear me, that your soul may live."

Questions

Friend, do you see it now? The water is in the Word of God. Drinking comes by listening. The Bible is our source of true refreshment and quenching of our thirst.

Question 2. According to verse 2 above, what is the result of drinking in the Word of God?

Question 3: According to verse 3 above, what is the result of listening to God's Word?

Question 4: Next, please provide your thoughts on this quote:

> "None but God can satisfy the longings of an immortal soul; that as the heart was made for Him, so He only can fill it." (**Richard Chenevix Trench**: *Notes on the Parables: Prodigal Son*).

Yesterday's lesson was about the woman at the well, who had been "drinking" from the wrong water. She was filling herself with one relationship after another (6 total), and she was obviously not satisfied. She was spending herself on what did not satisfy. But Jesus offered her living water, which she could receive as a free gift, and would satisfy her thirst forever. Today we are admonished to stop spending our time, energy and money on what will never satisfy us, and to drink the water that brings delight, joy and life to our souls. See what we have been missing while involved in medicating ourselves?

Question 5. How does the following verse relate to what we are studying?

> Death and Destruction are never satisfied, and neither are the eyes of man (Proverbs 27:20).

Chuck wrote, "The destruction and spiritual death that I have been living in just goes on and on. There is no end to it. I never will reach a place in my sin where, all of a sudden, the misery stops and I find fulfillment and peace in it. But this sometimes has been the deception that my eyes see. In my drunkenness and deceived mind, I think that maybe this time it will be different, but it never is. The end result is the same."

Friend, I was trapped in alcoholism for 17 years and I never found satisfaction. I continued to want excitement and the "belonging" that partying and drinking alcohol offers. I would look at television ads and see people my age drinking "socially" and having the best time imaginable. Why couldn't I find that kind of joy in beer and liquor? By the end of those 17 years, I found out that I had been drinking from a putrid, impure source of water that not only never satisfied, but it also left me defiled and unclean. But since September of 1999, I have been drinking the clean, refreshing, satisfying, life-giving, thirst-quenching water of Jesus Christ. The teaching of these two days is foundational to overcoming alcoholism and drug addiction. Switch water sources! No substance will ever satisfy us. Beer and liquor companies make billions of dollars off customer dissatisfaction. They know that once we are hooked, we will return time and time again for more—never to be satisfied. It is like salt water giving more thirst than satisfaction.

Question 6. How does the following verse go with today's teaching?

> Having lost all sensitivity, they have given themselves over to sensuality so as to indulge in every kind of impurity, with a continual lust for more (Ephesians 4:1).

Chuck wrote, "Turning away from God, and instead continually filling my thirst with things that make me drunk and cloud my mind, makes me lose the sensitivity of hearing from God or sensing His touch. With a mind that is cloudy and so out of touch with reality, it is no wonder I automatically go after everything that I want in my flesh, because in that state, I don't want God. I want my lusts to be fulfilled instead of His presence."

Question 7. Write your thoughts on this verse:

> My people have committed two sins: They have forsaken me, the spring of living water, and have dug their own cisterns, broken cisterns that cannot hold water (Jeremiah. 2:13). (Note a cistern is a well)

Questions

Note: God describes Himself as the "Spring of living water." He alone is the Source of life, refreshment, joy and nourishment for us. He is ever fresh and new, like a spring, and to "drink" of God is to receive life and be satisfied! Turning to cocaine is like trying to get water from a jar with holes in it.

Chuck wrote, "If I don't have God filling me, I will naturally go after the lusts of my flesh. These lusts will not fulfill me, though, these lusts are broken cisterns, that cannot provide God's living water."

Question 8. Please read this quote from the famous preacher, **Charles Spurgeon**, and record your comments about it:

"Men are in a restless pursuit after satisfaction in earthly things. They will exhaust themselves in the deceitful delights of sin, and, finding them all to be vanity and emptiness, they will become very perplexed and disappointed. But they will continue their fruitless search. Though wearied, they still stagger forward under the influence of spiritual madness, and though there is no result to be reached except that of everlasting disappointment, yet they press forward. They have no forethought for their eternal state; the present hour absorbs them. They turn to another and another of earth's broken cisterns, hoping to find water where not a drop was ever discovered yet." Write your thoughts here:

Carol wrote, "That certainly sums up the mental, emotional, and spiritual deformity of mankind. Today is the only thing that seems to be of utmost importance and what it can offer me. It's like chasing a whirlwind, and never finding the beginning or the end—a weary and futile exercise that never brings any semblance of happiness."

Chuck wrote, "Even though exhausted by pursuit of my sins, and with little sleep, I am soon on to my next pursuit. It is spiritual madness to continually go after these things that can never bring me peace. He talks about the 'present hour' absorbing me. That is what it is all about in my sin. I am not thinking about any time, but right then. It is a cycle of going after my lusts, letting them push me or really pushing myself into just living for the moment—and then as soon as possible, doing it again, but never being filled."

Vickie wrote, "I can totally relate to the term 'spiritual madness.' That is exactly how it feels to be driven to drink time and time again, even when you know it's not good for you, and each time you say you won't do it again, but you know you will."

Yesterday we studied the story of the woman at the well. We noticed how she had been "drinking" of the "water" of multiple relationships (6 total) and yet she was still "thirsty." Jesus offered her "living water" that would quench her thirst eternally. Today, I want to add one final thought about this story, and show how it relates to our involvement with alcohol or drug addiction. Please read the following verses in John 4—from the passage we studied yesterday.

Then, leaving her water jar, the woman went back to the town and said to the people, "Come, see a man who told me everything I ever did. Could this be the Christ?" They came out of the town and made their way toward him (John 4:28 - 30).

Question 9. After speaking with Jesus, the woman at the well went back into town. What did she do with her water jar?

Question 10. Yesterday we saw that Jesus Christ compared the water in that well to what?

a. Spring water

b. Living Water

Question 11. The woman at the well leaving her water jar behind could have meant that…

a. She had begun drinking of the water Jesus gave her and no longer needed the other water.

b. She had a short memory.

Scripture does not specifically say why the woman left her water jar with Jesus and so we cannot know for certain why she left it. Obviously she did indeed need to continue to drink physical water even after her encounter with Christ. However, the following truths are seen in the passage: First, Jesus compared the physical thirst of the woman with her attempts to quench the thirst of her soul by having multiple and sinful relationships; and secondly, Jesus offered her "living water" which would quench the thirst of her soul once and for all. Oh, dear friend, here is good news for us! As we learn how to drink living water, that only Jesus can give, we can leave our "water jar" behind.

Questions

Question 12. Please read this quote from **Arthur Pink** and give your comments:

"She left her water pot because she had now found a well of 'living water.' She had come to the well for literal water and that was what her mind was set on. But now that she had obtained salvation, she did not think any more about her water pot. It is always this way. Once our souls truly perceive Christ, once we know Him and receive Him as our personal Savior, we turn away from what we used to think about. Her mind was now fixed on Christ, and she had no thought of well, water, or water pot."

Granted, even after we come to Christ and learn to drink of His living water, there can be a time when we must learn how to leave the other "water behind" and it is certainly not always an instantaneous exchange of water, as it was for the woman at the well. We are not saying that it always happens in this manner, but that as we drink of Christ's living water we are able to leave behind the sinful water.

How well I remember that day when I realized that God had taken away my desire for alcohol and drugs. I will tell you more about what happened next as we continue this course, but let me say that my life has been completely different since then. I began drinking of the living water of Jesus Christ and I never want to go back to that filthy, stagnant, putrid sewer water again. My heart's desire is to see you, Friend, drinking along with me from the living water—the water that delights the soul and gives it life, and the water that satisfies forever!

Question 13. Please provide your closing thoughts on this day of teaching, and summarize the main thought of the lesson. Have you learned anything new, or re-learned something you have forgotten? Will anything change in your life as a result of this teaching?

Scripture to Consider

Nothing in all creation is hidden from God's sight. Everything is uncovered and laid bare before the eyes of him to whom we must give account (Hebrews 4:13).

Jesus said: "The Spirit of the Lord is on me, because he has anointed me to preach good news to the poor. He has sent me to proclaim freedom for the prisoners and recovery of sight for the blind, to release the oppressed, to proclaim the year of the Lord's favor" (Luke 4:18 - 19).

Did you feast on God's Word in the last 24 hours?

      Yes   No

If so, how did you feast? In other words, circle the ways you enjoyed God today. Reading? Prayer? Worship? Fellowship? Witnessing?

Were you free from drug and alcohol abuse since you did the last lesson?

      Yes   No

Did you spend personal time with the Lord since you did the last lesson?

      Yes   No

If you answered "no" to any of the above questions, describe what led to your fall.

If you answered "yes" to the above questions, you may use this area for additional comments.

Course member Teresa writes, "I have not had a drink in 8 days. My soul is in the process of healing. My husband and several friends are standing with me giving hope and encouragement. I will be telling our church about my sin on Sunday and I am very scared to do so. Yet, I know it is what is best for my soul. My sin needs to be brought out of the darkness and exposed to the light. I need Christ's strength and courage."

DAY 4 - THE POVERTY OF DRUNKENNESS

Dear Friend, welcome back for today's lesson. My prayer is that you are beginning to get a glimpse of hope like a light at the end of the tunnel. There is hope in Jesus Christ, and He is the light that will set us free from sin! Today we are going to look at a very important teaching that answers the question, "What does the Bible say about drunkenness?" Read through the following passage from Proverbs 23:20-21

> ²⁰Do not join those who drink too much wine
> or gorge themselves on meat,
> ²¹for drunkards and gluttons become poor,
> and drowsiness clothes them in rags.

As we look at this passage, the result of being a 'drunkard' really hits home. We don't really need a definition of the word 'drunkard' because it is given in verse 20. Notice the definition: "those who drink too much wine." So this is saying that "those who drink too much wine" will come to poverty. The word "poor" here has a much bigger meaning than just losing money, though that is certainly a part of it. The word also means to devour, destroy, or bring to ruin.

How well I remember the poverty of my 17-year drunken state. I spent every dime I could get my hands on to become drunk. The spending of money wasn't all, though, I was committing suicide daily—the toll on my body and health was incredible. I would wake up with terrible hangovers and have bruises and aches that I had no clue where they came from. The risk of driving while intoxicated was a menace to myself and others. I knew that my behavior would eventually kill me, but I just kept coming back for more. At the end of 17 years I was broke financially as well as broken physically.

Questions

Question 1: In what ways has drunkenness or drugs left you "poor?"

Course Member Teresa writes, "I have abused my body and brought about poor health. I have betrayed Christ, friends and family by my secret life. I have shamed the name of Christ. I have sinned against my Lord, family, friends and church family. I have been hurt by a recent fall down a flight of stairs. I have brought much, much sorrow to others and myself."

Chuck wrote, "Drunkenness has left me poor, both financially and spiritually. And the paranoia that goes with this is insane at times. I play scenarios in my head about what people think of me that probably comes more out of guilt than truth. The constant waking up and asking for mercy, but not really meaning it in my heart, leaves me feeling dead inside, like I'm just going through the motions."

Questions

Chris wrote, "I have been ruined financially, socially, mentally, and spiritually. At a time when I was exceptionally poor, I began to sell everything I could to get money for drugs. I sold my guitar amp, bass guitar, drum machine, four track, and a few rare rifles that my grandfather had given me as a gift, which were of great sentimental value. Selling these things caused me to feel a great amount of guilt. I also would lie to my spouse about money that I had spent and I would spend money meant for bills on drugs, and then lie to her about the money. I've lost the trust of friends and relatives due to my behavior and my dishonesty. I have also jeopardized my connection with Christ in that I chose my will over His repeatedly, and for selfish reasons."

Look at the conclusion of this chapter. Proverbs 23:29-35,

> ²⁹Who has woe? Who has sorrow? Who has strife? Who has complaints? Who has needless bruises? Who has bloodshot eyes?
> ³⁰Those who linger over wine, who go to sample bowls of mixed wine.
> ³¹Do not gaze at wine when it is red, when it sparkles in the cup, when it goes down smoothly!
> ³²In the end it bites like a snake and poisons like a viper.
> ³³Your eyes will see strange sights and your mind imagine confusing things.
> ³⁴You will be like one sleeping on the high seas, lying on top of the rigging.
> ³⁵'They hit me,' you will say, 'but I'm not hurt! They beat me, but I don't feel it! When will I wake up so I can find another drink?'

Question 2: Write out the "results" of drunkenness listed in verse 29 above.

Look at verse 35: Even after all of the problems that accompany drunkenness, the beaten man seeks after another drink. It is always one more drink to try and kill the pain that only worsens each time.

Oh, how I remember that, Friend! I would wake up in such a shape—nauseated and physically hurting, but emotionally I was battered as the cycle kept going over and over. I was truly circling the drain and about to go down. Yet as I woke up, the thing that came to mind first was that I thought drunkenness was the only cure for the pain I felt - to numb the hurt one more time. Yet that "cure" only led to more pain and the cycle had begun again.

Read the following quote by **Matthew Henry**:

> "All sin will be bitterness in the end, and this sin particularly. It bites like a serpent, when the drunkard is made sick by his surfeit, thrown by it into a dropsy or some fatal disease, beggared and ruined in his estate, especially when his conscience is awakened and he cannot reflect upon it without horror and indignation at himself, but worst of all, at last, when the cup of drunkenness shall be turned into a cup of trembling, the cup of the Lord's wrath, the dregs of which he must be forever drinking, and shall not have a drop of water to cool his inflamed tongue. To take off the force of the temptation that there is in the pleasure of the sin, foresee the punishment of it, and what it will at last end in if repentance prevent not. In its latter end it bites (so the word is); think therefore what will be in the end thereof." [1]Henry, M. 1996, c1991. *Matthew Henry's commentary on the Whole Bible: Complete and Unabridged in One Volume (Proverbs 23:29). Hendrickson: Peabody*

Question 3: Provide your thoughts on Matthew Henry's quote below:

Course Member Teresa writes, "I am indeed tasting the bitterness of my sin. Yet I have hope that I will not experience the torment of hell. God has removed much of the temptation for me because of the sorrow I have inflicted upon others and myself. My search for 'pleasure and numbness' has brought much damage and sorrow."

Friend, we must see drunkenness as a sin. It is hard to look in the mirror and see that a behavior that is so much a part of us could be that ugly in God's sight. The fact remains, though, that God hates sin. This means, as well, that God hates drunkenness.

Verse 31 above tells us not to gaze at wine while it sparkles in the cup, nor to think of it as it goes down so smoothly. In other words, compare the allurement of alcohol or drugs with its reality. The allurement is the sparkle and the smoothness, the promise of excitement and satisfaction; the reality is the inevitable poverty and ruin. Next time you see the sparkle of alcohol, or think of its smoothness (verse 31), let that be a reminder to you of its poverty and destruction (verses 29-32).

Question 4. Please write down what the "allurement" of alcohol or drugs has been for you. How has it "sparkled" and been "smooth" to you?

Chris wrote, "For me, the allurement of using drugs was the escape from boredom and everyday problems. I found comfort and solace in the numbing effect and distraction that drugs provided. No wonder that I found myself imprisoned by them when I was not properly equipped with the wisdom and discernment of Christ to know better. I remember how excited and desperate I would get when I was about to or had just acquired drugs. Everything else in my life would pale in comparison to that moment, and that moment would shine and 'sparkle' with the promise of pleasure and escape from the things in my life with which I didn't want to deal."

Question 5. Now write down all the ways your substance of choice has bitten you like a serpent, and poisoned you like a viper.

Remember how our motivation MUST be for the glory of God? In light of this, read the following verses and provide your comments on them below as to how they relate to drunkenness:

> Let us behave decently, as in the daytime, not in orgies and drunkenness, not in sexual immorality and debauchery, not in dissension and jealousy. Rather, clothe yourselves with the Lord Jesus Christ, and do not think about how to gratify the desires of the sinful nature (Romans 13:13-14).

Questions

Question 6. Please write your comments:

For you have spent enough time in the past doing what pagans choose to do living in debauchery, lust, drunkenness, orgies, carousing and detestable idolatry (1 Peter 4:3).

Question 7. Please write your comments:

Scripture to Consider

Do not get drunk on wine, which leads to debauchery. Instead, be filled with the Spirit (Ephesians 5:18).

Question 8. Please write your comments:

. . . being confident of this, that he who began a good work in you will carry it on to completion until the day of Christ Jesus (Philippians 1:6).

Did you feast on God's Word in the last 24 hours?

     Yes   No

If so, how did you feast? In other words, circle the ways you enjoyed God today. Reading? Prayer? Worship? Fellowship? Witnessing?

Were you free from drug and alcohol abuse since you did the last lesson?

     Yes   No

Did you spend personal time with the Lord since you did the last lesson?

     Yes   No

As important as this teaching is in seeing how God views drunkenness, it is also important to know that He forgives us for our drunken behavior when we turn from our sin. It does hurt to look at sin from His perspective, but God is faithful to forgive. Once again, here is hope for us: God's grace is sufficient, Friend!

Question 9. Finally, share any ways today's lesson changed the way you view drunkenness.

If you answered "no" to any of the above questions, describe what led to your fall.

If you answered "yes" to the above questions, you may use this area for additional comments.

DAY 5 - THE CROSS

Welcome Friend! You know that we are following the story of Pastor Jeff Perry, but also a course member named Teresa, and from time to time, others. To introduce the teaching of this day, I wanted to share with you a letter (by permission) that Teresa wrote when she had completed her fifth day in the course. Here it is:

Dear loved ones,

I am specifically asking for prayer for my husband Bob and I both today and tomorrow. The outpouring of love and forgiveness that has been shown to me by my friends has been almost unbelievable. My daughter and her husband have been loving, forgiving and supportive. I feel such guilt! I am not sure whether their love brings feeling of guilt out in me because of my sin and my pattern of having a hard time accepting love, or whether it is a good thing given to me by Christ. I hope that makes some sort of sense.

I believe the Lord will enable me to stand before the congregation tomorrow and confess my sin with courage. However, I am at times almost in despair because my husband will be facing consequences for my sin. The knowledge that I have caused this is so sorrowful I can hardly breathe. It was my sin and my sin alone. He is such a loving, patient, kind, and godly man. Yet I feel he will be "punished" (not sure that's the right word) far more severely than I who actually committed the sin of drunkenness. At times I can't believe how far-reaching my sin has been. How ignorant of me to believe I was only hurting myself and that it would affect no one else.

Please pray that the Lord will give me the discernment I need. I am so confused about whether my feelings are truly from Christ or the enemy of my soul taunting me. I am very confused. This is such a very dark time right now.

As a side note, I saw my doctor yesterday for a follow up visit. He told me 'You are very lucky you woke up. You might have lain there and bled to death.' I know that this was for my good. The Lord loved me enough to get my attention to stop my sin. I am now on day 11 of sobriety. When I look at the sorrow my sin has caused, alcohol is absolutely the furthest thing from my mind.

Thank you for your help.

Teresa

Well, today we want to examine the gospel, and see how it relates to drunkenness and bondage to alcohol or drugs. Let's examine the following passages of Scripture:

> But your iniquities have separated you from your God; your sins have hidden his face from you, so that he will not hear (Isaiah 59:2).

> Friend, when I was involved in drunken behavior I was separated from God and God did not hear my prayers. In fact, my constant sinning caused Him to hide His face from me because He cannot look on sin. I felt like my prayers stopped at the ceiling and then fell to the floor. Even though I may have been a Christian I was "darkened in my understanding and separated from the life of God . . ." (Ephesians 4:18).

Indeed this was a very dark time in my life.

Question 1. Can you identify with the feelings of separation from God while involved in drunkenness? Write your answers here:

Please read the following passage:

> [21]Once you were alienated from God and were enemies in your minds because of your evil behavior. [22]But now he has reconciled you by Christ's physical body through death to present you holy in his sight, without blemish and free from accusation [23]if you continue in your faith, established and firm, not moved from the hope held out in the gospel. This is the gospel that you heard and that has been proclaimed to every creature under heaven, and of which I, Paul, have become a servant (Colossians 1:21-23).

As I came out of drunkenness, the above verses showed my past, my present and my future. I used to be "alienated from God" and was His "enemy" because of my "evil behavior." This was my past as I lived in the darkness of secret sins. I may have claimed to be God's friend, but the reality is that I was alienated from God, and was His enemy because of my habitual sinning in drunkenness.

But God took action on my behalf. He "reconciled me by Christ's physical body through death." I am no longer His enemy; I am reconciled to God through the death of Jesus Christ. This is the work that He did; it is nothing that I have done.

Now, please understand that not everyone who has been involved in drunkenness is an enemy of God. You may be a Christian who has fallen into this trap and are eager to be released. For me, I concluded that though I would profess Christ, I did not truly know Him in a saving way. I knew about Him, but did not truly know Him through genuine repentance.

Questions

These verses in Colossians 1 describe not only how we are saved, but how we come to leave alcohol or drugs behind as well. So let us look at the above verses from the perspective of how to be free from drunkenness. These verses present three things:

1. The Problem

2. The Solution

3. The Results

1. The problem. Sin, in our case drunkenness or drug addiction, separates and alienates us from God. We can become so distanced from God that we feel that our prayers are not heard, and they may not be. The abuse of any substance, because it causes us to love the world, eventually leads us to hate God. I remember so well how I became very critical and even angry with anyone who would talk to me about God or try to encourage me to seek His help. I felt like He had abandoned me to this hurt. I felt as if He did not care about me and I considered it a cruel joke on His part to create me as such a hurting and angry person. The truth was that I had turned my back on Him and walked down this destructive path, yet I blamed God for all my problems. Sin had so hardened my heart, and deceived my very soul, that I was becoming a very hateful and angry person.

Question 2. Have you experienced this hatred for God?

Some may say yes, others no. Let me assure you that if you continue in the path of sin you will eventually get to the place where you do indeed hate God.

> "No man can serve two masters: Either he will love the one and hate the other, or he will be devoted to the one and despise the other" (Matthew 6:24).

2. The Solution. God has reconciled us by putting Jesus to death. Because amphetamines or drunkenness causes us to eventually hate God, God took the initiative to reconcile us. He took all our sins off of us and put them onto Jesus, who died to pay for them. On the cross, Jesus was treated as a drunkard, a God-hater, an enemy of God, in order to bring us back to God. On the cross, Jesus removed our sin that prevented us from having a relationship with God. **The solution to the problem is Jesus Christ.**

Question 3. Please write out verse 22 from the Colossians 1 passage from the previous page:

Question 4. What has Jesus Christ done to deal with the problem of sin? What is the result for those who continue in the faith (v. 23)?

Course Member Teresa writes, "I have tried 'will-power', asking humans for help (which did not come), 'vowing' each day to not drink, setting up guidelines regarding drinking. I never kept them for more than a day or two. I felt too ashamed to go to Christ. Yet, I knew that there was absolutely nothing hidden from His sight. My reasoning abilities were definitely warped."

Dear friend, beware of any teaching, program, or method for finding freedom from alcohol or drug addictions that does not have Jesus Christ at the center, for there is no other way to solve the sin/problem than Jesus. There is no other way to be reconciled to God, to be changed from His enemy to His friend, to cease the evil behavior, than through Jesus.

I remember the treatments so well! Counseling, drugs . . . I was given anti-depressants that left me in such a fog that I could barely remember who I was. After a period, it was decided that perhaps I needed a stimulant because of another diagnosis. The only result of this was that now I couldn't sleep! Doctors, counselors, psychiatrists emptied the pharmacy into me over the years, but none of the medicines ever helped or took the torment away. It was like I was willing to take anything or try any method other than the one thing that would help me, Jesus Christ!

Question 5. Have you tried other methods to be free from alcohol or drugs? If so, what were they?

Questions

Carol wrote, "I have gone to AA faithfully, but always felt that they were still worshiping alcohol. I tried in-patient counseling for almost a year. I went to psychiatrists, who thought that I was a very interesting specimen of humanity! Of course, I tried will power but that was absolutely useless. I had none."

3. The Results. The death of Jesus Christ tells us that God has done something about our sin problem. It tells us that He is committed to eradicating sin and has taken radical action to dispose of it, by putting His Son to death in our place.

Notice the results of what Jesus did for us on the cross. "But now he has reconciled you by Christ's physical body through death to present you holy in his sight, without blemish and free from accusation." Oh friends, this is a marvelous truth with practical results. Because of Jesus' death on the cross, we who have been reconciled to God are *holy, without blemish, and free from accusation.*

Question 6. By way of reflection, please list (1) how your sin has impacted your relationship with God, (2) God's provision for sin (3) how this will change your life?

God made him who had no sin to be sin for us, so that in him we might become the righteousness of God (2 Corinthians 5:21).

Question 7. Please provide your comments on the preceding verse:

For God so loved the world that he gave his one and only Son, that whoever believes in him shall not perish but have eternal life. For God did not send his Son into the world to condemn the world, but to save the world through him (John 3:16 - 17).

Yet to all who received him, to those who believed in his name, he gave the right to become children of God, children born not of natural descent, nor of human decision or a husbands will, but born of God (John 1:12, 13).

Question 8. Please provide your comments:

For what I received I passed on to you as of first importance: that Christ died for our sins according to the Scriptures, that he was buried, that he was raised on the third day according to the Scriptures, and that he appeared to Peter, and then to the Twelve. After that, he appeared to more than five hundred of the brothers at the same time, most of whom are still living, though some have fallen asleep (1 Corinthians 15:3 - 6).

Question 9. Please provide your comments:

Friend, perhaps you are still an enemy of God in your mind because of your evil behavior. Maybe it is time to put up the white flag of surrender and ask God to reconcile you to Himself. If you know that you need to be holy, without blemish and free from accusation then why not ask God right now for help.

Question 10. Here is a place to put your thoughts and prayers to Him in writing:

Questions

Healing did come for me and the pain began to turn to joy. You see, God led my wife and me to that little church on that particular Sunday for a reason. It turns out that I had not committed the unpardonable sin and I was not hopeless. I had come to the end of myself, but God was just warming up. I want to share with you how God began to heal and restore me that day and what followed. Much the same as a canvas that had been soiled and stained, the Master was fixing the damage one brush stroke at a time! It all began with a step—a turn of the head from the drunken world to which I had become enslaved. A turn in the direction of a loving God and the healing that He was about to give. That day was like a sip of water—living water that was so refreshing and so satisfying! It was indeed the **New Wine** of Jesus Christ that I had been seeking all along, the satisfying, cleansing, and healing waters that He provides.

Read and think about Deuteronomy 4: 25-31 for a moment. This passage states that the children of God would become corrupt, make themselves idols to worship, assimilate into the practices of the surrounding nations, and do evil against the Lord for many years. Look at verse 29, which says:

> "But if from there, you seek the LORD your God, you will find him if you look for him with all your heart and with all your soul. When you are in distress and all these things have happened to you, then in later days you will return to the LORD your God and obey him. For the LORD your God is a merciful God; he will not abandon or destroy you or forget the covenant with your forefathers, which he confirmed to them by oath."

These words are medicine for our souls: "But if from there . . ." But if from there, you seek the Lord with all your heart, you will find Him. Wherever your "there" is, if you will seek the Lord from "there" you will find Him. And He will make you holy, without blemish, and free from accusation.

Question 11. Please summarize the teaching of today. I'm specifically looking for your understanding of any changes that will be made in your life because of the Scripture that you have read today.

Scripture to Consider

Ask and it will be given to you; seek and you will find; knock and the door will be opened to you. For everyone who asks receives, he who seeks finds, and to him who knocks, the door will be opened (Matthew 7:7).

Did you feast on God's Word in the last 24 hours?

     Yes   No

If so, how did you feast? In other words, circle the ways you enjoyed God today. Reading? Prayer? Worship? Fellowship? Witnessing?

Were you free from drug and alcohol abuse since you did the last lesson?

     Yes   No

Did you spend personal time with the Lord since you did the last lesson?

     Yes   No

If you answered "no" to any of the above questions, describe what led to your fall.

If you answered "yes" to the above questions, you may use this area for additional comments.

DAY 6 – BROKENNESS: KEY TO VICTORY

Today's lesson comes out of my own experience and the experience of others, of discovering what it takes to truly be done with habitual sin. Today we will study a truth that absolutely must be experienced in the soul if there is to be real, lasting victory over alcohol or any substance. The truth is, Friend, that God must break us! "Well, that is not very encouraging or hope-inspiring" you say. Actually it is. Read below what several men of God have said on this subject:

"The kingdom of God is a kingdom of Paradox, where through the ugly defeat of a cross, a holy God is utterly glorified. Victory comes through defeat; healing through brokenness; finding self through losing self." **Charles Colson**

"God will never plant the seed of his life upon the soil of a hard, unbroken spirit. He will only plant that seed where the conviction of his spirit has brought brokenness, where the soil has been watered with the tears of repentance as well as the tears of joy." **Alan Redpath**

"Deliverance can come to us only by the defeat of our old life. Safety and peace come only after we have been forced to our knees. God rescues us by breaking us, by shattering our strength and wiping out our resistance." **A. W. Tozer**

"True prayer is born out of brokenness." **Francis J. Roberts**

(Quotations taken from Edith Draper's Book of Quotations for the Christian World - Wheaton: Tyndale House Publishers, Inc. 1992)

So why are we devoting a whole day's study to this subject of brokenness? Because as the authors state above, brokenness brings healing, life, revival, rescue, and true prayer. So becoming broken before the Lord is indispensable.

Please read the following passage and answer questions below:

> Psalm 51 (A psalm of David. When the prophet Nathan came to him after David had committed adultery with Bathsheba.)
>
> Have mercy on me, O God, according to your unfailing love; according to your great compassion blot out my transgressions. Wash away all my iniquity and cleanse me from my sin. For I know my transgressions, and my sin is always before me. Against you, you only, have I sinned and done what is evil in your sight, so that you are proved right when you speak and justified when you judge. Surely I was sinful at birth, sinful from the time my mother conceived me. Surely you desire truth in the inner parts; you teach me wisdom in the inmost place. Cleanse me with hyssop, and I will be clean; wash me, and I will be whiter than snow.
>
> Let me hear joy and gladness; let the bones you have crushed rejoice. Hide your face from my sins and blot out all my iniquity. Create in me a pure heart, O God, and renew a steadfast spirit within me. Do not cast me from your presence or take your Holy Spirit from me. Restore to me the joy of your salvation and grant me a willing spirit, to sustain me. Then I will teach transgressors your ways, and sinners will turn back to you. Save me from bloodguilt, O God, the God who saves me, and my tongue will sing of your righteousness. O Lord, open my lips, and my mouth will declare your praise. You do not delight in sacrifice, or I would bring it; you do not take pleasure in burnt offerings. The sacrifices of God are a broken spirit; a broken and contrite heart, O God, you will not despise (Psalm 51).

Note: This is a prayer for forgiveness and cleansing, made by David. The prophet Nathan had confronted him about his sin with Bathsheba and he was now broken-hearted over it.

Questions

Question 1. Write the words David uses to ask God to do something. The first ones are "cleanse me," and "wash me." What are the others? Write them here:

Question 2. What are the sacrifices that God accepts?

Note: David is saying that God receives brokenness as the only acceptable sacrifice for sins committed. The previous verse states that God does not take pleasure in burnt offerings. The reason for this is obvious: someone could give burnt offerings (or tithes, or church-work, etc.) without the heart being involved.

Question 3. Hebrews 3:13 states, "But encourage one another daily, as long as it is called today, so that none of you may be hardened by sin's deceitfulness." What does sin do to our hearts?

Those of us who have spent many years in bondage to substances have become hardened by sin's deceitfulness. Hearts turn cold, brittle, unfeeling and desensitized by this sin. Since God disciplines those he loves, he will break our hard hearts, cold and unyielding spirits, and harsh attitudes. God breaks us so that he can remake us (Jeremiah 18.) Friend, if you are experiencing genuine brokenness over your sin before God, know that God is working. If you are not broken before the Lord, will you pray that God would do this miraculous work in your heart lest you die in a hard-hearted condition?

Questions

Question 4. Honestly assess the condition of your heart and life. Where are you in the process of offering the acceptable sacrifice of brokenness before the Lord? Ask the Lord to reveal your heart's condition to you right now. Write it here:

Today we are going to read some very instructive writings on this important subject: one from Matthew Henry, several from Charles Spurgeon, and one from John Bradford. Please give your thoughts after each writing.

Matthew Henry writes about the Passover Lamb: "It was to be eaten with bitter herbs in remembrance of the bitterness of their bondage in Egypt. We must feed upon Christ with sorrow and brokenness of heart, in remembrance of sin; this will give an admirable relish to the lamb. Christ will be sweet to us if sin be bitter."

Question 5. Your comments about Matthew Henry's quote above:

Charles Spurgeon hits the nail on the head as usual. Read this carefully: "True repentance has a distinct and constant reference to the Lord Jesus Christ. If you repent of sin without looking to Christ, away with your repentance. If you are so lamenting your sin as to forget the Savior, you have a need to begin all this work over again. Whenever we repent of sin, we must have one eye upon sin and another upon the cross; or, better still, let us have both eyes upon Christ, seeing our sin punished in him, and by no means let us look at sin except as we look at Jesus. A man may hate sin just as a murderer hates the gallows but this does not prove repentance if I hate sin because of the punishment, I have not repented of sin; I merely regret that God is just.

"But if I can see sin as an offense against Jesus Christ, and loathe myself because I have wounded him, then I have a true brokenness of heart. If I see the Savior and believe that those thorns upon his head were put there by my sinful words; if I believe that those wounds in his heart were pierced by my heart-sins; if I believe that those wounds in his feet were made by my wandering steps, and that the wounds in his hands were made by my sinful deeds, then I repent after a right fashion. Only under the cross can you repent. Repentance elsewhere is remorse, which clings to the sin and only dreads the punishment. Let us then seek, under God, to have a hatred of sin caused by a sight of Christ's love."

Question 6: Please comment on Spurgeon's quote above:

Charles Spurgeon tells us what 'normal' should be: "When I sat on this platform on Monday night, and marked your sobs, in tears, and heard the suppressed sighs and groans of the great multitude then assembled, I could not but say, 'Behold!' And yet it ought not to be a wonder, it ought not to be a strange thing for God's people to be in earnest, or for sinners to feel brokenness of heart."

Question 7. Please write your comments on Spurgeon's quote above:

John Bradford said that when he was in prayer, he never liked to rise from his knees till he began to feel something of brokenness of heart. Get up to your chamber, then, poor sinner, if you would have a broken and contrite spirit, and come not out until you have it. Remember, you will never feel so broken in heart as when you can see Jesus bearing all your sins; faith and repentance are born together, and aid the health of each other.

> Law and terrors do but harden,
> All the while they work alone;
> But a sense of blood-bought pardon,
> Will dissolve a heart of stone.

Spurgeon writes: "Go as you are to Christ, and ask him to give that tenderness of heart which shall be to you the indication that pardon has come; for pardon cannot and will not come unattended by a melting of soul and a hatred of sin. Wrestle with the Lord! Say, I will not let you go except you bless me. Get a fast hold upon the savior by a vigorous faith in his great atonement. Oh! May his spirit enable you to do this! Say in your soul, here I will abide, at the horns of the altar; if I perish I will perish at the foot of the cross. From my hope in Jesus I will not depart; but I will look up and still say, Savior, your heart was broken for me, break my heart! You were wounded, wound me! Your blood was freely poured forth, for me, Lord, let me pour forth my tears that I should have nailed you to the tree. Oh Lord, dissolve my soul; melt it in tenderness, and you will be forever praised for making your enemy your friend.

"May God bless you, and give you repentance, if you have not repented; and if you have, may he enable you to continue in it all your days, for Jesus Christ sake. Amen."

Questions

Question 8. Please write your comments on the above quote here:

Scripture to Consider

"Psalm 51 is the photograph of a contrite spirit. Oh, let us seek after the like brokenness of heart, for however excellent our words may be, yet if the heart is not conscious of the blackness and Hell-deservingness of sin, we cannot expect to find mercy with the Judge of all the earth. If the Lord will break your heart, consent to have it broken; asking that he may sanctify that brokenness of spirit to bring you in earnest to a savior, that you may yet be numbered with the righteous ones."
Charles Spurgeon

Question 9. Please provide your comments here:

For this is what the high and lofty One says, he who lives forever, whose name is holy: "I live in a high and holy place, but also with him who is contrite and lowly in spirit, to revive the spirit of the lowly and to revive the heart of the contrite" (Isaiah 57:15).

Did you feast on God's Word in the last 24 hours?

      Yes   No

If so, how did you feast? In other words, circle the ways you enjoyed God today. Reading? Prayer? Worship? Fellowship? Witnessing?

Were you free from drug and alcohol abuse since you did the last lesson?

      Yes   No

Did you spend personal time with the Lord since you did the last lesson?

      Yes   No

If you answered "no" to any of the above questions, describe what led to your fall.

If you answered "yes" to the above questions, you may use this area for additional comments.

Course Member Teresa writes, "I need to embrace brokenness over sin as a wonderful gift of God. It is evident of the work He is doing in my life. It actually should give me hope because it is evidence of God's mercy in my life. Mercy in that I realize how ugly my sin is to Christ. This is to be more precious to me than anything."

Friend, this time may seem to be full of gloom and sorrow. I just want to encourage you by sharing that as I went through this same thing, forgiveness follows swiftly on the heels of repentance. It hurts to look into the mirror and see yourself from God's point of view. But the reason that God gives us this "look" at ourselves is to break us in preparation for forgiveness and that is the roadmap to freedom!

DAY 7 - RUNNING LIGHT

Therefore, since we are surrounded by such a great cloud of witnesses, let us throw off everything that hinders and the sin that so easily entangles, and let us run with perseverance the race marked out for us (Hebrews 12:1).

Friend, this passage of Scripture describes the Christian life as a foot race, and the author tells us that in order to run fast we must run light. We are here instructed to "throw off everything that hinders and the sin that so easily entangles." Here, temptation and sin are described as those things that hinder and entangle, and they must be thrown off.

The first thing that I knew I had to do was to get rid of all the alcohol and cocaine in our house. Freedom would not come with that temptation in the refrigerator or on the counter! The next thing was to avoid situations where I might be tempted to "take a drink" such as bars, parties, even some restaurants that served alcoholic beverages. I knew that these could be potential areas to fall so I got rid of the alcohol and cocaine and refused to go into those places that could tempt me. In other words, I "threw off" all of those things so that I could run the race to win!

Questions

Question 1. Please describe what things have hindered you from running this race to win:

> **Course Member Teresa writes,** "One of my first hindrances was that I kept my sin in the dark. I would not risk telling others. Another hindrance was that I did not reach out for help from the church body. My self-sufficiency was one of the biggest hindrances. I had convinced myself that I was strong enough on my own to overcome my bondage."

Question 2. What are we commanded to do with these things that hinder us?

As you can imagine, life was much different. I even took a good deal of "flack" from friends who wanted me to go out with them or join them for a drinking "party." I found out, though, that as I began to stay away and to deny myself access to alcohol, that I did not miss the drunkenness or the hangovers or the lost hours in a blackout. The fact was, I liked being a sober, clear-minded man! The temptation was still there and Satan did not want to let go that easily. I still had moments when I thought the temptation was too much to bear. Had I kept any access to cocaine or alcoholic beverages I may very well have fallen, but by the Lord's grace I did not!

Questions

Then came that day when I realized God had taken the need and the desire away. There was freedom from alcohol and drugs—freedom from my sin that had plagued me for so long. The work of God had begun in my life and He was about to pour blessings upon my family that I could not even imagine. I look back at that time and realize how God had led me step by step down this path to freedom. Had I skipped over this important step of "throwing off" these potential pitfalls, I might have missed the blessings and the healing that He provided.

Do you see the importance of applying this principle to your own life? As we have been working with people at Setting Captives Free, we have discovered that those who apply this teaching to their lives begin to walk in victory over sin. We have also noticed, unfortunately, that those who will not rid their lives of that which is causing them to stumble, just never seem to get free. They confess to falling, getting back up and telling us they are sorry and won't be doing that again. We instruct them that they need to remove that which caused them to fall. They make excuses and say that they have learned their lesson, and because temptations are weak right after a fall they think that they "have a handle" on it now. We know that it is just a matter of time before they fall again, and sure enough usually within two weeks down they go. This will continue unless and until they throw off that which causes them to stumble.

Question 3. So, what things will you throw off so you can run light? Please only list those things that you will get rid of RIGHT NOW.

Course member Teresa writes, "Bob and I did not keep alcohol in the house. I had to go to the store to buy it each time I drank. Because of this, I will not be going to the grocery store alone for a while. Also, we have gotten rid of the wine glasses that I used and the wine bottle openers. I am curtailing my viewing of cooking shows for the time being because there are shows that use wine either in the recipe or as an accompaniment with the meal."

But put ye on the Lord Jesus Christ, and make not provision for the flesh, to fulfill the lusts thereof (Romans 13:14).

Notice the above verse tells us to "make no provision for the flesh." You see, when I had access to alcohol and cocaine, I could pray or resolve not to drink or use all day long, but then I would always end up giving in and cracking open that bottle. I would have a bad day or even a good day and somehow I would justify "celebrating." The next day I would groan and say "never again." All the resolve in the world would crumble as that bottle or that "fix" would be beckoning and I would fall again. Any weakness or "bump" in the road of life would send me back into oblivion. This is such a key principle to freedom because if we allow ourselves access to that which causes us to sin, we will inevitably find ourselves giving in during a weak moment.

Question 4. Now, please list any area that you currently still have provision for your flesh to be gratified:

Friend, if you listed anything in the space above, those areas are where your next fall will be. It is just a matter of time. You can be drinking the living water, exposing your sin and asking for help, praying to be reconciled to God, but in a weak moment you WILL fall because there is provision made to fulfill your lusts. So, it is imperative that right now you eradicate that from your life. It has got to go. If you keep it around, you are trying to run a race with a huge burden on your back, and every time you fall in that area you add weight to the burden. Eventually you will not be able to run the race but will have fallen down off to the side of the road in the thorns and weeds.

Question 5. Are you willing to part with that which will make you fall? Will you get rid of it right now?

Right about now is when we start getting objections. They usually go something like this: "But it is not heroin or prescription meds that is the problem, it is my heart. Jesus says that out of the heart come the things that defile us, so I don't want to just deal with the symptom, which is having access to the substance, I need to get my relationship right with Jesus so I can be strong enough to say 'No' to my temptation."

This is true! We have no quarrel with the above statements. However, what we are talking about in this lesson is the manner in which we get our hearts right with God so that we can say "no" to drugs or alcohol when we are tempted by them. And there is only one Scriptural way to do this—the total removal of anything that causes us to stumble. This is a principle of truth, that in order to run this race we must remove anything that entangles us. Our hearts will continue to be defiled if we continue to intoxicate ourselves at the devil's bar, and the way to be free initially is to remove the temptation.

You see, I wanted to be able to look temptation in the face and say "no." I thought that I would be strong when I have temptation and be able to stand up against it. In reality, I wanted to be strong rather than pure. This is not the way to victory over sin.

Notice this next passage:

If your right eye causes you to sin, gouge it out and throw it away. It is better for you to lose one part of your body than for your whole body to be thrown into hell. And if your right hand causes you to sin, cut it off and throw it away. It is better for you to lose one part of your body than for your whole body to go into hell (Matthew 5:29-30).

Friend, the above verses could be summarized by the words "radical amputation." Now Jesus was not referring to a physical cutting off of our hands or an actual plucking out of the eyeball. Handicapped and blind men still drink and lust. What He was saying was to deal radically with whatever causes us to sin: cut it off, pluck it out, hack it off. Some have stated a desire to be "reasonable" and "balanced" in the approach to overcoming sin. We agree. It is only reasonable to destroy those things in our lives that seek to destroy us. Radically amputating cocaine from my home was one way of dealing with sin. Jesus' method of dealing with sin is radical amputation.

Question 6. Will you, right now, cut off and pluck out anything that is causing you to stumble?

Yes   No

Questions

There are many ways that you can go about radically amputating substances from your life! Some may choose to not carry credit cards or extra money so that they cannot buy alcohol. Or perhaps a different route home must be taken to avoid driving by a bar or store where alcohol is present. There is one fact that is unavoidable—substances are available everywhere we turn. We must do everything we possibly can to avoid them. I know that I used a lot of creative energy figuring out ways to drink and to hide it when needed. Try using that same creative thought and energy to "cast off" and "pluck out" access to alcohol and drugs!

Dear friends, run the race to win. Remove that which hinders you, and anything that entangles you. It's worth it to be running light! I am no longer encumbered with the heavy and growing burden of habitual sin. I can actually run the race marked out for me and know that I am running to win, because God has enabled me to throw off the sin that so easily besets me.

Please, Friend, take this teaching of Scripture seriously. We have seen some students who delay in removing that which trips them up, and some who only remove it part way. In every instance of a half-done job, there is a fall that is soon to come. Don't hesitate to be radical in dealing with this. After all, God was radical in dealing with sin. He gave His one and only Son to suffer and die on the cross. That's radical! Be willing to part with that which you have loved in the past. Be willing to sacrifice it to be free from it.

Question 7. Record how things are going for you today.

Course Member Teresa writes, "I am beginning to feel freedom. Last night, however, I attended a movie with a group of my sisters from church. There were parts of the movie where alcohol was either being consumed or was shown at restaurants and celebrations. I began to think 'I could handle having an occasional glass of wine.' Almost instantly, the Lord said 'No! You cannot.' When I came home I told my husband about the temptation. This morning I emailed my accountability partners to tell them about the temptation. I know if I don't do this, I will begin to slowly 'live in secret and darkness' again. I believe I have to be honest and transparent about my temptations."

Scripture to Consider

Therefore, if anyone is in Christ, he is a new creation; the old has gone, the new has come! (2 Corinthians 5:17).

For what I received I passed on to you as of first importance: that Christ died for our sins according to the Scriptures, that he was buried, that he was raised on the third day according to the Scriptures (1 Corinthians 15:3 - 4).

The thief comes only to steal and kill and destroy; I have come that they may have life, and have it to the full (John 10:10).

Did you feast on God's Word in the last 24 hours?

> Yes   No

If so, how did you feast? In other words, circle the ways you enjoyed God today. Reading? Prayer? Worship? Fellowship? Witnessing?

Were you free from drug and alcohol abuse since you did the last lesson?

> Yes   No

Did you spend personal time with the Lord since you did the last lesson?

> Yes   No

If you answered "no" to any of the above questions, describe what led to your fall.

If you answered "yes" to the above questions, you may use this area for additional comments.

DAY 8 - STRENGTH THROUGH CONFESSION

This aspect to fighting substance abuse is very important: confession of sins. We'll examine this today and you will discover that spiritual strength to overcome sin is directly tied to confession of sins. Read the following verses and answer the questions about the passage that follows.

> When I kept silent, my bones wasted away through my groaning all day long. For day and night your hand was heavy upon me; my strength was sapped as in the heat of summer (Psalm 32:3-4).

Questions

Question 1. The above verses describe someone in a lethargic condition. His bones were "wasting away," and his strength was "sapped" as in the heat of summer, and God's hand was against him. What was the reason for his affliction?

Question 2. The context of this passage makes it clear that David was keeping silent about a sin he had committed. So what happens when people hide their sin? And do you now, or have you ever felt like the person above?

Questions

Course Member Teresa writes, "Absolutely! I have recently come out of that very situation. When your sin is hidden many things happen. First, there is the deception that you can 'handle' this yourself (pride). When you are at that point, you no longer look to the Lord for your help. Then there is shame because you are living a deceptive dual life. I had gotten to the point that I could not even look another Christian in the eye. Their walk with Christ was convicting to me. Because of the overwhelming shame and guilt I felt, I ran to alcohol to numb myself because I didn't want to feel the very things the Lord was using to get my attention. The shame and guilt came from Him because I was in sin. My heart began to get harder and harder."

Note: Sin is debilitating, exhausting, paralyzing. This "sapping of strength" keeps us powerless to fight the Enemy, and ineffective in serving God. It is the opposite of "I can do all things through Christ who strengthens me," and it leaves us spent, tired, and emotionally drained. But there is a way out!

> Then I acknowledged my sin to you and did not cover up my iniquity. I said, "I will confess my transgressions to the Lord"—and you forgave the guilt of my sin. Therefore let everyone who is godly pray to you while you may be found; surely when the mighty waters rise, they will not reach him. You are my hiding place; you will protect me from trouble and surround me with songs of deliverance (Psalm 32:5-7).

Notice that when David "kept silent" his bones wasted away and his strength was "sapped" as in the heat of summer. But, we will see that there were four specific benefits to when David "acknowledged" his sin and "did not cover up" his iniquity and "confessed" his transgressions to the Lord. They are:

1. Forgiveness (v.5). God "forgave the guilt of my sin." Before David "confessed his sin" God did not forgive him; indeed God's hand was "heavy upon him."

Questions

2. Discovering God (v.6). "Let everyone who is godly pray to you while you may be found." This verse teaches that the only way to "find God" is through forgiveness of sins. And forgiveness of sins only comes through acknowledgment and confession of sin.

3. Spiritual Strength (v.6). ". . . surely when the mighty waters rise, they will not reach him." You know what this is like: At times, sin comes rushing in like a flood. It overwhelms us and we sink. But notice that confession of sin is immediately followed by this promise of victory. In owning up to our sins we will find that God will protect us from being overcome by the floods of sin.

4. Spiritual Protection (v.7). "You are my hiding place; you will protect me from trouble and surround me with songs of deliverance."

So, to summarize: hiding our sins (we actually cannot hide them from God, He knows) and refusing to confess them brings about spiritual sickness, loss of strength against further sin attacks, and the anger of God. Confession of sin brings forgiveness, knowing God, spiritual strength and protection.

Friend, even though this may be difficult, it is important that you make a full confession and disclosure of your sins. This must first be to God, as all sins are against God. But it also must be to the person, or people against whom you have sinned. If you are hiding your bondage from a spouse, then this is deception, it is a sin. This needs to be confessed before you can expect real and lasting victory. However, while confessing it to God must be total, complete and immediate, confessing it to others requires wisdom and discernment as to timing and detail. If you are now contemplating making a confession to someone, you might be apprehensive. Most times confession is not an easy thing to do.

If you have felt the consequences of hiding sin, and now see the value of fully confessing, but are just a bit scared and need to talk to someone, please feel free to ask your accountability partner for help. We want your victory in the Lord, and we pray for it. Confession is a necessary part of that victory. Don't put it off. Next, we will look at how confession brings strength and victory.

Please read 1 Samuel 7:2-11 below to discover how the Israelites were victorious over their enemies. They employed several of the teachings that we have been studying through this course in the past few days.

> ²It was a long time, twenty years in all, that the ark remained at Kiriath Jearim, and all the people of Israel mourned and sought after the LORD. ³And Samuel said to the whole house of Israel, "If you are returning to the LORD with all your hearts, then rid yourselves of the foreign gods and the Ashtoreths and commit yourselves to the LORD and serve him only, and he will deliver you out of the hand of the Philistines." ⁴So the Israelites put away their Baals and Ashtoreths, and served the LORD only.

> ⁵Then Samuel said, "Assemble all Israel at Mizpah and I will intercede with the LORD for you." ⁶When they had assembled at Mizpah, they drew water and poured it out before the LORD. On that day they fasted and there they confessed, "We have sinned against the LORD." And Samuel was leader of Israel at Mizpah.

> ⁷When the Philistines heard that Israel had assembled at Mizpah, the rulers of the Philistines came up to attack them. And when the Israelites heard of it, they were afraid because of the Philistines. ⁸They said to Samuel, "Do not stop crying out to the LORD our God for us, that he may rescue us from the hand of the Philistines." ⁹Then Samuel took a suckling lamb and offered it up as a whole burnt offering to the LORD. He cried out to the LORD on Israel's behalf, and the LORD answered him.

> ¹⁰While Samuel was sacrificing the burnt offering, the Philistines drew near to engage Israel in battle. But that day the LORD thundered with loud thunder against the Philistines and threw them into such a panic that they were routed before the Israelites. ¹¹The men of Israel rushed out of Mizpah and pursued the Philistines, slaughtering them along the way to a point below Beth Car (1 Samuel 7:2-11).

Question 3. Can you find and name the ways the Israelites were victorious over their enemies? Write your findings in the space below.

Question 4. Write out what the Israelites said in verse 6 above:

Questions

Notice how "radical amputation" in verses 3 and 4 is followed by "confession" in verses 5 and 6, and "victory" in verse 11. Now, let us note the steps to victory. Write them next to each verse.

Question 5. 1 Samuel 7:2: First step:

Question 6. 1 Samuel 7:3, 4: Second step:

Question 7. 1 Samuel 7:5: Third step:

Question 8. 1 Samuel 7:6: Fourth step:

Question 9. Friend, where are you in the above scenario? Have you radically amputated? Or are you rationalizing and excusing? Have you made all necessary confessions (or at least planning to as the Lord opens doors for you)? If you have done these things, please share the victories the Lord is giving you.

> **Course Member Teresa writes,** "I confessed my sin to Christ and asked for forgiveness. I confessed my sin to my family (husband, daughter and son-in-law) and asked for forgiveness. I then did the same thing with my pastor and also asked for help. I did the same with my daughter's mother and father-in-law. Sunday, I confessed my sin to my church family and asked for their forgiveness. Then I did the same with my sister-in-law and brother-in-law with whom we are close.
>
> The victories are almost too many to list. I once again have peace and joy. I feel that even at the age of 46, I am completely new. My husband and I have been tremendously blessed with the love, forgiveness and support of all those to whom I have made confession. Their acts of service and love to us continue as I am recuperating from a fall down the stairs. I see things so much more clearly now. I honestly believe that my fall down the stairs was for my good. I was told by my doctor that I could have died that night. But I understand that Christ loved me so much, he didn't want me to die in the sinful state I was in. It has been interesting to hear of how the confession of my sin has impacted our church body. Not only has it been for my personal good, but apparently for the good of those who know us. Just as my sin was far-reaching, Christ's forgiveness and restoration have been also. The only term that comes to my mind is that I have been "blown away" by God's goodness and mercy along with the love and forgiveness of our family and church body.
>
> I realize, though, that I have a long way to go. The struggles and temptations will come. But because of exposing my sin and struggles, I know that I will receive much help from the body of Christ."

Finally, note this very well-worded and impassioned commitment to confession:

"I have been reflecting on God's wonderful grace and the sin from which He has so lovingly delivered me. I had tried so many times to stop myself from my sin, I had thought that I had failed too many times and that God had given me up to my lusts.

"If we confess our sins, he is faithful and just to forgive us our sins, and to cleanse us from all unrighteousness" (1 John 1:9). I thought and hoped—desperately hoped—that I would never have to confess this sin, except to God Himself. But that is pride. I was not broken enough, not contrite enough, not desirous of Him enough to confess my sin to others. And it defeated me. My unwillingness to do everything, to completely submit, undid me.

"I now want God and His Forgiveness, His Love, His Grace and His Mercy more than anything else. I know now that I can't hide. I need Him. I am willing to do anything and everything to secure my portion of Him. I will risk all and forsake all that I previously held too dear to endanger by my confession.

"God gave Himself for me. I am nothing, but I willingly give myself to Him. Not in return for what He did, because that would be futile and ridiculous. I can't ever repay or compensate Him. Just because He Loves me and paid the price for me, I am His without reservation or condition."

Editors Note: Friends, words are not enough, for "the kingdom of God is not a matter of talk but of power" (for action): 1 Corinthians 4:20. Unfortunately, the man who wrote that beautifully articulated letter above, failed to confess his sin to his wife as he knew he should, and has now returned to the slavery of sin "as a dog returns to its vomit" (2 Peter 2:22). Please pray that God would genuinely recover him and grant him true repentance.

Many of us hide our drunkenness from our families and friends. We lie to our bosses at work and cover up the fact that we are intoxicated or suffering from a hangover when we go in to work. There may be some in the ministry that hide their drinking from the church or their pastors. Many of us also deceive ourselves that we are okay and that we just need to 'slow down.' Whatever the case, stating "I have this hidden sin in my life" is very important. We are not seeking to hurt, but to heal and cast off that weight of deception that has burdened us. It is also important to note that while our spouses or others may know that we are involved in drunkenness, there may be hurt that we have caused or inflicted on them that we need to ask for forgiveness. This confession and admission of wrong may be the first step in healing.

Besides that, dear friends, although we have confessed to ignorance, in many sins we did not know a great deal. Come; let me quicken your memories. There were times when you knew that such an action was wrong, when you started back from it. You looked at the gain it would bring you, and you sold your soul for that price and deliberately did what you were well aware was wrong. Are there not some here, saved by Christ, who must confess that, at times, they did violence to their conscience? They quenched the light of heaven, and drove the Spirit away from them, distinctly knowing what they were doing.

"Let us bow before God in the silence of our hearts and own to all of this. We hear the Master say, Father; forgive them; for they know not what they do. Let us add our own tears as we say, And forgive us, also, because in some things we did know;" (**Charles Spurgeon**, *Jesus, The Pleading Savior*).

Scripture to Consider

When anyone is guilty in any of these ways, he must confess in what way he has sinned (Leviticus 5:5).

Did you feast on God's Word in the last 24 hours?

      Yes   No

If so, how did you feast? In other words, circle the ways you enjoyed God today. Reading? Prayer? Worship? Fellowship? Witnessing?

Were you free from drug and alcohol abuse since you did the last lesson?

      Yes   No

Did you spend personal time with the Lord since you did the last lesson?

      Yes   No

If you answered "no" to any of the above questions, describe what led to your fall.

If you answered "yes" to the above questions, you may use this area for additional comments.

DAY 9 – HAPPY ARE THE HELPLESS

Now when he saw the crowds, he went up on a mountainside and sat down. His disciples came to him, and he began to teach them, saying: "Blessed are the poor in spirit, for theirs is the kingdom of heaven. Blessed are those who mourn, for they will be comforted" (Matthew 5:1-4).

When Christ began this Sermon on the Mount, He began at the narrow gate of the basic need of man before God. Man needs what only God can give him—life. Without God, man is hopelessly lost and eternally condemned.

I have been amazed at the published material (sometimes Christian) caressing the pride of man today. Such things like, *"Choosing Your Own Greatness"*; or *"You're Nature's Greatest Miracle";* or *"You've Got What It Takes";* or *"Unlocking Your Potential."* All these are misdiagnoses!

You've heard it said, "God helps those who help themselves." This is not true. According to Scripture, God helps the helpless!

We are studying an important subject today that will help us overcome drunkenness and substance abuse. Blessed are the poor in spirit. Or, happy are the helpless!

So, let us seek to understand what "Poor in Spirit" is. Here are some definitions:

*   Bankrupt in Self

*   Self-worth is nothing without God

*   All I am, have, and do is worthless without God

*   I understand my total inability before God.

This word "poor" has to do with "one who crouches or cowers," and refers to one who is beggarly. Let's see an example:

Jesus sat down opposite the place where the offerings were put and watched the crowd putting their money into the temple treasury. Many rich people threw in large amounts. But a poor widow came and put in two very small copper coins, worth only a fraction of a penny (Mark 12:41-42).

The above example is actually an illustration of what poverty is NOT. This widow was poor, not a beggar.

Questions

Question 1. Have you approached God as a beggar? Or have you come like this widow, with something to give?

The following truths will help us see the importance of coming to God spiritually bankrupt.

*   This spiritual poverty is in reality the foundation of all graces. God gives grace to the humble, not to the proud. The humble, or those who recognize their own impoverished condition, are given grace.

*   Emptiness Precedes Fullness. We cannot receive from God until we have empty hands. He who recognizes he has nothing to offer God will receive everything from God.

Questions

*   Self must be done away with for Christ to be wanted. If we are setting out in life to honor ourselves, Christ will be far from us. But he who honors God will himself be honored.

*   A starving heart will give all to have the Bread of Life. It is only the hungry who sense their need of Jesus, not the full.

Question 2. Can you see the benefits of being poor in spirit? From the above thoughts, please list the blessings that come to a spiritually poor person:

Friend, in order to overcome life-dominating sins, such as drunkenness, one must be poor in spirit. Overcoming the abuse of prescription medications takes the presence of God and the power of God, and these are only given to the destitute ones, the broken and empty ones, and the poor in spirit. God blesses those who are poor in spirit.

Notice four ways in which He blesses the poor in spirit:

1. God is near to the poor in spirit: "The LORD is close to the broken-hearted and saves those who are crushed in spirit" (Psalm 34:18).

2. God will not despise the poor in spirit: "The sacrifices of God are a broken spirit; a broken and contrite heart, O God, you will not despise" (Psalm 51:17).

3. God dwells with the poor in spirit: "For this is what the high and lofty One says- he who lives forever, whose name is holy: 'I live in a high and holy place, but also with him who is contrite and lowly in spirit, to revive the spirit of the lowly and to revive the heart of the contrite'" (Isaiah 57:15).

4. God esteems the poor in spirit: "This is the one I esteem: he who is humble and contrite in spirit, and trembles at my word" (Isaiah 66:2).

Take a moment and write out all the blessings the poor in spirit receive, from the above four items. As you are writing these, ask God to work poverty of spirit deep within you, that He might bless you in these ways.

Question 3. Number 1 blessing to the poor in spirit:

Question 4. Number 2 blessing to the poor in spirit:

Question 5. Number 3 blessing to the poor in spirit:

Question 6. Number 4 blessing to the poor in spirit:

Please read the following quote:

"A castle that has been long besieged and is ready to be taken will deliver up on any terms to save their lives. He whose heart has been a garrison for the devil and has held out long in opposition against Christ, when once God has brought him to poverty of spirit and he sees himself damned without Christ, let God propound what articles He may, he will readily subscribe to them. 'Lord, what will you have me to do?'" (**Thomas Watson**).

Question 7. Please write your thoughts on the above quote from Thomas Watson:

Note: Watson connected the attitude "Lord, what will you have me to do?" with one who is poor in spirit. We have also noticed that those who come to the **New Wine** course in humility, wanting to learn, asking questions for the purpose of implementing the answers, will always get free from bondage. But those who think they have something to give and contribute, who come in to this course teaching and instructing, will usually fall often. It is the "poor in spirit" who are blessed with freedom from habitual sin.

Next, please read the following passage, paying particular attention to which of the praying men received the blessing from God:

> To some who were confident of their own righteousness and looked down on everybody else, Jesus told this parable: Two men went up to the temple to pray, one a Pharisee and the other a tax collector. The Pharisee stood up and prayed about himself: "God, I thank you that I am not like other men—robbers, evildoers, adulterers—or even like this tax collector. I fast twice a week and give a tenth of all I get."
>
> But the tax collector stood at a distance. He would not even look up to heaven, but beat his breast and said, "God, have mercy on me, a sinner."
>
> I tell you that this man, rather than the other, went home justified before God. For everyone who exalts himself will be humbled, and he who humbles himself will be exalted (Luke 18:9-14).

Question 8. It is obvious that the tax collector was the one who was poor in spirit. Please write out the evidences of his poverty of spirit. What things did he do and say that show us he was spiritually impoverished?

Question 9. From Luke 18:9-14 above, what blessing did the man who was poor in spirit receive?

Questions

Next, let us notice additional rewards and blessings of those who are poor in spirit.

1. God thinks on and delivers the poor in spirit: "Yet I am poor and needy; may the Lord think of me. You are my help and my deliverer; O my God, do not delay" (Psalm 40:17).

2. God hears and does not despise the poor in spirit: "The LORD hears the needy and does not despise his captive people" (Psalm 69:33).

3. God spares and saves the poor in spirit: "He will take pity on the weak and the needy and save the needy from death" (Psalm 72:13).

4. God gives success to the poor in spirit: "But he lifted the needy out of their affliction and increased their families like flocks" (Psalm 107:41).

Again we find that the poor in spirit are blessed. Please write down the four ways that God blesses them from the four verses above. Also, record any thoughts you have while thinking through these verses:

Question 10. Number 1 blessing to the poor in spirit:

Question 11. Number 2 blessing to the poor in spirit:

Question 12. Number 3 blessing to the poor in spirit:

Question 13. Number 4 blessing to the poor in spirit:

Question 14. Psalm 107:41 from above says, "But He lifts the needy out of their affliction…" Please describe how this verse shows that the poor in spirit will be rescued from drunkenness, etc.

> **Course Member Teresa writes,** "As I have begun to cry out to Christ for forgiveness and asked Him to soften my heart, He has shown me that I had turned to alcohol to meet my needs instead of Him. He has now filled my heart with a new love for Him and a desire to serve Him. He has shown me the extent of damage and hurt my sin has caused. Because of His Spirit, I am enabled to turn from my idol and turn to Christ. This will be a process, but I have much hope because I am not alone, Christ is with me."

Friend, I have shared with you all throughout this course that it was not until I became poor in spirit that I received the blessing of God in being lifted out of my affliction. I came before God with nothing, broken and helpless. He responded by picking me up and dusting me off. He set me free from that which I could not escape. But it had to come in His timing and in His way. All the times I tried to break free by myself, I was saying, "I can do this, I am strong enough." Only when I came before God completely helpless and with nothing at all to give did He pick me up and break the chains! Have you come to **New Wine** as a helpless and poor sinner? If you have, then I have news of great joy for you: God helps those who are helpless!

Finally, please note the evidences and applications of the Poor in Spirit, and take the time to look up the Scripture references sometime.

Poverty of spirit brings about a:

- Weaning from self (Galatians 2:20; Philippians 1:21)

- Delighting in God's glory (2 Corinthians 3:18)

- Seeking God's fingerprints (Romans 8:17, 18, 28)

- Seeing the best in others and the worst in yourself (Matthew 7:3)

- Praying like a beggar and praising like a son (Luke 18:9-14)

- Serving like a slave (James 1:1, 2 Peter 1:1)

Questions

Question 15. Can you see any or all of the above evidences of spiritual poverty in your life? If so, which ones?

Course Member Teresa writes, "It makes so much sense. As I have been stripped clean these past several weeks, there has been an eagerness in my heart to obey Christ and learn. I feel like a child sitting at the feet of my father. I find myself quieter in Bible studies, more receptive to listening. I am more eager for instruction and for fellowship with believers. I am experiencing peace. The things that seemed so important that I became frazzled, although they are important, don't command so much of my attention."

Scripture to Consider

Guard your steps when you go to the house of God. Go near to listen rather than to offer the sacrifice of fools, who do not know that they do wrong. Do not be quick with your mouth; do not be hasty in your heart to utter anything before God. God is in heaven and you are on earth, so let your words be few (Ecclesiastes 5:1, 2).

Did you feast on God's Word in the last 24 hours?

      Yes   No

If so, how did you feast? In other words, circle the ways you enjoyed God today. Reading? Prayer? Worship? Fellowship? Witnessing?

Were you free from drug and alcohol abuse since you did the last lesson?

      Yes   No

Did you spend personal time with the Lord since you did the last lesson?

      Yes   No

If you answered "no" to any of the above questions, describe what led to your fall.

If you answered "yes" to the above questions, you may use this area for additional comments.

DAY 10 - TURNING

Today we are going to discuss the subject of repentance, and see from Scripture exactly what repentance is.

> [4]For we know, brothers loved by God, that he has chosen you, [5]because our gospel came to you not simply with words, but also with power, with the Holy Spirit and with deep conviction. You know how we lived among you for your sake. [6]You became imitators of us and of the Lord; in spite of severe suffering, you welcomed the message with the joy given by the Holy Spirit. [7]And so you became a model to all the believers in Macedonia and Achaia. [8]The Lord's message rang out from you not only in Macedonia and Achaia, your faith in God has become known everywhere. Therefore we do not need to say anything about it, [9]for they themselves report what kind of reception you gave us. They tell how you turned to God from idols to serve the living and true God, [10]and to wait for his Son from heaven, whom he raised from the dead—Jesus, who rescues us from the coming wrath (1 Thessalonians 1:5-10).

Please answer the following questions as we think through this most important issue of repentance together.

> For, He that would love life, And see good days, Let him refrain his tongue from evil, And his lips that they speak no guile: and let him turn away from evil, and do good; let him seek peace, and pursue it (1 Peter 3:10 - 11).

Question 4. How does the above verse define repentance? What are the aspects of true repentance, as shown from this verse?

Questions

Question 1. According to verse 5, in what manner did the gospel come to the Thessalonians?

Question 2. According to verses 8 and 9, what things were being reported about these Thessalonian believers?

Friend, here is true repentance summarized: "They tell how you turned to God from idols to serve the living and true God." Repentance has often been described as "doing a 180" meaning we turn away from sin and turn to God. This is the very reason that psychology and humanistic programs fall short of truly assisting people who are trapped in sin. They attempt to get the person to turn away from sin, but cannot instruct them to turn to God, so they are in essence instructing us to do a 90-degree turn. This half-turning is never sufficient to truly eradicate sin from our lives. True repentance is not only turning from sin, it is turning to God and serving Him.

Question 3. Write the words from verse 9 that define true repentance:

I was involved in drunkenness and use of cocaine for many years, but when God granted me genuine repentance I turned away completely and have not ever returned. I'm not saying that I didn't want to stop before, but I hadn't learned how to walk away from the sin, and my motive was not God's glory.

We can see from Scripture that genuine repentance is a complete turnaround from our previous course. For me, that meant totally turning away from the sin of drunkenness using cocaine, and turning to God. The turn must be complete! We must put our backs to the sin and walk away from it, never to return again. And we must face Christ and walk towards Him. No half-hearted turning will free us from the power of sin; no partial turning will enable us to escape the trap of the devil.

Oh, the pain in my heart during those long years where I was not truly turning away from the substances. I was like Lot's wife, who did indeed leave the burning city, but longed for it in her heart and turned back just to have a look. Her turning away from the sin of that city was not complete, and she perished in her sin, turning to a pillar of salt. We should remember Lot's wife, for she is a monument to all who will not fully turn away from sin. God has now granted me the repentance that makes me hate my previous way of life and therefore turn completely away from it.

This is my hope and prayer for you too, Friend. That God would enable you to truly turn away from sin for good, and to begin to walk away from it as fast as you can, and to get as far away from it as possible.

Questions

Now, here is another excellent passage that describes the attitude of genuine repentance:

> Come near to God and he will come near to you. Wash your hands, you sinners, and purify your hearts, you double-minded. Grieve, mourn and wail. Change your laughter to mourning and your joy to gloom. Humble yourselves before the Lord, and he will lift you up (James 4:8-10).

Here is how we can tell when God is granting somebody repentance. They not only make a 180-degree turn around, but they also lose their silliness, their hollow laughter, their joking, and their pride. They become earnest in being rid of their sin.

They feel sorrow over their sins and even become somewhat gloomy, as the above verses mention. This does not mean that they live like this the rest of their lives, because joy comes into the life that is committed to purity. But there is a time where all the levity is gone, and there comes a need to be done with sin for good.

I remember the gloom of looking back on my life of drunkenness and drug use. I had done so many horrible things and hurt so many people. How could God ever forgive me for being so awful? As I looked into the mirror and was granted true repentance for my sin, I saw myself from God's point of view and I realized that the real sin was against Him. I hung my head in shame and could only say, "I am so sorry, Lord, please forgive me." He did forgive me and He gave me the joy of having all of that weight removed as He began to restore my life—to rebuild what I had torn down. But this only followed sorrow, and that was His gift to me, in His grace!

Question 5. Please read the following quote and give your comments below:

> "Conviction of sin is one of the rarest things that ever strikes a man. It is the threshold of an understanding of God. Jesus Christ said that when the Holy Spirit came He would convict of sin, and when the Holy Spirit rouses a man's conscience and brings him into the presence of God, it is not his relationship with men that bothers him, but his relationship with God, ". . . against Thee, Thee only, have I sinned, and done this evil in Thy sight" (Psalm 51:4). Conviction of sin, the marvel of forgiveness, and holiness are so interwoven that it is only the forgiven man who is the holy man, he proves he is forgiven by being the opposite to what he was, by Gods grace. Repentance always brings a man to this point: I have sinned. The surest sign that God is at work is when a man says that and means it. Anything less than this is remorse for having made blunders, the reflex action of disgust at himself.

> "The entrance into the Kingdom is through the panging pains of repentance crashing into a man's respectable goodness; then the Holy Ghost, Who produces these agonies, begins the formation of the Son of God in the life. The new life will manifest itself in conscious repentance and unconscious holiness, never the other way about. The bedrock of Christianity is repentance. Strictly speaking, a man cannot repent when he chooses; repentance is a gift of God. The old Puritans used to pray for the gift of tears. If ever you cease to know the virtue of repentance, you are in darkness. Examine yourself and see if you have forgotten how to be sorry" (**Oswald Chambers**, *My Utmost For His Highest*, December 7th Devotional).

What is repentance? It is sorrow for what we have done against a holy God and turning around, doing a 180, if you will, in the other direction. It is knowing inside that what we have done is wrong and wanting to get it right! It is truth . . . given by God in His grace.

This passage made quite an impact on me:

> And a servant of the Lord must not quarrel but be gentle to all, able to teach, patient, in humility correcting those who are in opposition, if God will perhaps grant them repentance, so that they may know the truth, and that they may come to their senses and escape the devil, having been taken captive by him to do his will (2 Timothy 2:24-26).

I begged God over and over and over to take away my sin of using cocaine and alcohol, but He waited. Why did He wait? He waited so that I might know the truth. Do you think if I did not completely fail in MY attempts to stop that I would not have somehow taken at least some of the credit? The truth is that I was a puppet on Satan's string doing his will just like the above verse says . . . ONLY by the grace of God am I free, and ONLY after HE granted me repentance like the above verse says. The freedom that He gives—SAVING me from the sin of drunkenness and drug use—means I never want to return to the pit I was in and by His grace I will not.

Why would God wait to grant us repentance? I think part of the answer can also be found in the above passage: "so that they may know the truth, and that they may come to their senses and escape."

Question 6. Are you escaping the trap? If so, can you see how God has granted you repentance? Explain a little about this repentance. Do you have it? If so, are you enjoying it? If not, will you seek God for it?

Questions

> **Jackie wrote,** "I am escaping the trap. God has granted me repentance. I have completely turned from Vicodin and turned to God. God has taken my desire for the Vicodin away, too. I am enjoying repentance. My goal is to learn something new about God each day and find a way or ways to apply it to my life."

> **Carol wrote,** "By Gods grace, I am escaping the trap. God has granted me repentance. I know the truth now and I have come to my senses, I do not want to be a captive of the devil, nor do I want to do his will. I want to do God's will. Repentance is a hard discipline, but I'm learning valuable insights. Seek God First. That is the most important thing that I have learned. I can't put Him on a shelf and take Him down when I want to. He has to be the center of my life every day, all the time."

Next, let us examine one final passage of Scripture and note the elements of repentance contained in it:

> Seek the LORD while he may be found;
> call on him while he is near.
> Let the wicked forsake his way
> and the evil man his thoughts.
> Let him turn to the LORD, and he will have mercy
> on him, and to our God, for he will freely pardon
> (Isaiah 55:6-7).

Question 7. Please list the four defining elements of repentance as stated in the verses above. The first one is "Seek the Lord".

Question 8. Please make an honest assessment of your life right now. Are you seeking the Lord, calling on Him, forsaking your sin, and turning to the Lord?

Friend, there is much good news to be found in repentance. It is not as if we were merely turning away from sin only to be left empty and with no excitement in life. You see, as you turn from substance abuse and turn to God there is a blessed life of satisfaction and joy to be found in Jesus Christ. In reality, we are leaving the lesser and temporary pleasures for the greater and eternal ones. Yes, we are giving up the pleasures of sin, but we are gaining the pleasures of Christ, and Psalm 16:11 describes the pleasures of Christ as "eternal."

Scripture to Consider

Or do you show contempt for the riches of his kindness, tolerance and patience, not realizing that God's kindness leads you toward repentance? (Romans 2:4).

Seek the LORD while he may be found;
call on him while he is near.
Let the wicked forsake his way
and the evil man his thoughts.

Let him turn to the LORD, and he will have mercy on him,
and to our God, for he will freely pardon (Isaiah 55:6-7).

Did you feast on God's Word in the last 24 hours?

     Yes   No

If so, how did you feast? In other words, circle the ways you enjoyed God today. Reading? Prayer? Worship? Fellowship? Witnessing?

Were you free from drug and alcohol abuse since you did the last lesson?

     Yes   No

Did you spend personal time with the Lord since you did the last lesson?

     Yes   No

If you answered "no" to any of the above questions, describe what led to your fall.

If you answered "yes" to the above questions, you may use this area for additional comments.

DAY 11 - NEW DIRECTION

Friend, please begin this lesson by reading the following Scripture and provide your thoughts and insight:

> [8]Even if I caused you sorrow by my letter, I do not regret it. Though I did regret it I see that my letter hurt you, but only for a little while [9]yet now I am happy, not because you were made sorry, but because your sorrow led you to repentance. For you became sorrowful as God intended and so were not harmed in any way by us. [10]Godly sorrow brings repentance that leads to salvation and leaves no regret, but worldly sorrow brings death. [11]See what this godly sorrow has produced in you: what earnestness, what eagerness to clear yourselves, what indignation, what alarm, what longing, what concern, what readiness to see justice done. At every point you have proved yourselves to be innocent in this matter. [12]So even though I wrote to you, it was not on account of the one who did the wrong or of the injured party, but rather that before God you could see for yourselves how devoted to us you are. [13]By all this we are encouraged (2 Corinthians 7:8-13).

Questions

There came a time when I was granted godly sorrow and I remember weeping over that. It felt as if my whole life had been a lie and a waste. Worst of all, I felt that I had hurt God because of my sin and my hard heart. I cried out in anguish to Him and begged Him to forgive me. This sorrow began working within me a resolve to never return to alcohol and cocaine again, and to this day I have not. Godly sorrow brings about repentance, and so this sorrow is our friend. Pray for it; seek after it.

Question 4. What does worldly sorrow bring about?

Questions

Question 1. From verse 11, write out the seven ways that godly sorrow showed itself in the life of the Corinthians.

1.

2.

3.

4.

5.

6.

7.

Question 2. Go through this portion of Scripture and count the number of times Paul uses the words "sorry," "sorrow" or "sorrowful."

Question 3. According to verses 9 and 10, what does godly sorrow over sin bring about?

Question 5. Godly sorrow is the mourning one goes through when he has grieved the Holy Spirit of God with sin. When you are only sorry about your sin because you got caught or because of its consequences, what kind of sorrow would you call it?

Note: We can see from this study on repentance that godly sorrow leads to and is a part of repentance that leads to life, whereas worldly sorrow leads to death.

Question 6. Honestly assess your heart right now. Ask the Holy Spirit to illuminate your understanding to know whether you have been granted godly sorrow and genuine repentance unto life, or if you only have worldly sorrow. What are your thoughts?

Note this well: True sorrowing over sin brings about real repentance. So, this being true, we need to pray for sorrow in our hearts that it might lead us to repentance.

Now we have seen that part of repentance is experiencing a godly sorrow over sins committed against God.

Questions

Question 7. How do the following verses define repentance?

> [14]And it will be said: "Build up, build up, prepare the road! Remove the obstacles out of the way of my people." [15]For this is what the high and lofty One says - he who lives forever, whose name is holy: "I live in a high and holy place, but also with him who is contrite and lowly in spirit, to revive the spirit of the lowly and to revive the heart of the contrite." (Isaiah 57:14-15).

Friend, my habitual drugged state hardened my heart and puffed me up with pride. Sin, pride and hardness of heart always go together (Hebrews 3:13). Genuine repentance brings with it lowliness and contriteness. I remember approaching the Bible and church with a quiet, humble attitude. I had always been so confident in my knowledge of life and my ability to overcome anything. I realized that I did not know nearly as much as I thought. My pride was gone. I began to learn and to grow by experiencing God through His Word—nothing will humble us more than that!

We can recognize this humility in people as they begin to ask questions, and ask for help, instead of presenting all their biblical knowledge and their viewpoints on everything. They become humble and teachable, lowly and contrite.

This repentance is the key to lasting victory over sin. Anything short of true repentance will leave one wanting to return to the sin. This is why real repentance is a must, and only God can grant repentance. So, please seek the Lord and ask Him for the gift of repentance, and then repent with horror and disgust at past sins.

Friend, the teaching of both yesterday and today define what true repentance is. It is a turning completely away from sin, doing an about-face, and then pursuing God with a reckless abandon. And it is also sorrowing over sin to such an extent that the heart begins to hate the sin and turn from it in disgust.

This is repentance, and if either of these elements are missing the "freedom" from sin will not be lasting. If one merely feels sorrow over the sin but does not turn from it then he is not free. Or if one merely turns from the sin but does not develop a heart-sorrow over it he is not free either. Freedom comes when both of these are present.

Question 8. Are both of these qualities of repentance becoming evident in your life? Are you turning away from sin toward God, and are you sorrowing in your heart over sin?

Course member Teresa writes, "Yes, I believe that I am doing both. Memories of how I have sinned against Christ and hurt others with my drunkenness bring me to tears. The Lord is beginning to open my eyes to other areas that (because of my hardness of heart) I was deceived about. My sin and hardness affected most areas, even things I would consider small. He has given me the realization of how deceived I was."

Next, notice how repentance works itself out in worship. These next few verses show what true worship looks like, and admonishes us to conform:

> Guard your steps when you go to the house of God. Go near to listen, rather than to offer the sacrifice of fools, who do not know that they do wrong. Do not be quick with your mouth, do not be hasty in your heart to utter anything before God. God is in heaven, and you are on earth, so let your words be few. Much dreaming and many words are meaningless. Therefore stand in awe of God! (Ecclesiastes 5:1-2, 7).

This passage of Scripture shows that worship of God from a repentant soul brings a quietness and an awe of God. I think back on my years in drunken bondage and they were loud years, with much talking and teaching and making myself out to be somebody. All my many words were evidence that I was not in awe of God, but was instead taken with myself. But when God brought me low, and caused my heart to fear Him, I immediately shut up, and began being in awe of God. He was in heaven and I was on earth. I finally saw Him for Who He was and myself for the loud-mouthed, irreverent man that I was.

Please note: I don't believe Scripture here is saying that just because we are in awe of God that we cannot talk. Some people are naturally more talkative than others, and do not necessarily sin when they do so.

What these verses refer to is the loud and obnoxious man who feels that what he has to say is most important. He is one who does not revere the Lord.

True repentance evidences itself in the worship of God. It shows us the Majestic Deity of God, His holiness and power, grace and love, and His awesome character. We begin to develop awe for Him and we listen more than talk.

Question 9. What is your life currently like in relationship to this truth? Are you discovering awe of God and becoming quiet before Him?

Questions

Please notice the definition of repentance from this verse: Therefore say to the house of Israel, "This is what the Sovereign Lord says: 'Repent! Turn from your idols and renounce all your detestable practices'" (Ezekiel 14:6). This can apply to us who have been involved with drunkenness or drug addictions. Substances have become an "idol" and we are to turn away from it as a "detestable practice" and we are to renounce it.

Question 10. Finally, please use this space to record how you are doing now. What are your struggles, victories, feelings, etc?

Course Member Teresa writes, "I'm anxious today because it will be the first time I will be alone overnight since my fall. Whenever my husband would go out of town I would view it as an opportunity to drink. Even when I would make a vow not to drink, I usually broke the vow. I have put many 'safety checks' into place for the night. I do not think 'I'm okay now, I can handle it, or I'm strong now, or this is not a problem anymore.' That is foolish. I am praying that through the strength given by Christ, the sorrow I've had over my sin, and the accountability I've asked that the Lord will enable me to be here alone tonight and wake up victorious in the morning. I am planning on meditating on 1 Corinthians 10:12: 'Therefore let him who thinks he stands take heed lest he fall. . . .'"

Scripture to Consider

If at any time I announce that a nation or kingdom is to be uprooted, torn down and destroyed, and if that nation I warned repents of its evil, then I will relent and not inflict on it the disaster I had planned (Jeremiah 18:7-8).

I tell you that in the same way there will be more rejoicing in heaven over one sinner who repents than over ninety-nine righteous persons who do not need to repent (Luke 15:7).

[46]When they sin against you—for there is no one who does not sin—and you become angry with them and give them over to the enemy, who takes them captive to his own land, far away or near; [47]and if they have a change of heart in the land where they are held captive, and repent and plead with you in the land of their conquerors and say, "We have sinned, we have done wrong, we have acted wickedly;" [48]and if they turn back to you with all their heart and soul in the land of their enemies who took them captive, and pray to you toward the land you gave their fathers, toward the city you have chosen and the temple I have built for your Name; [49]then from heaven, your dwelling place, hear their prayer and their plea, and uphold their cause. [50]And forgive your people, who have sinned against you; forgive all the offenses they have committed against you, and cause their conquerors to show them mercy; [51]for they are your people and your inheritance, whom you brought out of Egypt, out of that iron-smelting furnace (1 Kings 8:46-51).

Did you feast on God's Word in the last 24 hours?

       Yes   No

If so, how did you feast? In other words, circle the ways you enjoyed God today. Reading? Prayer? Worship? Fellowship? Witnessing?

Were you free from drug and alcohol abuse since you did the last lesson?

       Yes   No

Did you spend personal time with the Lord since you did the last lesson?

       Yes   No

If you answered "no" to any of the above questions, describe what led to your fall.

If you answered "yes" to the above questions, you may use this area for additional comments.

DAY 12 - ACCOUNTABILITY

There is an aspect to overcoming drunkenness, or any sin, that is extremely important: one alone may be overcome; two can be victorious.

Read and observe the following passage from Ecclesiastes 4:

> ⁹Two are better than one, because they have a good return for their work: ¹⁰If one falls down, his friend can help him up. But pity the man who falls and has no one to help him up! ¹¹Also, if two lie down together, they will keep warm. But how can one keep warm alone? ¹²Though one may be overpowered, two can defend themselves. A cord of three strands is not quickly broken (Ecclesiastes 4:9-12).

Today we will see the value and necessity of finding and maintaining an accountability partner.

Questions

Question 1. According to verse 9 above, why are two better than one?

A study was done with horses to determine the true value of team effort. The study revealed that one horse pulling alone was able to pull 2,500 pounds. The test was then repeated with two horses pulling together; the two horses were able to pull 12,500 pounds! The two horses together were able to pull 5 times the amount of weight that the one horse alone could pull!

Ecclesiastes 4:9 is about spiritual fruit. Teamwork is critical in overcoming any type of substance abuse. As I have told you, I was in bondage to alcohol and cocaine for several years, all of which I was living as a Christian. I even had an accountability partner during a very dark period of sin in my life. I deceived him the entire time. I remember so well how I went to his house one Sunday afternoon and poured out my whole life to him in a flood of tears and grief. I am not sure what I expected, but the response that he gave was simply, "I love you, my friend." There was such freedom in this! I continue to maintain an accountability relationship with him as well as with my wife and my pastor. I can always count on them to pick me up or strengthen me in times of need, plus I know that I must answer their questions honestly. The importance of this principle cannot be overstated!

"Two are better than one, and happier jointly than either of them could be separately, more pleased in one another than they could be in themselves only, mutually serviceable to each other's welfare, and by a united strength more likely to do good to others." (**Matthew Henry**)

Have you ever read Pilgrim's Progress? It is a wonderful allegory of the Christian life. In the 9th scene a man by the name of "Hope" finds himself desiring to take a nap in the land of Enchantment. But Christian reminds him of 1 Thessalonians 5:6 that says, "let us not sleep, as do others; but let us watch and be sober." Hope, being reminded of the truth of Scripture, becomes very thankful for Christian. He says these words: "I acknowledge that I was wrong; and if I would have been here alone, by my sleeping I would have been in danger of death. I see it is true what that wise man said, 'Two are better than one.' Therefore you being here has been a mercy to me; and you will have a good reward for your labor."

Questions

Friend, an accountability partner should, by love of the Scriptures and care for your soul, be able to detect when you are about to "sleep" in the "land of enchantment," which, in our case, may be prescription meds, alcohol or pot. "Hope" is restored when another "Christian" helps to wake us up. That accountability partner is indispensable.

> If one falls down, his friend can help him up. But pity the man who falls and has no one to help him up (Ecclesiastes 4:10).

Question 2. Can you recall a time when you've "fallen" into drunkenness and then had no strength to "get up?" What were the results? What happened? What did you do?

Course Member Teresa writes, "Yes. I would usually sleep for a long period of time unable to stay awake. When I would wake, the feelings of disgust, shame and guilt were overwhelming. Often I could not look at my own reflection in the mirror."

Brothers, if someone is caught in a sin, you who are spiritual should restore him gently. But watch yourself, or you also may be tempted (Galatians 6:1).

Question 3. We all need an accountability partner. From Galatians 6:1 above, what qualifications does your future partner need to possess in order to help you?

Question 4. What about you? Have you had anyone to come along side and "help you pull more?" Have you had anyone to "help you up" when you fell into sin?

> But encourage one another, as long as it is called "Today," so that none of you may be hardened by sin's deceitfulness (Hebrews 3:13).

Question 5. Notice how "daily encouragement" is an antidote to sin. According to this verse, how often should you and your accountability partner communicate?

If we are serious about overcoming, we must utilize an accountability partner. Here's how:

1. Church is important. If you are involved in church, speak with someone in church leadership. Simply request his help in overcoming alcohol or drug addictions, and ask if he can be an accountability partner with you. If you do not have a church, please consider finding a good church that exalts the name and word of God.

2. Your spouse, if you are married, should eventually become your number one accountability partner. Have you shared your struggles with him or her and asked for their help? If not, possibly this may be the time to do so.

3. Perhaps you can organize a group of Christians who desire to study this workbook together and you can determine accountability partners.

Here are some guidelines to follow when you initiate accountability with your partner:

1. You agree to openness and honesty. Bondage to heroin or alcohol, for example, brings deception with it; some of us have been deceptive for years. If we want to lose the slavery to sin, we start with honesty, even if it is humbling. If your accountability partner asks how you are doing, and you have just fallen, you must honestly admit this.

2. You agree to prepare and share with your accountability partner your "break the chain" plan as taught in this course. Ask your accountability partner to help you by making suggestions to your plan and holding you accountable to it.

3. You agree to give your partner freedom to ask the hard questions, without taking offense. For instance, "Have you had any alcohol or amphetamines today?"

4. You agree to initiate communication daily for the first 30 days, as much as possible.

"It is good for two to travel together, for if one happens to fall, he may be lost for want of a little help. If a man falls into sin, his friend will help to restore him with the spirit of meekness; if he falls into trouble, his friend will help to comfort him and assuage his grief." (**Matthew Henry**)

> Also, if two lie down together, they will keep warm. But how can one keep warm alone? (Ecclesiastes 4:11).

Question 6. How does this statement "Also, if two lie down together they can keep warm" apply to our topic of study?

Note: In Revelation 3 Jesus tells the church of Laodicea that it had grown "lukewarm." They needed to repent of their sin and open the door to Jesus Christ and restore fellowship.

Question 7. How is your spiritual zeal?

> **Course Member Teresa writes,** "I am beginning to see my heart soften. I find myself thinking about the Lord most of the day and turning not only to prayer more often, but to the scriptures. I want to be around other believers much more rather than avoiding them. We discuss on a regular basis the spiritual aspects of what has and is taking place in my life. How the Lord is and will continue to bring good from my sin. I am 'allowing' other believers to love me and to help me. I did not believe I was loved for most of my life. Letting others help me has meant putting aside my pride (I can do it myself). It is a gradual, steady change."

"If two lie together, they have heat. So virtuous and gracious affections are excited by good society, and Christians warm one another by provoking one another to love and to good works." (**Matthew Henry**)

And now, we will examine the final verse in this important "accountability" section. Ecclesiastes 4:12 says, "Though one may be overpowered, two can defend themselves."

We have discovered that two working together can produce spiritual fruit (v. 9), that it can provide spiritual restoration (vs. 10), prompt spiritual zeal (v. 11), and now we will see that two working together can provide spiritual protection.

Questions

Question 8. What does verse 12 teach that "two together" can provide?

Question 9. Has this spiritual protection been missing in your life in the past?

Question 10. Have you contacted someone yet to be an accountability partner with you?

To be honest, if you are unwilling to maintain an accountability relationship then most likely you will not win the battle against alcohol or any drug addiction for any length of time. Remember, "one can be overpowered." (I proved the truth of this fact in my life for 17 years. I did not have accountability and I was overpowered again and again.) However, if you will contact your church leadership, spouse, or others, then "two can defend themselves" and you can experience victory too, Friend! (Man, is it ever good to be done with drunkenness and cocaine usage!) We are in a battle, dear friend. We can either be "overpowered" or we can "defend ourselves," depending on our willingness to find a partner.

"United strength. If an enemy find a man alone, he is likely to prevail against him; with his own single strength he cannot win, but, if he has a second, he may do well enough: two shall withstand him." (**Matthew Henry**)

Notice this story from Scripture which reinforces the truth we have been studying:

> ⁹Joab saw that there were battle lines in front of him and behind him; so he selected some of the best troops in Israel and deployed them against the Arameans. ¹⁰He put the rest of the men under the command of Abishai his brother and deployed them against the Ammonites. ¹¹Joab said, "If the Arameans are too strong for me, then you are to come to my rescue; but if the Ammonites are too strong for you, then I will come to rescue you. ¹²Be strong and let us fight bravely for our people and the cities of our God. The LORD will do what is good in his sight" (2 Samuel 10:9-12).

The end result of this battle was victory for the Israelites. Joab in essence said, "You help me with my enemy and I'll help you with yours." And so together they were victorious whereas separately they would have been conquered. This is an important aspect of an accountability relationship. We should provide one another with spiritual protection from our mutual enemy.

The way we do this is to pray for each other, share "battle tips" that helped us, take each other to the Word of God, and help each other amputate the causes of sin. This is a winnable war, but it takes two!

"We Christians need each other. There is strength in numbers. When isolated and separated from our brothers, we are easy pickings for the Enemy of our souls" (**Robert Daniels**, *The War Within*).

Please provide your comments on the following passages of Scripture:

> Let us hold unswervingly to the hope we profess, for he who promised is faithful. And let us consider how we may spur one another on toward love and good deeds. Let us not give up meeting together, as some are in the habit of doing, but let us encourage one another—and all the more as you see the Day approaching (Hebrews 10:23-25).
>
> As iron sharpens iron, so one man sharpens another (Proverbs 27:17).

Question 11. What are your comments on the above verses?

Now, as a special bonus for this day's teaching, we have secured permission from Chuck Colson's Prison Fellowship Ministries to reprint one of their articles on accountability. This is an excellent article; please take the time to read through it.

> A person standing alone can be attacked and defeated, but two can stand back-to-back and conquer. Three are even better, for a triple-braided cord is not easily broken (Ecclesiastes 4:12, NLT).

I urge all Christians not only to attend church services regularly but also to establish small groups of other Christians to whom they are accountable. I've seen this simple practice work wonders in my own life. In fact, I would never have developed real Christian maturity merely by staying home,

Questions

reading religious books and attending church once a week; no more than an athlete can develop by shooting baskets alone in the driveway. We're all parts of a larger Body, and as parts we can't operate alone. Nor is the Body fully formed when some of its parts are not fully integrated.

After I became a Christian, I was surrounded by some loving Christian brothers. I credit my early spiritual growth to that prayer group. They made it clear from the beginning that they would meet with me regularly, and we agreed that I wouldn't make decisions without them.

Why is this necessary? Even if Christ lives in you, and even if you're a committed disciple, there will be times when temptation will be nearly overpowering. We need to remember that we're self-deluding creatures who are fully capable of rationalizing the worst sins, even as Christians. Remember the story of David and Nathan? David, a man after God's own heart, couldn't see his own considerable sin, so Nathan told him the story of a man's obvious sin. David was enraged and told Nathan the man should be punished. Only then could Nathan say, "You are the man!"

A group can tell us when we're off base. A group has the wonderful ability to get us to focus on God rather than on ourselves. We may resist this, but without a group we will likely never recognize how out of focus we're becoming.

Let me be the first to admit that over the years I've been tempted to sin, and I've done things wrong without even knowing it. Because the human heart is deceitful, the accountability of a small group is indispensable. (**Charles W. Colson**)

Reprinted with permission of Prison Fellowship, P.O. Box 17500 Washington, DC 20041-7500

Scripture to Consider

The way of a fool is right in his own eyes, but a wise man is he who listens to counsel (Proverbs 12:15).

So then every one of us shall give account of himself to God (Romans 14:12).

Did you feast on God's Word in the last 24 hours?

    Yes   No

If so, how did you feast? In other words, circle the ways you enjoyed God today. Reading? Prayer? Worship? Fellowship? Witnessing?

Were you free from drug and alcohol abuse since you did the last lesson?

    Yes   No

Did you spend personal time with the Lord since you did the last lesson?

    Yes   No

If you answered "no" to any of the above questions, describe what led to your fall.

If you answered "yes" to the above questions, you may use this area for additional comments.

DAY 13 - PURE GRACE

For the next several days, we are going to examine a pivotal teaching of the Scriptures. The necessity of understanding this cannot be overstated. Simply put, grace is what saves us, sanctifies us and will ultimately glorify us. The grace of God is responsible for rescuing us from our dependence on substances and for keeping us free from their grip until the end. The value of this truth is that grace can do what the law cannot. In other words, if I am caught in the trap of drug abuse, I cannot escape through obeying the law. The law condemns my behavior as sinful but provides no power to help me stop. On the other hand, the grace of God actually releases us from the trap of the devil, redeems us from slavery to the devil, and rescues us from the kingdom of the devil.

"To run and work the law commands, but gives us neither feet nor hands. But better news the gospel brings, it bids us fly and gives us wings." (origin unknown)

I wonder if you are familiar with the strangle-knot. It is an excellent knot to be used as a running-knot for a snare because the more force that is applied from inside the loop the more firmly the running-knot prevents the opening of the loop. In short, the harder you pull against the knot the tighter the knot becomes! The only way to break free of this snare is by cutting the rope with a knife.

Mind altering substances are a strangle-knot for us. All of our own efforts to break free from sin only serve to increase its death-grip on us. The truth is that only the grace of God can break our bondage and free us from certain death. God's grace is like the knife that can free from the strangle-knot.

Please read the following story from Scripture of "Pure Grace", and answer the questions below.

> But Jesus went to the Mount of Olives. At dawn he appeared again in the temple courts; where all the people gathered around him, and he sat down to teach them. The teachers of the law and the Pharisees brought in a woman caught in adultery. They made her stand before the group and said to Jesus, "Teacher, this woman was caught in the act of adultery. In the Law Moses commanded us to stone such women. Now what do you say?" They were using this question as a trap, in order to have a basis for accusing him. But Jesus bent down and started to write on the ground with his finger. When they kept on questioning him, he straightened up and said to them, "If any one of you is without sin, let him be the first to throw a stone at her."
>
> Again he stooped down and wrote on the ground. At this, those who heard began to go away one at a time, the older ones first, until only Jesus was left, with the woman still standing there. Jesus straightened up and asked her, "Woman, where are they? Has no one condemned you?" "No one, sir," she said. "Then neither do I condemn you," Jesus declared. "Go now and leave your life of sin" (John 8:1-11).

Nothing is more humiliating than being caught in an act of disobedience! Whether it's a child with his hand in the cookie jar or an adult driving over the speed limit, we all know the sinking feeling of being caught. In John 8, a woman is caught in the act of adultery. Let us study her story and learn. (Some of the following questions are taken from Lesson Builder by Logos.)

Questions

Question 1. From the early verses of the above passage, what do we know about the character and motive of those who bring this woman to Jesus?

Question 2. How do you think the woman feels when the men make her "stand before the group" and publicly expose her sin?

Question 3. While it is obvious that this woman is guilty, what elements of injustice can you find in this situation?

Note: The Pharisees and scribes continued to press their point. They were not after the poor woman as much as they were after Jesus. They were saying this to test Jesus (v. 6). They wanted grounds for "accusing" Jesus. He is the one they are really after here.

This self-righteous, self-appointed group of Pharisees were acting as judge and jury and wanting to stone this woman; but don't mistake it, their ultimate goal was the death of Jesus. They were filled with self-righteous hatred toward Jesus. They kept stressing their point. "They persisted in asking Him" (v. 7a). They kept the pressure on Jesus. "Come on, tell us teacher, what do You say? Will you kill the woman or kill the Law?"

Scripture makes no definitive statement as to what Jesus wrote in the dirt. Here is a thought: There are only two other times in Scripture where God is shown to write something with His hand or finger, and both times what was written condemned those to whom He wrote. The first time was when God wrote

Questions

the Law on tablets of stone, the second time was when He wrote on the wall of King Belshazzar. One scholar says that "an ancient opinion is that he wrote the sins of the accusers." Note Job 13:26: "For you write down bitter things against me and make me inherit the sins of my youth."

Question 4. The Pharisees and teachers were often very self-righteous. Why did they go away instead of stoning the woman?

Question 5. Was Jesus condoning the woman's sin by not condemning her? Please explain.

Thoughts: As these religious leaders persisted in questioning him, Jesus stood up and invited any one among them who was sinless to throw the first stone. By this statement they could not possibly say Jesus rejected the law. Jesus specifically told them to throw the first stone. Go ahead, you are right, the Law says stone her. She is guilty. Now, you, which one of you, is sinless?

Question 6. Why are we tempted to condemn other people's sins rather than our own?

Question 7. How would you describe Jesus' attitude towards the woman? (Notice Jesus was the only one who talked to her; the others only talked about her).

Please notice the last statement of Jesus: "Neither do I condemn you..." This is pure grace, Friend. The law required punishment and death of the woman caught in the act of adultery, Jesus forgave her and gave her life. The woman did not make any excuses (v. 11). She was guilty. She knew it. She stood condemned. She didn't have to be convinced of that fact. She needed grace. She did not deserve it. "The wages of sin is death" (Romans 6:23). "The soul that sins will surely die." (Ezekiel 18:4). She couldn't earn it. She was a spiritual pauper in the need of the riches of God's marvelous grace.

Jesus said to her, "Neither do I condemn you; go your way; from now on sin no more" (v. 11). Let those words soak in. "Neither do I..." "Neither do I condemn you."

How could Jesus offer such a sinner no condemnation? He did it the same way He does to us. He knew that He was going to the cross to die for her sins. That is the way all sinners are—helpless. A helpless sinner doesn't merit forgiveness. A helpless sinner doesn't earn forgiveness. "For while we were still helpless [sinners], at the right time Christ died for the ungodly" (Romans 5:6).

Moreover, "God demonstrates His own love toward us, in that while we were yet sinners, Christ died for us" (v. 8).

To every guilt-ridden sinner who puts their trust in Jesus Christ as their Savior, the LORD God comes today and whispers in your ear "neither do I condemn you." "There is now no condemnation for those who are in Christ Jesus" (Romans 8:1).

But Jesus' statement of grace is immediately followed up by an admonition to "go and sin no more." Theologians have made terms that describe what Jesus did here: Justification and Sanctification. Justification is: "Neither do I condemn you." Sanctification is: "Go and sin no more." And it is critical to see the order of Jesus' statements, for He did not say, "Go and sin no more, neither do I condemn you." "Clean up your act and then I will forgive you." Jesus Christ here uses grace as the motive for pure living.

Question 8. If you were the woman, how would you feel as you left Jesus' presence?

Friend, let us bring this teaching home. Drunkenness is sin. Ephesians 5:18 says "And do not get drunk with wine, for that is dissipation, but be filled with the Spirit." This sin is against God and we are rightly condemned, according to His law, just as this woman was condemned of adultery. So, like her, we stand accused before Jesus Christ, deserving death.

And yet, there is a place where sinners can go to find pardon and forgiveness. It is in Jesus, who "justifies the wicked" (Romans 4:5). It is in Jesus, who was "pierced for our transgressions, and crushed for our iniquities." And it is also in Jesus where we find grace to live differently. "For it is the grace of God (not the law of God) that teaches us to say no to ungodliness" (Titus 2:12). Pure grace. We need it. He has it.

Questions

In summary, a snare was set for this woman; she was in a strangle-knot with no way to break free. But Jesus cut the knot by the knife of pure grace. He can do the same for us!

Meditate on the following words from the hymn by Charles Wesley:

Grace Alone

Every promise we can make,
Every prayer and step of faith,
Every difference we will make,
Is only by His grace.
Every mountain we will climb,
Every ray of hope we shine,
Every blessing left behind,
Is only by His grace.

Grace alone which God supplies,
Strength unknown He will provide,
Christ in us our Cornerstone,
We will go forth in grace alone.
Every soul we long to reach,
Every heart we have to teach,
Everywhere we share His peace,
Is only by His grace.
Every loving word we say,
Every tear we wipe away,
Every sorrow turned to praise,
Is only by His grace.

Question 9. Do you know the life-transforming power of the grace of God? Do you know the joy of having an Advocate like Jesus Christ?

Scripture to Consider

"I, even I, am he who blots out your transgressions, for my own sake, and remembers your sins no more" (Isaiah 43:25).

John testifies concerning him. He cries out, saying, "This was he of whom I said, 'He who comes after me has surpassed me because he was before me.'" From the fullness of his grace we have all received one blessing after another. For the law was given through Moses; grace and truth came through Jesus Christ" (John 1:15-17).

If we confess our sins, he is faithful and just and will forgive us our sins and purify us from all unrighteousness (1 John 1:9).

Did you feast on God's Word in the last 24 hours?

　　　　Yes　　　No

If so, how did you feast? In other words, circle the ways you enjoyed God today. Reading? Prayer? Worship? Fellowship? Witnessing?

Were you free from drug and alcohol abuse since you did the last lesson?

　　　　Yes　　　No

Did you spend personal time with the Lord since you did the last lesson?

　　　　Yes　　　No

If you answered "no" to any of the above questions, describe what led to your fall.

If you answered "yes" to the above questions, you may use this area for additional comments.

DAY 14 – SURPRISING GRACE

There was once a great and noble King whose land was terrorized by a crafty dragon. Like a massive bird of prey, the scaly beast delighted in ravaging villages with his fiery breath. Hapless victims ran from their burning homes, only to be snatched into the dragon's jaws or talons. Those devoured instantly were deemed more fortunate than those carried back to the dragon's lair to be devoured at his leisure. The King led his sons and knights in many valiant battles against the dragon.

Riding alone in the forest one day, one of the King's sons heard his name purred low and soft. In the shadows of the ferns and trees, curled among the boulders, lay the dragon. The creature's heavy-lidded eyes fastened on the prince, and the reptilian mouth stretched into a friendly smile.

"Don't be alarmed," said the dragon, as gray wisps of smoke rose lazily from his nostrils.

"I am not what your father thinks."

"What are you, then?" asked the prince, warily drawing his sword as he pulled in the reins to keep his fearful horse from bolting.

"I am pleasure," said the dragon. "Ride on my back and you will experience more than you ever imagined. Come now. I have no harmful intentions. I seek a friend, someone to share flights with me. Have you never dreamed of flying? Never longed to soar in the clouds?"

Visions of soaring high above the forested hills drew the prince hesitantly from his horse. The dragon unfurled one great webbed wing to serve as a ramp to his ridged back. Between the spiny projections, the prince found a secure seat. Then the creature snapped his powerful wings twice and launched them into the sky. The prince's apprehension melted into awe and exhilaration.

From then on, he met the dragon often, but secretly, for how could he tell his father, brothers or the knights that he had befriended the enemy? The prince felt separate from them all. Their concerns were no longer his concerns. Even when he wasn't with the dragon, he spent less time with those he loved and more time alone.

The skin on the prince's legs became calloused from gripping the ridged back of the dragon, and his hands grew rough and hardened. He began wearing gloves to hide the malady. After many nights of riding, he discovered scales growing on the backs of his hands as well. With dread he realized his fate were he to continue, and so he resolved to return no more to meet the dragon.

But, after a fortnight, he again sought out the dragon, having been tormented with desire. And so it transpired many times over. No matter what his determination, the prince eventually found himself pulled back, as if by the cords of an invisible web. Silently, patiently, the dragon always waited.

One cold, moonless night their excursion became a foray against a sleeping village. Torching the thatched roofs with fiery blasts from his nostrils, the dragon roared with delight when the terrified victims fled from their burning homes. Swooping in, the serpent belched again and flames engulfed a cluster of screaming villages. The prince closed his eyes tightly in an attempt to shut out the carnage.

In the pre-dawn hours, when the prince crept back from his dragon trysts, the road outside his father's castle usually remained empty. But not tonight. Terrified refugees streamed into the protective walls of the castle. The prince attempted to slip through the crowd to close himself in his chambers, but some of the survivors stared and pointed toward him.

"He was there," one woman cried out, "I saw him on the back of the dragon." Others nodded their heads in angry agreement. Horrified, the prince saw that his father, the King, was in the courtyard holding a bleeding child in his arms. The King's face mirrored the agony of his people as his eyes found the prince's. The son fled, hoping to escape into the night, but the guards apprehended him as if he were a common thief. They brought him to the great hall where his father sat solemnly on the throne. The people on every side railed against the prince.

"Banish him!" he heard one of his own brothers angrily cry out.

"Burn him alive!" other voices shouted.

As the king rose from his throne, bloodstains from the wounded shone darkly on his royal robes. The crowd fell silent in expectation of his decree. The prince, who could not bear to look into his father's face, stared at the flagstones of the floor.

"Take off your gloves and your tunic," the King commanded. The prince obeyed slowly, dreading to have his metamorphosis uncovered before the kingdom. Was his shame not already enough? He had hoped for a quick death without further humiliation. Sounds of revulsion rippled through the crowd at the sight of the prince's thick, scaled skin and the ridge growing along his spine.

The King strode toward his son, and the prince steeled himself, fully expecting a back-handed blow, even though he had never been struck so by his father.

Instead, his father embraced him and wept as he held him tightly. In shocked disbelief, the prince buried his face against his father's shoulder.

"Do you wish to be freed from the dragon, my son?"

The prince answered in despair, "I wished it many times, but there is no hope for me."

"Not alone," said the King. "You cannot win against the dragon alone."

"Father, I am no longer your son. I am half beast," sobbed the prince.

But his father replied, "My blood runs in your veins. My nobility has always been stamped deep within your soul."

With his face still hidden tearfully in his father's embrace, the prince heard the King instruct the crowd, "The dragon is crafty. Some fall victim to his wiles and some to his violence. There will be mercy for all who wish to be freed. Who else among you has ridden the dragon?"

The prince lifted his head to see someone emerge from the crowd. To his amazement, he recognized an older brother, one who had been lauded throughout the kingdom for his onslaughts against the dragon in battle and for his many good deeds. Others came, some weeping, others hanging their heads in shame.

The King embraced them all.

"This is our most powerful weapon against the dragon," he announced. "Truth. No more hidden flights. Alone we cannot resist him."

(Melinda Reinicke, Parables for Personal Growth (San Diego, CA: Recovery Publications, Inc., 1993), pp. 5-9, Used by Permission.)

Questions

Question 1. What are your thoughts on this story? Do you see parallels with your own life? What are your comments?

Have you been so disgusted and shame-filled over your slavery to alcohol or heroin that you resolved to never do it again, only to find yourself pulled back, as if by the cords of an invisible web? I have. I resolved over and over to stop, to never do that again, and yet all my resolve melted in the heat of the temptation. I was receiving God's grace in vain.

Friend, it is possible to "receive the grace of God in vain" (2 Corinthians 6:1); that is, with no associated heart and life change. So, let us examine Scripture and see that the grace and love of God is the cure for any bondage. Sin is a spiritual problem, and requires a spiritual solution. God's grace, given to us at the cross of Jesus Christ, is the solution.

For if, by the trespass of the one man, death reigned through that one man, how much more will those who receive God's abundant provision of grace and of the gift of righteousness reign in life through the one man, Jesus Christ. (Romans 5:17)

Question 2. According to this passage, what will those who receive grace do?

> ⁹For I am the least of the apostles and do not even deserve to be called an apostle, because I persecuted the church of God. ¹⁰But by the grace of God I am what I am, and his grace to me was not without effect. No, I worked harder than all of them—yet not I, but the grace of God that was with me (1 Corinthians 15:9-10).

Question 3. Paul says that the grace God gave to Paul was not without effect. What was the effect of God's grace to Paul?

> Now this is our boast: Our conscience testifies that we have conducted ourselves in the world, and especially in our relations with you, in the holiness and sincerity that are from God. We have done so not according to worldly wisdom but according to God's grace (2 Corinthians 1:12).

Question 4. How did Paul conduct himself while he was among the Corinthians?

Question 5. What was the source of Paul's ability to conduct himself in "holiness and sincerity" (according to . . . what)?

Question 6. They acted in holiness according to what?

> And God is able to make all grace abound to you, so that in all things at all times; having all that you will need, you will abound in every good work (2 Corinthians 9:8).

Question 7. What does it take in order to "abound in every good work?"

> ¹¹For the grace of God that brings salvation has appeared to all men. ¹²It teaches us to say "No" to ungodliness and worldly passions, and to live self-controlled, upright and godly lives in this present age (Titus 2:11-12).

Question 8. If we are ever to learn to say "No" to ungodliness, if we are ever to deny worldly passions, if we are ever to live a self-controlled life, what will it take?

Friend, hopefully these verses have taught us one very basic, but essential truth: the grace of God alone will enable us to conquer any sin habit. While we acknowledge that grace is a sovereign gift of God which cannot be earned, Scripture does instruct us on how we can put ourselves into a position to enjoy grace from Him. Let's look at four actions which promote the grace of God in our lives.

1. Humble ourselves: God opposes the proud but gives grace to the humble. Submit yourselves, then, to God. Resist the devil, and he will flee from you. Come near to God and he will come near to you. Wash your hands, you sinners, and purify your hearts, you double-minded. Grieve, mourn and wail. Change your laughter to mourning and your joy to gloom. Humble yourselves before the Lord, and he will lift you up (James 4:6-10).

2. Rid our lives of idols: Those who cling to worthless idols forfeit the grace that could be theirs (Jonah 2:8). Whatever is between God and us must be given up in order to experience grace. Either forfeit the idols, or forfeit grace.

3. Seek after it: Ask and it will be given to you; seek and you will find; knock and the door will be opened to you. For everyone who asks receives; he who seeks finds; and to him who knocks, the door will be opened (Matthew 7:7-8).

Questions

4. Don't miss it: See to it that no one misses the grace of God and that no bitter root grows up to cause trouble and defile many (Hebrews 12:15). See to it. Make it your primary objective. Do not miss the grace of God. Humble yourself, rid your life of any idol, and seek after the grace of God. What is the result? God gives grace; grace makes us more than conquerors through Him who loves us; we reign in life; and we overcome our bondage to substances.

Overcoming and conquering drunkenness or any drug addiction takes hard work! So hard, in fact that we find that we are unable to do so apart from the grace of God. That is why seeking Him with all our being is so important. I still remember how it felt to fail miserably over and over. Each failure seemed to further drain my resolve and I was defeated before I even began. The grace of God is different because His grace not only allows us to "work harder than the rest" but God also overcomes all of the obstacles! Did you catch that part? He overcomes all obstacles no matter how high or how deep or how impossible they may seem. My whole life has changed because of the work He has done. His grace penetrated down inside the deepest recesses of my being and "changed" me. I had ridden the dragon so many times and was scarred and wounded. But just like the king, God has given grace where there was none deserved.

I will be sharing the rest of my story with you as we go, but let me say this much today; God's grace has met every expectation and then surpassed anything I could have imagined. Oh friend, seek His grace with all your heart and being! There is freedom from persistent sin in God's grace; like the famous hymn, "Amazing grace, how sweet the sound that saved a wretch like me." Wretched? Yes, I was but now His grace has saved me from drunkenness and a crack addiction!

Often recall the proverb: "The eye is not satisfied with seeing nor the ear filled with hearing" (Ecclesiastes 1:8b). Try, moreover, to turn your heart from the love of things visible and bring yourself to things invisible. For they who follow their own evil passions stain their consciences and lose the grace of God.

A point of clarification may be warranted here. I am not saying that by doing these things you can earn God's grace, for grace is undeserved. What I am saying is that these actions put you in a place to receive grace. All that is good or ever will be good in us is preceded by the grace of God. While one might claim to have humbled himself, it is God's grace which enables him to do so. It is God who grants grace so that we may turn in repentance away from idols. Men do not seek God first; He seeks them for Jesus tells us, "You did not choose me, but I chose you and appointed you to go and bear fruit" (John 15:16). Ours is the response to His initial work. It is our duty to humble ourselves, repent and seek Him. And He gives us grace upon grace.

Question 9. Are you truly committed to receiving God's grace? Will you employ the above four principles? Please list those four principles and tell how you will practically apply them:

1.

2.

3.

4.

Question 10. Write out anything you have learned in this lesson, or any new thoughts or ideas you have had today.

Course member Teresa wrote, "The story of the dragon was both a sad and beautiful analogy of my sin and the mercy and grace of Christ. The theme seems to be grace, grace, grace. Oh, how I forget that often! I will only be delivered when I believe in God's grace without doubt. Every time I tried to get free from alcohol on my own, I would wake up resolving not to drink again and would eventually do just that. I felt hopeless, trapped and fearful. The wounds and hardness of heart allowed me to think that I could conquer this in my own strength. How glad I am that my 'strength' failed one night at the bottom of a staircase where I was bleeding and wounded. The Lord used that fall to jolt me out of my self-sufficiency and showed me I was incapable of becoming free apart from Him. This lesson is very powerful."

Scripture to Consider

[8] For it is by grace you have been saved, through faith - and this not from yourselves, it is the gift of God, [9]not by works, so that no one can boast (Ephesians 2:8-9).

Did you feast on God's Word in the last 24 hours?

    Yes   No

If so, how did you feast? In other words, circle the ways you enjoyed God today. Reading? Prayer? Worship? Fellowship? Witnessing?

Were you free from drug and alcohol abuse since you did the last lesson?

    Yes   No

Did you spend personal time with the Lord since you did the last lesson?

    Yes   No

If you answered "no" to any of the above questions, describe what led to your fall.

If you answered "yes" to the above questions, you may use this area for additional comments.

DAY 15 – ONGOING FREEDOM

¹Therefore, I urge you, brothers, in view of God's mercy, to offer your bodies as living sacrifices, holy and pleasing to God; this is your spiritual act of worship. ²Do not conform any longer to the pattern of this world, but be transformed by the renewing of your mind. Then you will be able to test and approve what God's will is - his good, pleasing and perfect will (Romans 12:1-2).

In the above passage, the apostle Paul teaches us that the receiving of God's grace should prompt us to offer our bodies up to the Lord as a living sacrifice. He shows us that God's grace motivates and enables us to offer ourselves to the Lord, which is why we placed this lesson after the two days of teaching on grace. Grace leads us to holiness, to pleasing the Lord with our bodies, and to true worship.

The language of Paul in these verses reminds us of animal sacrifices that God's people in the Old Testament used to offer unto the Lord. If a member of God's family sinned, they were required to bring a lamb and present it to the priest as an offering. The priest would sacrifice the animal, which pointed forward to the death of Jesus Christ to pay for our sins, and the person presenting the sacrifice would be released from guilt, and in presenting this sacrifice he was supposed to be worshiping God.

In the same manner we are to present to God, not an animal sacrifice, but the sacrifice of our own body. And just as the member of God's family in the Old Testament would present the entire animal as a sacrifice, holding no part back, so we are to offer God our entire being: heart, mind, hands and feet; indeed all of us are to be presented to God.

In light of God's grace, it is time for us to begin offering up our bodies as living sacrifices to God. He gave His all for us, now we are to give our all for Him. I remember how this hit me several years ago. I prayed, "Oh God, I have abused and nearly destroyed this body. I have used it for everything except serving you. I have filled my body with alcohol and cocaine and spent so much time with its poison coursing through my veins. I am so sorry that I have counted all that you did for me as nothing and now I want to serve you. I want to use all of my mind, body and soul for you. I want to be a living sacrifice to you, the God who gave me grace when I deserved death."

Questions

Question 1. You may want to take a moment and write out a prayer to God and present Him with your body. If so, here is a place for you to do this:

Right here some clarity may be helpful as to what it means to worship God. Is worshiping God going to church and singing songs? Is it hearing a sermon and receiving the Word planted in our hearts? Is it singing in the choir, or participating in prayer? It sure can be. But the above verses tell us that presenting our bodies as living sacrifices to God is our "spiritual act of worship." If you want to experience worship in the most powerful way, just offer up your body to God for Him to live in, work through and use to draw others to Himself.

Friend, right now it will be wise for you to develop a daily habit of presenting your body to the Lord as soon as you awake. The first thing each morning, let us present our bodies to the Lord as a living sacrifice. This takes the grace of God to accomplish, as we have already discussed.

Question 2. Will you seek God for grace to offer yourself to Him daily?

Next, the above verses describe precisely how we can overcome the habitual habit of drug abuse. Notice verse 2: "Do not conform any longer to the pattern of this world, but be transformed by the renewing of your mind." We are not to be conformed but transformed. And this is accomplished by renewing our minds. What does this look like in the life of one who has been enslaved to heroin, for instance?

I remember how it was when I would think about what my day was going to consist of. No matter what else I might be doing, alcohol had to be a part of it! I could not imagine life without it! I would dwell on drinking and think about it so much that I was in a frenzy with desire. Just thinking about alcohol is like pouring gas on the fire and this is very frustrating for people who wish to be free from habitual sin because these thoughts torment our minds. It is like the devil is mocking us, or worse yet, it is as if he is raping our souls.

I would be so stirred up by afternoon or evening time that drinking was inevitable and soon I would be drunk.

Questions

Just remembering drinking experiences from the past would be powerful enough that I could almost taste the alcohol as I thought about it. It was overwhelming! So how do we combat this?

Well, first we "radically amputate" (more on this tomorrow) by "cutting off" and "plucking out" the source of this desire, and second we "radically transform" our minds by renewing them.

The first thing I do in the morning is present my body to the Lord as a living sacrifice. Then I sit down with my Bible and I read it. As I meditate over the truths, I undergo a change in my thinking. I begin dwelling on Jesus Christ and His perfect sacrifice on the cross, and how I am to die to my flesh. I then begin planning out the day from a spiritual perspective. What will I do to avoid temptation completely? What will I do if I have a "surprise attack?" How will I handle this situation, and that situation, etc. . .

This "renewing my mind" is really just "thinking differently" and thinking differently leads to acting differently.

Question 3. What will be some ways that you will begin to "renew your mind" by the grace of God? Please be specific.

Do not conform any longer to the pattern of this world, but be transformed by the renewing of your mind (Romans 12:2).

Notice here that renewing our minds leads to a transformation. The Greek word for transformation is where we get our word "metamorphosis." This metamorphosis, which comes by renewing our minds, makes a total change in our nature, and is what enables us to be free on a daily basis. Therefore it is critical to renew our minds. We do this by reading the Bible, and earnestly seeking the Lord in prayer. This gives us "the mind of Christ" (1 Corinthians 2:16) and enables us to think differently, which pro0duces a real change in our character. Metamorphosis is the same word we use to describe what happens to a caterpillar that changes into a butterfly. What has previously inched along the ground in the mud and dirt can now soar heavenward in perfect freedom of flight.

Friend, I was crawling in the dirt and mud of drunkenness and cocaine use for 17 long years, inching my way along the road that goes nowhere. But in September of 1999, a metamorphosis began to take place in my heart and life by the grace of God. I began actually applying biblical principles to my life and the truths affected my heart, not just my head. God made me serious about eradicating all drugs from my life. As I began offering my body as a living sacrifice every morning, and renewing my mind in His Word, I have been experiencing changes in my thoughts, my desires, my goals in life—everything! Everything is changing, and I feel as though I have been given wings of grace to soar to the presence of God.

I love this metamorphosis, and don't ever want to go back to crawling in the mud. How about you? This is day 15 for you, and most people begin to see real and ongoing victory just up ahead. But also about this time period, the devil begins stomping his feet and throwing a temper tantrum over his captives leaving. The hardest part for most people is the period from the 14th day up to and including the 30th day. I'm telling you this as a warning that things may get harder before they get easier, and to be forewarned is to be forearmed.

Question 4. Are you sensing a "metamorphosis" in your life? What are some of the changes taking place in the following areas: heart, life, marriage (if married), work environment, home environment, etc. . . Write your answer here.

Course member Teresa writes, "I pray daily for my heart to be softened and I see real evidence of that. As others have talked with me about their own struggles I have much more compassion. My prayer time is richer than previously and as I read the Word, I no longer see 'just the words on the page.' I let it soak in. A major change for me is that I am reaching out to others more often rather than isolating myself. It seems small but this is an area that was dangerous for me in many ways. When temptations come or I am struggling I ask others (accountability partners, friends, and husband) to pray and come alongside me.

God has revealed to me how much power I had given my pride (I can do it myself, I don't want to bother other people, they won't love me if they know what I'm really like, etc.). God has given me discernment regarding areas of temptation and creative ways to overcome them (give my husband the keys to my van when he leaves, not going to the grocery store alone, allowing friends to pick up anything I need at the store, etc.) I have had a strong and loving marriage the last 25 years, but it also has been strengthened and made richer. We work on this together, everyday. I used to try and handle my problem without my husband because I thought 'he was busy' or 'he doesn't drink and wouldn't understand' or 'he'd be so disappointed if he knew what I was doing.' (See, PRIDE!) I have 'allowed' my daughter to be of help to me and have begun to be totally honest with her about my sin and struggle. Since I work at home I now listen to Christian music most of the day. My home has been stripped of any items that would cause me to stumble. In general, not only is my heart changing, but I realize the seriousness of my fleshly lusts. It is not something I regard flippantly anymore. For me, this is HUGE."

Questions

To review, we learned or reviewed two key principles to overcoming drunkenness today.

1. Offer up our bodies as living sacrifices.
2. Renew our minds, and be metamorphosed as a result.

And we can only do these things "in view of God's mercy." In other words, Jesus Christ offered up His body as a sacrifice to the Father, to satisfy God's hatred toward sin, and to forgive us our sins. He held nothing back, but presented all of who He is to God. His back was whipped, His beard was pulled off, His hands and feet were nailed to the cross, His head was crowned with thorns, His heart imploded, and then He died. Jesus' death on the cross was the demonstration of God's mercy, and in light of that mercy we too should offer our own bodies as living sacrifices, and renew our minds to be transformed.

Question 5. What are your final thoughts on this teaching today? Did you learn anything new, or were you reminded of any truths that may have been neglected before? Please answer here:

Scripture to Consider

[8]For you were once darkness, but now you are light in the Lord. Live as children of light. [9](for the fruit of the light consists in all goodness, righteousness and truth) [10]and find out what pleases the Lord (Ephesians 5:8-10).

[18]The LORD is near to all who call on him, to all who call on him in truth (Psalm 145:18).

Did you feast on God's Word in the last 24 hours?

     Yes   No

If so, how did you feast? In other words, circle the ways you enjoyed God today. Reading? Prayer? Worship? Fellowship? Witnessing?

Were you free from drug and alcohol abuse since you did the last lesson?

     Yes   No

Did you spend personal time with the Lord since you did the last lesson?

     Yes   No

If you answered "no" to any of the above questions, describe what led to your fall.

If you answered "yes" to the above questions, you may use this area for additional comments.

DAY 16 – RADICAL AMPUTATION

If your hand causes you to sin, cut it off. It is better for you to enter life maimed than with two hands to go into hell, where the fire never goes out. And if your foot causes you to sin, cut it off. It is better for you to enter life crippled than to have two feet and be thrown into hell. And if your eye causes you to sin, pluck it out. It is better for you to enter the kingdom of God with one eye than to have two eyes and be thrown into hell (Mark 9:43-47).

Friend, we need to separate ourselves completely from whatever has caused our abuse of substances. This may not seem reasonable, but in dealing with sin being radical is only reasonable.

After 17 years of being enslaved, I desperately needed and wanted to be free. My wife and I decided to completely rid our lives of any and all access to alcohol and cocaine.

The first thing I did was to get rid of any alcohol in the house. There was no room for any of it, even those "special" bottles or cans with sentimental significance. Who wants to get sentimental over something that has you in chains!? The second thing was to stay out of bars completely. This was a huge step for me because I played in rock bands and our gigs were in bars. This had been a part of my life for many years, but it had to go. There was no way I could go into a bar and not drink—the temptation was too great. Oh, I might have done it once or twice, but eventually my resolve would crumble and I would give in. Parties, social "get-togethers" at friend's houses, Monday night football, all of it had to go. I lost friends who did not understand or scoffed at me because of this, but I knew deep down inside that I could not be free with access to alcohol.

Jesus said that we should "cut off" and "pluck out" whatever causes us to sin, and He warned us that if we don't radically amputate the source of our sin we could end up in Hell. Friend, do not take this lightly. We are talking life and death here; Heaven and Hell. If you thought you were "just playing" with alcohol or drugs please know this: it will take you farther than you want to go, keep you longer than you want to stay, and cost you more than you want to pay. If you doubt this, just look around at the devastation substance abuse has caused in the lives of people all around us!

Jesus is not referring to a physical cutting off of your foot or a plucking out of your eyeball. Blind men still lust. He's referring to the complete removal of the source of your sin. He's saying that if we want to be free from this, some things in our lives have to go, and we must do whatever it takes. For me, this meant getting rid of the alcoholic beverages in my home and not going into bars or places where drinking was going on.

Course member Teresa writes, "Getting rid of my favorite wine glasses and openers. Since we did not keep alcohol in the house, we had none to get rid of. There had been times when I purchased two or three bottles of wine at a time just to 'have on hand.' Every time I did that, I couldn't stay away from them and would end up drinking them. I knew I couldn't keep a stock in my house. There was a 'cool' wine bottle wrapped in burlap from Australia that was above my kitchen cabinets for 'decoration.' I asked my husband to get rid of it. The openers are gone. I do not go to the grocery store alone; I've stopped watching my favorite cooking shows because wine was used extensively as an ingredient. I've begun to replace white wine with apple juice in recipes that call for wine, avoiding community gatherings where alcohol is prevalent, and avoiding the drink menus at restaurants."

Question 2. Please list here what things have caused you to sin in the area of substance abuse.

Question 3. Above we looked at Mark 9:43-47: What did Jesus say to do with things that cause us to sin?

Question 1. Please list what "complete removal" means to you.

Questions

Question 4. Truth time: Have you totally "amputated" everything that has caused you to sin?

This teaching may seem less than reasonable; indeed it may come across as quite radical. Some people, rather than cut off the causes of sin, want to stare it in the face and say "no." (We will read about this on Day 19.) That would be true victory for them. However, this desire to be strong rather than pure will not result in victory.

I am enjoying freedom. It is precious and God has given so much in His grace, my marriage is strong and loving, we have two beautiful children, I am on staff at my church doing full-time ministry and reaching out to help those in bondage. I have found peace after 17 long years of hard labor at the hands of Satan—a slave to cocaine and alcohol. I am not bragging here for it is only by the grace of God that I even survived. The point I want to make is that none of this would have happened if any access to either substance remained. In fact, I would most likely be dead. Friend, please take this to heart as you consider what things need to be amputated in your life.

Today is the day to clean house! Are you hiding anything anywhere that can cause you to sin? If so, go throw it away. Get rid of it. Have a "smash party" where you get rid of all alcohol and drugs for good. View it as crushing the old sin in your life with God's love.

Question 5. Please comment on Hebrews 12:1 as it relates to our study today: "Therefore, since we are surrounded by such a great cloud of witnesses, let us throw off everything that hinders and the sin that so easily entangles, and let us run with perseverance the race marked out for us."

Course member Teresa writes, "I cannot succeed in becoming free from the bondage of alcohol if I keep something around that will cause me to sin again. This is not 'play-time,' it is serious—dead serious. I cannot think that I am strong enough to look my temptations in the eye and believe I can overcome. There can be no excuses. If I am not willing to get rid of everything that helps to keep me in bondage, then I am not really serious about changing and becoming more Christ-like. BUT, I AM!!!"

The Case for being Radical (Adapted from Matthew Henry)

1. The case supposed that (if) our own hand, or eye, or foot, offend us; the impure corruption we indulge in is as dear to us as an eye or a hand, or that which is to us as an eye or a hand may become an invisible temptation to sin, or occasion of it. Suppose the beloved may become a sin, or the sin a beloved. Suppose we cannot keep that which is dear to us because it will be a snare and a stumbling-block; suppose we must part with it, or part with Christ and a good conscience.

2. The duty prescribed in that case: Pluck out the eye, cut off the hand and foot, mortify the darling lust, kill it, crucify it, starve it, make no provision for it. Let the idols that have been delectable things, be cast away as detestable things. Keep at a distance that which is a temptation, though ever so pleasing. It is necessary that the part which is gangrened should be taken off for the preservation of the whole. The part that is incurably wounded must be cut off, lest the parts that are sound be corrupted. We must put ourselves to pain, that we may not bring ourselves to ruin; self must be denied, that it may not be destroyed.

3. The necessity of doing this: The flesh must be mortified, that we may enter into life (Mark 9: 43, 45); into the kingdom of God, v. 47. Though, by abandoning sin, we may for the present feel as if we were maimed, yet it is for life. All that men have they will give for their lives. It is for a kingdom—the kingdom of God—which we cannot otherwise obtain. These maims will be the marks of the Lord Jesus; they will be in that kingdom scars of honor.

4. The danger of not doing this: The matter is brought to this issue, that either sin must die, or we must die. If we will lay this Delilah in our bosom, it will betray us. If we be ruled by sin, we shall inevitably be ruined by it. If we must keep our two hands, and two eyes, and two feet, we must with them be cast into hell. Our Savior often pressed our duty upon us, from the consideration of the torments of Hell, which we run ourselves into if we continue in sin. With what an emphasis of terror are those words repeated three times here, "Where their worm dieth not, and the fire is not quenched!" The words are quoted from Isaiah 66:24. The reflections and reproaches of the sinner's

Questions

own conscience are the worm that dieth not; which will cleave to the damned soul as the worms do to the dead body, and prey upon it, and never leave it till it is quite devoured. Will you say, "…How have I hated instruction, and my heart despised reproof…" (Proverbs 5:12, 23). The soul that is food to this worm, dies not; and the worm is bred in it, and one with it, and therefore neither doth that die. "He shall die without instruction, and in the greatness of his folly he shall go astray" (Proverbs 5:23). Damned sinners will be to eternity accusing, condemning, and upbraiding themselves with their own follies, which, however much they are now in love with them, will at the last bite like a serpent, and sting like an adder. (**Matthew Henry**)

Question 6. Comments?

Scripture to Consider

[17]Therefore do not be foolish, but understand what the Lord's will is. [18]Do not get drunk on wine, which leads to debauchery. Instead, be filled with the Spirit. [19]Speak to one another with psalms, hymns and spiritual songs. Sing and make music in your heart to the Lord, [20]always giving thanks to God the Father for everything, in the name of our Lord Jesus Christ (Ephesians 5:17-20).

[10]The thief comes only to steal and kill and destroy; I have come that they may have life, and have it to the full (John 10:10).

Did you feast on God's Word in the last 24 hours?

      Yes   No

If so, how did you feast? In other words, circle the ways you enjoyed God today. Reading? Prayer? Worship? Fellowship? Witnessing?

Were you free from drug and alcohol abuse since you did the last lesson?

      Yes   No

Did you spend personal time with the Lord since you did the last lesson?

      Yes   No

If you answered "no" to any of the above questions, describe what led to your fall.

If you answered "yes" to the above questions, you may use this area for additional comments.

DAY 17 –
SETTING CAPTIVES FREE I

[31]To the Jews who had believed him, Jesus said, "If you hold to my teaching, you are really my disciples. [32]Then you will know the truth, and the truth will set you free."

[33]They answered him, "We are Abraham's descendants and have never been slaves of anyone. How can you say that we shall be set free?"

[34]Jesus replied, "I tell you the truth, everyone who sins is a slave to sin. [35]Now a slave has no permanent place in the family, but a son belongs to it forever. [36]So if the Son sets you free, you will be free indeed" (John 8:31-36).

This passage contains amazing truth for us who have been involved with the abuse of prescription meds or other substances. Let's examine it, by answering some questions.

Question 3. Have you had this type of "slavery" experience?

Questions

Question 1. According to verse 31 and 32, what will be the result of holding to Jesus' teachings?

Here we see a very important reason for Bible study. How can we know the truth if we do not study the teachings of Jesus? And if we do not know the truth, we will not be set free. But it is not only Bible study that is important. I studied the Bible all throughout the years that I was a captive to drunkenness. Many people come to this New Wine course knowing much Scripture because of having studied much. No, it is not just studying the Bible that frees us from sin's captivity. Jesus said "If you hold to my teaching..." indicating that it is not merely studying the Scriptures but embracing them that brings freedom. Holding Jesus' teachings has to do with keeping them ever before me so that when I am tempted I recognize the lie in the temptation, and flee from it so as to not indulge in it. This is what it means to hold on to Jesus' teaching and is the truth that sets us free.

Question 2. What did Jesus say would happen when we know the truth?

According to verses 34-36 Jesus stated that the truth sets us free from sin's slavery. Slaves are not free people, but rather, they have a master and must do his bidding. I remember how I would take that first drink even though I had resolved not to the night before or that morning. "One drink won't hurt" would be the argument, but one would turn to three and then five or six and I was soon in a drunken stupor . . . AGAIN!!! This is slavery to sin.

> He feeds on ashes, a deluded heart misleads him; he cannot save himself, or say, "Is not this thing in my right hand a lie?" (Isaiah 44:20).

Course member Teresa writes, "Yes, I have. I, too, made promises to myself to not drink. When I bought groceries I would end up buying a bottle of wine telling myself 'It is not wrong. Having ONE glass of wine is not forbidden by Scripture.' (I was using my liberty in Christ as an excuse for my sin). Then one glass led to two and then I would become careless and uninhibited, throwing caution out the window, followed by glass three and then four. I would wake up again in the morning making the same oath, and eventually broke the vow. It is similar to an overweight person vowing to 'start my diet on Monday' and then over the course of the next few days eating everything in sight viewing it as 'my last time.'"

But notice it is the truth that sets us free. You see, Friend, if we are slaves to sin we are deceived. We believe a lie. The lie may be that alcohol or drugs will satisfy us, or that somehow the problems would just go away or be magically solved while I was drunk. They were always there when I sobered up, however, and they just got worse! I even believed the lie that I could quit using anytime I wanted to—that there was no problem there. The problem was sin and the lies were from the devil, keeping me in slavery.

Questions

Question 4. What are some lies you have believed?

So, part of our leaving substances behind is to embrace truth. Examine every temptation and ask, "Is this true?" Will indulging in this sin bring the satisfaction it promises? Will it satisfy me eternally, or will it leave me with guilt and regret?

Question 5. Compare verse 32 and 36. What do they have in common?

Friend, Jesus Christ is the Truth that sets us free. When we embrace HIM, we know the truth which sets us free. Jesus says in John 14:6, "I am the Way, the Truth, and the Life. No man comes to the Father but through Me." And in Proverbs 8 Jesus Christ is portrayed as "wisdom" and is shown to be the "way" (vs. 1-2), the "truth" (v. 7) and the "life" (v. 35).

Question 6. The above makes it clear that Jesus Christ is the Truth that sets us free! He declares: "So if the Son sets you free, you will be free indeed." Do you long to be "free indeed"?

Yes   No

Let's be clear about this, Friend. There is no program, or system, or counseling technique that can set us free from the slavery to sin. This course will not set you free, apart from Christ. Only Jesus, the Truth, can release us. "Salvation is found in no one else, for there is no other name under heaven given to men by which we must be saved" (Acts 4:12). And the way He sets us free is by enabling us to embrace the Truth, rather than deception and lies. Involving ourselves in drunkenness is the same as believing lies, and living in a world of deception. Drugs do not satisfy, as they promise to do. It is like drinking from a stream of polluted water, which leaves one "thirstier" than before. In order to overcome this sin we must drink the living water which quenches our thirst eternally, and we begin to embrace the truth as it is in Jesus.

Begin to speak the truth, to forsake lies, to refuse to live in any form of deception. Drag your sin into the light, and begin to be honest in all your dealings with others. You see, it is because of our sins that we are taken captive and are made slaves. Notice the following verses from the New Living Translation: The LORD asks, "Did I sell you as slaves to my creditors? Is that why you are not here? Is your mother gone because I divorced her and sent her away? No, you went away as captives because of your sins. And your mother, too, was taken because of your sins" (Isaiah 50:1).

It is the main mission of the Messiah to release men and women from their chains of captivity. Jesus declares His mission in Luke 4:18-19: "The Spirit of the Lord is on me, because he has anointed me to preach good news to the poor. He has sent me to proclaim freedom for the prisoners and recovery of sight for the blind, to release the oppressed, to proclaim the year of the Lord's favor." He came to release us from captivity to our sins, and to bring freedom from bondage and slavery. His freedom is real. He breaks the power of sin, and releases us from the prison of sin. I testify that I have been free from alcohol and cocaine for several years, not to brag about my own strength to overcome for I have none, but rather to glorify Jesus who came to earth for this very purpose.

Question 7. Please provide your thoughts on the following verses:

"Then you will call upon me and come and pray to me, and I will listen to you. You will seek me and find me when you seek me with all your heart. I will be found by you," declares the LORD, "and will bring you back from captivity" (Jeremiah 29:12-14).

Yet even now, you can be free from your captivity! Leave Babylon and the Babylonians, singing as you go! Shout to the ends of the earth that the LORD has redeemed his servants, the people of Israel (Isaiah 48:20).

So now the Sovereign LORD says: "I will end the captivity of my people; I will have mercy on Israel, for I am jealous for my holy reputation!" (Ezekiel 39:25).

Questions

So, to summarize: drunkenness, indeed all sin, makes us slaves. It deceives us so that as we partake of it we believe a lie. But Jesus came to break the power of sin, to release us from slavery to sin, to set the captives free! This is why Jesus came to earth.

Question 8. Finally, it is reflection time. Where are you with the above teaching? Is Jesus releasing you from sin's captivity? Do you see how you've believed lies, and are you seeking to embrace truth now? Write your thoughts here:

Friend, I can recall my captivity very clearly even today, years later. If my "master", alcohol, told me to go and get drunk, I would have to obey. If he told me to get involved with sin at a bar, then I followed his orders. I was a slave to my lusts, and captive to evil desires. But now Jesus Christ has freed me, by causing me to embrace the truth. And freedom is very precious to me, and I never want to return to my slavery again. Jesus made me His prisoner now: But thanks be to God, who made us his captives and leads us along in Christ's triumphal procession. Now wherever we go he uses us to tell others about the Lord and to spread the Good News like a sweet perfume. Our lives are a fragrance presented by Christ to God" (2 Corinthians 2:14-15). And when God makes us captives of Christ we also become prisoners of hope: "Come back to the place of safety, all you prisoners of hope, for there is yet hope!" (Zechariah 9:12).

So let us be clear: With Jesus Christ freedom is not only possible, it is inevitable. We must beg Christ to do His work in our hearts, for when He does, we will be free. No more slavery to sin, no more giving in just because the impulse comes to do so, no more drunken parties and reliving the guilt and stress each time. Freedom from habitual sin is real. My prayer is that you will experience and enjoy it!

Scripture to Consider

When the LORD brought back the captives to Zion, we were like men who dreamed. Our mouths were filled with laughter, our tongues with songs of joy. Then it was said among the nations, "The LORD has done great things for them." The LORD has done great things for us, and we are filled with joy" (Psalm 126:1-3).

The Spirit of the Sovereign LORD is upon me, because the LORD has appointed me to bring good news to the poor. He has sent me to comfort the brokenhearted and to announce that captives will be released and prisoners will be freed (Isaiah 61:1).

God, the LORD, created the heavens and stretched them out. He created the earth and everything in it. He gives breath and life to everyone in all the world. And it is he who says, "I, the LORD, have called you to demonstrate my righteousness. I will guard and support you, for I have given you to my people as the personal confirmation of my covenant with them. And you will be a light to guide all nations to me. You will open the eyes of the blind and free the captives from prison. You will release those who sit in dark dungeons" (Isaiah 42:5-7).

Did you feast on God's Word in the last 24 hours?

      Yes   No

If so, how did you feast? In other words, circle the ways you enjoyed God today. Reading? Prayer? Worship? Fellowship? Witnessing?

Were you free from drug and alcohol abuse since you did the last lesson?

      Yes   No

Did you spend personal time with the Lord since you did the last lesson?

      Yes   No

If you answered "no" to any of the above questions, describe what led to your fall.

If you answered "yes" to the above questions, you may use this area for additional comments.

DAY 18 - SETTING CAPTIVES FREE II

Precisely how does salvation work? Who is it for? What does it look like in the everyday life of someone who used to be in bondage to alcohol or amphetamines?

These are the questions we will seek to answer today. And there will be much encouragement from the Scriptures as we dig into God's Word.

We are about to embark on a fascinating study, Friend! You will discover that God had a purpose in your addiction. Read through the following verses and answer the questions below.

> ¹⁰Some sat in darkness and the deepest gloom, prisoners suffering in iron chains, ¹¹for they had rebelled against the words of God and despised the counsel of the Most High. ¹²So He subjected them to bitter labor; they stumbled, and there was no one to help. ¹³Then they cried to the Lord in their trouble, and He saved them from their distress. ¹⁴He brought them out of darkness and the deepest gloom and broke away their chains. ¹⁵Let them give thanks to the Lord for his unfailing love and his wonderful deeds for men, ¹⁶for he breaks down gates of bronze and cuts through bars of iron (Psalm 107: 10-16).

Today, let us do a verse-by-verse study and notice together the spiritual condition of the above people, and also let us note the reason why things were so bad for them.

> Verse 10: "Some sat in darkness and the deepest gloom, prisoners suffering in iron chains"

This verse states 5 things about these people. They were:

1. In darkness
2. In deepest gloom
3. Prisoners
4. Suffering
5. In iron chains

There may not be a better description of the spiritual condition of a drunkard in all of Scripture. Note:

1. <u>They are in darkness.</u> It is spiritually pitch black in the life of drunkards. Their lusts are continually stirred up by experiences and images that have been burned into their minds; their mind is dark because of the sin that dominates them; they lack genuine spiritual light, which is wisdom and understanding. Life is dark for the alcohol or drug addict.

2. <u>They are in deepest gloom.</u> Oh, not at the beginning, or the middle when the excitement of parties and euphoric memories floods their hearts and minds, but as the addiction continues, the gloom increases. And this is not just "ordinary" gloom, this is "deepest gloom," spiritual gloom, dread, fear, pessimism, hopelessness.

3. <u>They are prisoners.</u> They are captivated by the "rush" of intoxication, imprisoned by the next impulse to drink, which they are unable to fight. They are not free to simply choose to stop, or "just say no" anymore than a prisoner is free to leave his prison any time he wants.

4. <u>They are suffering.</u> Substance abuse causes suffering. Examine the end of anyone who has been addicted, and you will see suffering in their lives. I personally suffer for my years of involvement with drunkenness.

5. <u>They are in iron chains.</u> This is a reference to the strength of the sinful habit patterns. Drunkenness is an "iron chain" addiction—too strong for man to break.

Question 1. As you read through the previous description of someone enslaved to sin, which number(s) described your past prison the most?

And now, let us notice the reason why these people were in such bad shape:

> ¹¹for they had rebelled against the words of God and despised the counsel of the Most High.

And look what God did next:

> ¹²So He subjected them to bitter labor; they stumbled, and there was no one to help.

Notice 3 things that happened to these people because of their rebellion:

1. **God subjected them to bitter labor.** Were your drug-induced habits ever "bitter labor" to you? Mine sure were. The words "bitter labor" are the same words used in Exodus 1, referring to the slavery of the Israelites. Amphetamines can reduce us to "slave labor."

2. **They stumbled.** Friends, please do not miss this: drunkenness will be your downfall if you do not totally forsake it. They stumbled and fell. So did I.

3. **There was no one to help them up.** You probably know this already, but it is possible to go so far into drugs that nobody can help you. I remember the hopeless grief of staring at the closed coffin of one of my closest friends as his body was being lowered into the ground. I remember thinking that all the second and third and fourth chances were over. No more chances. The finality of his choice to get drunk at a bar was staggering. I could see myself in the same situation or in

Questions

prison because I had killed someone. I could feel that same hopeless end breathing down my neck. There is no doubt that I would have gone that far if God had not rescued me from slavery.

Question 2. Are you identifying with all this? Have you ever felt that you were in this very predicament? Explain please:

Course member Teresa writes, "Yes, I have. I had wondered several times whether I would be in an auto crash because I had too much to drink. (I never imagined that I would fall down a flight of stairs.) As I have stated before, after two or three glasses of wine, I would become careless and make foolish decisions. I know there were times I shouldn't have been driving, but I was compelled to go to the store for more alcohol. Most of the time after I had two to three glasses, I felt a little 'fuzzy' but that was all (my tolerance had become greater). I believed that I was okay—not drunk at all. Most of the time with the next glass it was as though I had been hit by a freight train. The state of drunkenness came suddenly without warning. There were many times that I would wake up and not have any remembrance of the night before. NONE! The fear of what I might have done was overwhelming. I would rack my brain trying to conjure up any memories and none came. I knew that I was out of control. After those times, I wondered what happened to the good sense God had given me. My body began to crave more and more. I felt trapped. Where would I go for help? Who could help me? Who would even want to help? Who would understand? How could I ask the Lord for forgiveness and then drink again hours later?"

Concentrate for just a moment on these words, "And there was no one to help them up." This is the place where God takes His children just before He saves them. He brings them to the point that they must cast themselves totally on His mercy. They cannot help themselves. Nobody else can help them. They are helpless and hopeless. And yet, what is impossible with man is possible with God!

"If the Son sets you free, you will be free indeed!" (John 8:36)

[13]Then they cried to the Lord in their trouble, and He saved them from their distress. [14]He brought them out of darkness and the deepest gloom and broke away their chains. [15]Let them give thanks to the Lord for His unfailing love and His wonderful deeds for men, [16]for He breaks down the gates of bronze and cuts through bars of iron (Psalm 107:13-16).

Oh, Friend, here is a prescription for freedom from bondage. Cry to the Lord. But you say, "I HAVE called to Him and I'm still falling." Keep crying out to Him! Have you ever noticed that when the Israelites first began calling to the Lord for help that their slavery increased?

God eventually delivered the Israelites by the blood of the lamb, and He can deliver you, too. It is the godless that won't cry to God. "The godless in heart harbor resentment; even when he fetters them, they do not cry for help" (Job 36:13).

Be like Jacob and wrestle with God in prayer until He blesses you with salvation from drunken sin. God purposely takes us to the place where we cannot help ourselves, and there is no one else to help us. In fact, in this same chapter that we are studying (Psalm 107) it says that certain people were "at their wits' end" (v. 27). They were at the end of their rope. But they cried to the Lord. And He saved them! Friends, when you are at the end of your rope, you are at the beginning of hope. Real hope. Call, call, call. And keep calling. He will answer, in His time.

Question 3. From verses 13-16, notice the 5 things that God does in response to people crying out to Him. Please write all five here.

1.

2.

3.

4.

5.

The above verses tell us that when God saves someone He destroys the work of the devil in their lives. He frees from the grip of the devil, removes oppression (though not temptation), rescues from slavery to sin and sets us free. We must ever pray for ongoing help and be on guard against backsliding, but the work of salvation is a thorough and ongoing deliverance from sin.

So, to answer the questions we asked at the beginning of Day 14:

1. **How does salvation work?** People rebel against God, God hands them over to slavery, they come to the end of their rope and nobody helps them, they cry to the Lord, He saves them.

Questions

2. Who is it for? Salvation is for those who have rebelled, those who have gone against the teaching of God's Word, those who have been in prison to sin.

3. What does it look like in the everyday life of someone who used to be addicted to drugs? We come to know that we are powerless to stop using. We see very clearly that we are enslaved and imprisoned by it. We hear that salvation is available through the cross and we begin to cry out. Oftentimes, God waits. We cry more, and louder. God hears, rescues, redeems, saves. We are no longer in bondage to the sin. The Son of God has set us free, and we are free indeed.

Question 4. Honesty time. Where are you in the above scenario? Enslaved? In prison? Calling? Or free indeed?

I look back and see where He has brought me and I can still remember how it felt to realize that God listens when we cry out! I thought I had gone so far that there was no hope of deliverance. I was so sure that I had contracted some "spiritual virus" that would only end in death. There is no doubt that God allowed me to walk right up to the precipice and stagger near the edge. But as I staggered on the brink of destruction He reached out a loving, compassionate, healing hand and gently pulled me back into His waiting arms. He delivered me from death itself. He heard me as I cried out in bondage. He came down the cellblock with keys in hand, opened the doors of my prison room and then led me out into the sunlight—permanently in His grace! Friend, God hears our prayers and the same freedom from bondage is there for you as well, even though you may feel that you are too bad, or have done too much wrong—He does hear!

Praise God, he sends deliverance to the captives and saves those that call out to Him in their distress. That makes me want to fall on my face before Him in humble adoration! What a merciful, great, and awesome God He is!

Does this lesson give you hope? Are you experiencing this freedom? Or are you still struggling and feel that there is still no hope for you? Have you found an accountability partner—a mentor—who will help you in the bad times as well as rejoice with you in the good times? We have found that students who faithfully submit lessons each day, meet God daily in prayer and Bible study, and communicate regularly with their accountability partner are much more successful than those who take shortcuts or lack commitment in these areas. Think of it as a reflection of your commitment to Christ!

Scripture to Consider

For there is no distinction between Jew and Greek, for the same Lord over all is rich to all who call upon Him. For "whoever calls on the name of the LORD shall be saved" (Romans 10:12-13).

Did you feast on God's Word in the last 24 hours?

     Yes   No

If so, how did you feast? In other words, circle the ways you enjoyed God today. Reading? Prayer? Worship? Fellowship? Witnessing?

Were you free from drug and alcohol abuse since you did the last lesson?

     Yes   No

Did you spend personal time with the Lord since you did the last lesson?

     Yes   No

If you answered "no" to any of the above questions, describe what led to your fall.

If you answered "yes" to the above questions, you may use this area for additional comments.

DAY 19 – SETTING CAPTIVES FREE III

In the Book of Exodus in the Bible, God's people were in slavery to the Egyptians. They had been in slavery for 400 years, and theirs was a very hard and bitter slavery. The Egyptians were "ruthless" and "harsh" taskmasters. Notice the wording in Exodus 1:11-14: "So they put slave masters over them to oppress them with forced labor...and worked them ruthlessly. They made their lives bitter with hard labor in brick, and mortar and with all kinds of work in the fields; in all their hard labor the Egyptians used them ruthlessly."

Friend, this is a picture of our condition in the grips of alcohol or drugs and drunkenness. We become "slaves" to that bottle, needle, or pill. Romans 6:20 illustrates this truth: "When you were slaves to sin, you were free from the control of righteousness." Alcohol made me a slave. If I had a thought to go to a bar or a store to buy some alcohol, it was just like I was a slave to that desire. My impulses controlled my actions for years. I was a slave. My master was alcohol. And it was a harsh master. Can you relate?

But the Israelites began to cry out to God in their slavery. Oh friend, God will not turn a deaf ear to "Help me, Oh God. Please. I beg you." And so He said to His people, "I have indeed seen the misery of my people in Egypt. I have heard them crying out because of their slave drivers, and I am concerned about their suffering. So I have come down to rescue them from the hand of the Egyptians and to bring them up out of that land into a good and spacious land..." (Exodus 3:7-8).

God "came down" to "bring them up." Friend, God never changes. The cross of Jesus Christ, where He died, was God "coming down" to "bring us up." He is now coming down to you . . . in the midst of your slavery. He has seen your misery, He's heard your cries for help, He's concerned about your suffering. His purpose in coming to you is to "rescue" you and "bring you up." Do you see that? In a little while we will see how He does that, and that will be an exciting discovery. But for now, please answer the following questions.

Questions

Question 2. Have you, yourself, gotten to the "slavery" part of substance abuse yet?

Steve wrote, "Yes. Being free from the compulsion to drink this past three weeks now has been much better. I am gradually learning how to find pleasure and satisfaction in life without alcohol—which was really required before—and while I still have thoughts about drinking, I find that I can get along just fine without it. There is a certain fear that drives the addiction . . . imagining being without the substance creates fear, which in turn drives one towards the substance."

Question 3. When the Israelites were slaves, what did they do to get help?

Question 4. Did God hear their cry for help?

Questions

Question 1. How is being addicted to a substance like being a slave? Write in your answer here:

How I hated that slavery! Outwardly it appeared that I loved getting drunk; after all, I did it all the time. The truth was that I hated the fact that it controlled me, day in and day out. I could almost feel the lashes of whips and the chains on my wrists. What a brutal taskmaster alcohol turned out to be! The only way that my drunkenness would ever be satisfied would be in destruction. In the meantime, neither personal problems nor physical sickness could stop the slave driver—alcohol controlled every part of my life. It never gave in or gave up. I was a slave in the truest sense of the word!

Questions

Question 5. Read the above verses. What words does the Bible use to describe how God felt about His people while they were in slavery?

Question 6. How has your drug of choice enslaved you in the past?

Course member Teresa writes, "It was slow and subtle. I didn't just wake up one day and say 'I think I will become a drunkard today.' As I felt the 'comforting' and numbing effect it had upon me, I began to use it as an escape from everyday problems instead of turning to Christ. As the addiction grew, I spent time 'mapping out' the stores I would purchase it from. I became secretive in my home, hiding my drinking from my husband. I stayed away from fellowship at church because I could not look anyone in the eye because I was so ashamed. My body and soul became addicted to it and all of the 'promises' it held. I became not only a drunkard, but a deceiver and a liar. All of my 'willpower' and 'promises' could not get me through more than one day."

Now for the life-changing part of this biblical story! The Israelites cried out to God and He came down to rescue the slaves. First He sent a series of plagues (frogs, hail, locusts . . . etc.) on the Egyptians to display His power. Finally, because Pharaoh's heart was hard and he would not let God's people go, God sent word that He would destroy the firstborn son of every Egyptian household. But, in order to protect His own people, He instructed them to kill a lamb and put its blood on the doorposts, and when the destroying angel "saw the blood" he would "pass over" that house and not destroy the firstborn.

Friend, the Bible says that Jesus Christ is our "Passover Lamb" (1 Corinthians 5:7). He was sacrificed on the cross 2000 years ago and His blood protects us from death. Oh Friend, ask that God would place the blood of His Son, Jesus, on the doorposts of your heart. LOVE the blood of Jesus, as your only protecting agent to save you from death. He died so we can live!

But now watch this! Not only were the Israelites told to put the blood of the lamb on their doorposts, they were also instructed to eat the lamb. And here are some of the most instructive words in Scripture: "This is how you are to eat it: with your cloak tucked into your belt, your sandals on your feet and your staff in your hand. Eat it in haste; it is the Lord's Passover" (Exodus12:11).

Question 7. Consider this for a moment, and please record your thoughts on why they were to eat the Passover Lamb with their cloaks tucked into their belts, their sandals on their feet, and their staffs in their hands:

The Israelites were to eat the lamb with their cloak tucked in, their sandals on, and their staff in their hands. In other words they were to be ready to go. God was saying to them: "Be ready to go, because as soon as you eat the lamb you will leave Egypt." Please don't miss this teaching for here is real and lasting help for us: The Israelites literally ate their way out of slavery! And so can we! This is the message that is taught to us today: When we feed on the Passover Lamb, we will leave slavery.

So, how do I "eat my way out of slavery?" Answer: Feed on the Word of God! Let's talk about that, and then we will have some questions for you.

The way that you and I, today, "eat the Lamb," is to take Scripture and chew on it. We take a small passage and eat it up, so to speak. Eating involves taking some food in to nourish us, and that is what Jesus Christ is: Food for the soul! Jesus Christ came not only to die for our sins, and give us eternal life by His death, but He also came to be eaten, and to provide nourishment for our hungry souls.

Question 8. How is meditating through a passage of Scripture like "eating the Lamb?"

There is a way out of your slavery to prescription meds! It is through feeding on Jesus Christ. As we become full of Him, through meditating on the Bible, we will discover our freedom. Freedom follows fullness.

Questions

Now, to be very practical with this teaching, we're going to ask you to "feed" on the following Scriptures. We will leave room after each one so you can "feed" us some of your "food." In other words, write down your thoughts as you think through the following Scriptures. And as you "feed" and get "full" you will leave the Egypt of dependence on substances behind. Always remember that freedom from alcohol or heroin, for instance, is a by-product of "feeding" on Jesus Christ by meditating on Scripture. We can't "try" our hardest not to drink and be successful; we will always fail. But we can "eat" our way out of slavery. Now, come do what Paul told Timothy to do: "Reflect on these things, and the Lord will give you insight" (2 Timothy 2:7).

Question 9. Please write your thoughts about the following verses:

> His delight is in the law of the Lord, and on His law He meditates day and night. He is like a tree planted by streams of water, which yields its fruit in season and whose leaf does not wither" (Psalm 1:2,3).

Question 10. Please write your thoughts about the following verse:

> Man does not live by bread alone, but by every word that comes from the mouth of God (Deuteronomy 8:3).

Question 11. Please write your thoughts about the following verse:

> "I am the bread of life. Your forefathers ate the manna in the desert, yet they died. But here is the bread that comes down from heaven, which a man may eat and not die. I am the living bread that came down from heaven. If anyone eats of this bread, he will live forever. This bread is my flesh, which I will give for the life of the world" (John 6:48-51).

Question 12. Please write your thoughts about the following verse:

> "When your words came, I ate them. They were my joy and my heart's delight" (Jeremiah 15:16).

Question 13. Please write your thoughts about the following verse:

> Sanctify them (set them apart from sin) by the truth: your Word is truth! (John 17:17).

Questions

Question 14. Please write your thoughts about the following verse:

Do not let this book of the Law depart from your mouth. Meditate on it day and night, so that you may be careful to do everything written in it. Then you will be prosperous and successful (Joshua 1:8).

Question 15. Have you learned something today? Does this teaching give you hope? How will you implement the teaching in your own life?

Scripture to Consider

Captives also enjoy their ease; they no longer hear the slave driver's shout. The small and the great are there, and the slave is freed from his master (Job 3:18-19).

When the LORD brought back the captives to Zion, we were like men who dreamed. Our mouths were filled with laughter, our tongues with songs of joy. Then it was said among the nations, "The LORD has done great things for them." The LORD has done great things for us, and we are filled with joy (Psalm 126:1-3).

Did you feast on God's Word in the last 24 hours?

      Yes   No

If so, how did you feast? In other words, circle the ways you enjoyed God today. Reading? Prayer? Worship? Fellowship? Witnessing?

Were you free from drug and alcohol abuse since you did the last lesson?

      Yes   No

Did you spend personal time with the Lord since you did the last lesson?

      Yes   No

If you answered "no" to any of the above questions, describe what led to your fall.

If you answered "yes" to the above questions, you may use this area for additional comments.

DAY 20 - TEMPTATION

Today we will study the subject of temptation. We want to discover the nature of temptation as well as how to combat it. Please read the following passage from Luke 4:

> Jesus, full of the Holy Spirit, returned from the Jordan and was led by the Spirit in the desert, where for forty days he was tempted by the devil. He ate nothing during those days, and at the end of them he was hungry. The devil said to him, "If you are the Son of God, tell this stone to become bread." Jesus answered, "It is written: 'Man does not live on bread alone.'"
>
> The devil led him up to a high place and showed him in an instant all the kingdoms of the world. And he said to him, "I will give you all their authority and splendor, for it has been given to me, and I can give it to anyone I want to. So if you worship me, it will all be yours." Jesus answered, "It is written: 'Worship the Lord your God and serve him only.'"
>
> The devil led him to Jerusalem and had him stand on the highest point of the temple. "If you are the Son of God," he said, "throw yourself down from here. For it is written: 'He will command his angels concerning you to guard you carefully; they will lift you up in their hands so that you will not strike your foot against a stone.'" Jesus answered, "It says: 'Do not put the Lord your God to the test.'" When the devil had finished all this tempting, he left him until an opportune time (Luke 4: 1-13).

The parallel passage in Matthew 4:1-11 records that this temptation of Jesus happened directly after he was baptized in the Jordan River, where Heaven was opened to Him and the Holy Spirit descended upon Him. He received the approval of His Father in Heaven who said, "This is my beloved Son in Whom I am well pleased." So the first thing we can learn about temptation is that it often happens directly after a high spiritual experience.

I have a friend who preaches weekly and he says that Sunday afternoon is usually a difficult time for him. Remember Paul who, after He experienced wonderful revelations from God, was given a "thorn in the flesh," a messenger of Satan for his humbling?

Questions

Question 1. If you are a Christian, have you been tempted after a special time of closeness with God, or after a high spiritual experience at a retreat, conference, church meeting, etc.? Please explain:

Questions

Next, let us notice that this temptation took place during a time of physical weakness. It says Jesus did not eat during those 40 days so there must have been a huge physical strain on Jesus' body. Temptations often transpire during a time of physical sickness, or when the body is in a weak state or when we are hungry or tired.

Question 2. Have you had an experience where you were hit with temptations during a time of physical weakness? Please explain:

Then let us note that Jesus was alone when He was tempted. He was not hit with these fierce onslaughts while in company with His disciples, but only as He was alone in the desert.

Question 3. Have you ever noticed that you can be with people all day long and be fine, but when you get alone you are beset by intense temptation?

Yes   No

Scripture warns us to expect it, and helps to remove our isolation when we are admonished: "Be self-controlled and alert. Your enemy the devil prowls around like a roaring lion looking for someone to devour. Resist him, standing firm in the faith, because you know that your brothers throughout the world are undergoing the same kind of sufferings" (1 Peter 5:8-9).

Questions

Question 4. What "alone time" is a temptation for you? Explain it here:

Question 5. If you are a Christian, do you see how the devil can use substances to get you to break your relationship from God and to declare your independence from Him? Please explain here:

Next, please notice the design of the temptations. The purpose was to get Jesus to sin against God, and to disqualify Him from being the ultimate Sacrifice for the sins of others. All through this temptation, Satan attempts to get Jesus to bypass the cross, by which He would save all believing mankind. Satan knew that if He could get Jesus to short-circuit the cross all mankind would be lost, and must suffer in eternal Hell to pay the price for their sins.

Learn this lesson well, Friend, for every temptation for us is designed by the enemy of our souls to cause us to disobey God, and to bypass our own cross. Satan's design is for us to give in and disobey rather than to resist and offer our bodies a living sacrifice; to indulge our flesh, rather than crucify it.

Next, let us note another design by Satan in tempting us. He wants us to doubt our relationship with God, and to become independent of Him in meeting our own needs.

Notice the first temptation: The devil said to him, "If you are the Son of God, tell this stone to become bread." Jesus answered, "It is written: 'Man does not live on bread alone.'" The devil said, "If you are the Son of God . . ." See how he attempts to cast doubt upon Jesus' identity and relationship with His Father? Notice again, that the devil said, "Tell these stones to become bread." He did not say, "Pray to your Father in Heaven and ask for bread," but rather "take matters into your own hands and provide for your own needs." The devil hates anything requiring humility and dependence upon God, and loves to tell us of our own self-sufficiency. The great thing that Satan aims at in tempting a Christian is to overthrow his relationship to God as a Father, so as to cut off his dependence on Him.

Let's apply this teaching for a moment. I know that there were so many times that I felt I couldn't live without co-caine. I also felt that I would be empty without the parties, the friends, and the activities that had become my life. I really felt that these were needs in my life that would just be a huge void without them. Are you willing to trust God to supply the fulfillment in your life, to supply the "bread" in His timing?

Course member Teresa writes, "I can honestly say that I have had to be stripped and broken by God in order to be able to say yes to this question. My 'pleasures' have come with a huge price to pay. God has brought me face to face with my inability to help myself. Because of the deceptiveness of my sin, there were many times that I did not want to be free from alcohol. I looked forward to it, I enjoyed it, I lusted after it. I had replaced the Lord with alcohol. It is hard to write that. Yet, if I am to be totally honest, that is precisely what I did. I placed it higher than Christ, my husband, family, friends, and my health."

Next, notice how the temptation was resisted and overcome:

1. Christ refused to comply with it. In this one aspect, the teaching of the world to "just say no" is correct, but it falls short because it does not teach the next point, which is:

2. He was ready to reply to it. He quoted from Scripture, saying, "It is written." Isn't it amazing that Christ answered and baffled all the temptations of Satan with "It is written." Not only was He the Living Word of God, but also God's Word lived in Him and He was strong and overcame the evil one by the Word of God.

Question 6. How does the following verse compare with our subject of study today?

"I write to you, young men, because you are strong, and the word of God lives in you, and you have overcome the evil one" (1 John 2:14).

Questions

Friend, it is not so much our knowing Scripture that gives us the victory, it is the Word of God living in us that enables us to "overcome the evil one." We see many people come to this course who have much knowledge of Scripture, yet they are habitually defeated by drunkenness. Scripture takes up residence in the heart only through obedience (Psalm 111:10).

Next, notice the second temptation:

> The devil led him up to a high place and showed him in an instant all the kingdoms of the world. And he said to him, "I will give you all their authority and splendor, for it has been given to me, and I can give it to anyone I want to. So if you worship me, it will all be yours."

In this temptation the devil showed Jesus all the splendor of the world. All the beauty, the glory, the power, the magnificence, the grandeur and the luxury of the world was shown to him. Friends, we don't have to be involved with alcohol long to see this same offer displayed on our television sets and magazine ads. The ads show us pictures of happy people who are finding their joy and fulfillment in a bottle. The ads promise the "time of your life."

The problem is that drunkenness is demonic (1 Corinthians 10:20), and that there is worship involved with it. Just as Jesus had to "worship" the devil if he was to enjoy the splendor and power of the world, so the devil is after our worship and offers us alcohol as the enticement.

Even though I was a professing Christian for the 17 years I was involved with cocaine and alcohol, I was unknowingly worshiping at a demonic altar. The truth is clear from this passage that the devil is after our worship, just as He was with Jesus.

Question 7. Please provide your thoughts on the following commentary by **Matthew Henry**:

> All this will I give thee. And what was all that? It was but a map, a picture, a mere phantasm, that had nothing in it real or solid, and this he would give him; a goodly prize! Yet such are Satan's proffers. Note, Multitudes lose the sight of that which is, by setting their eyes on that which is not. The devil's baits are all a sham; they are shows and shadows with which he deceives them, or rather they deceive themselves.

Notice how Jesus warded off this assault and conquered the enemy:

1. With abhorrence and detestation. A parallel passage says, "Get away from me, Satan" (Matthew 4:10). If we are ever going to win this battle against drunkenness or drug abuse, we must ask God to give us a holy detestation of it, as if we cannot bear the thought of it.

2. With Scripture. "It is written: 'Worship the Lord your God and serve him only.'" When dealing with fierce and intense temptations, answer from Scripture, and answer in brief.

Finally, the third temptation:

> The devil led him to Jerusalem and had him stand on the highest point of the temple. "If you are the Son of God," he said, "throw yourself down from here. For it is written: 'He will command his angels concerning you to guard you carefully; they will lift you up in their hands, so that you will not strike your foot against a stone.'" Jesus answered, "It says: 'Do not put the Lord your God to the test.'"

Here, the devil tempts Jesus to presume upon the promises of God. We presume upon the promises of God when we purposely sin, while clinging to a promise of God. If Jesus had purposely sinned by throwing Himself down from the temple, He would have been testing God to try to rely on God's promise to not let Him fall.

This has direct application to us who have been involved in drunkenness. If I purposely get drunk while claiming God's promise to forgive sin I am testing God. It's the same as praying, "God, please forgive me for this sin I am about to commit . . ." which presumes upon God's grace.

Please get this principle, Friend: The devil will throw all kinds of Scripture our way to get us to sin against God in drunkenness. "I will forgive your sins, and remember your wickedness no more," "All manner of sin and blasphemy will be forgiven among men," "Nothing can separate us from the love of God," "The evil I do not want to do, this I keep on doing," "If we confess our sins, He is faithful and just to forgive us our sins . . ." and so on. How do we know it is the devil using Scripture and not our own minds? If that Scripture is being used to lure us into sin, it is coming from the evil one.

Questions

Question 8. What did you learn today, and how are you doing now?

Scripture to Consider

No temptation has seized you except what is common to man. And God is faithful; he will not let you be tempted beyond what you can bear. But when you are tempted, he will also provide a way out so that you can stand up under it (1 Corinthians 10:13).

Did you feast on God's Word in the last 24 hours?

      Yes   No

If so, how did you feast? In other words, circle the ways you enjoyed God today. Reading? Prayer? Worship? Fellowship? Witnessing?

Were you free from drug and alcohol abuse since you did the last lesson?

      Yes   No

Did you spend personal time with the Lord since you did the last lesson?

      Yes   No

If you answered "no" to any of the above questions, describe what led to your fall.

If you answered "yes" to the above questions, you may use this area for additional comments.

DAY 21 - RETURN TO THE LORD

Scripture records that Solomon's Temple was radiant in its splendor, and brilliant with the Shekinah glory of the Lord. "...the cloud filled the temple of the LORD. And the priests could not perform their service because of the cloud, for the glory of the LORD filled his temple" (1 Kings 8:10-11). This Temple was the house of God, "I have indeed built a magnificent temple for you, a place for you to dwell forever" (1 Kings 8:12) and was meant to be a "light for all nations." It was "imposing" (1 Kings 9:8) and magnificent, a holy and glorious dwelling place for God.

It served several purposes: It was a place of worship, a place to find forgiveness of sins, a place where the presence of God was seen, a place where unbelievers could find God and learn how to worship Him. God's presence made it glorious, pure, holy, radiant with splendor and majestic in beauty.

But the book of Ezekiel in the Old Testament records the slow departure of the glory of the Lord from the nation of Israel. The Shekinah glory cloud (which symbolized the presence of God) left the Most Holy Place of the Temple, then left the Temple itself, then finally the entire land of Israel. The departing of God and His glory brought about monumental changes to the nation of Israel. They no longer had the presence of the Lord. Their enemies ransacked their nation, taking captive men, women and children, and they were left without a witness to the nations. They became "Ichabod" which means, "The glory of the Lord has departed." Why did God depart and leave Israel as Ichabod?

To answer our questions, let us take a tour of the book of Ezekiel and I believe we can discover what it was that drove the presence of God from the Temple and the nation. Please note what these verses say about why He withdrew from the Temple, and record your thoughts below each verse.

Questions

"As surely as I live," declares the Sovereign LORD, "because you have defiled my sanctuary with all your vile images and detestable practices, I myself will withdraw my favor; I will not look on you with pity or spare you" (Ezekiel 5:11).

Question 1. Please record your thoughts below:

Questions

"But as for those whose hearts are devoted to their vile images and detestable idols, I will bring down on their own heads what they have done," declares the Sovereign LORD (Ezekiel 11:21).

Question 2. Please record your thoughts below:

"I said to them, each of you, get rid of the vile images you have set your eyes on, and do not defile yourselves with the idols of Egypt. I am the LORD your God. But they rebelled against me and would not listen to me; they did not get rid of the vile images they had set your eyes on, nor did they forsake the idols of Egypt" (Ezekiel 20: 7).

Question 3. Please record your thoughts below:

This is what the Sovereign LORD says: "Will you defile yourselves the way your fathers did and lust after their vile images?" (Ezekiel 20:30).

It becomes obvious from reading these verses that the people of God were "setting their eyes on vile images" and "defiling themselves with vile images" and "detestable practices." They were idolatrous and this is why God withdrew His presence. Sin that is tolerated in the nation, or the home, or the individual always drives the Holy Spirit of God away.

So what does this teaching on the Temple have to do with alcohol and us? The following passages are taken from Paul's letter to the Corinthian church. Paul was teaching on sexual immorality, but we can also look at this teaching in regard to any idolatry including drunkenness! Again, please record your thoughts on the following verses, writing your comments immediately below the verse. The following verses are from 1 Corinthians chapter 6:

> The body is not meant for sexual immorality, but for the Lord, and the Lord for the body (1 Corinthians 6:13).

Question 4. Please record your thoughts below:

Question 5. According to verse 13 above, for what is your body intended?

Question 6. In your own words, please tell what you think the statement that our bodies are meant for the Lord actually means.

> By his power God raised the Lord from the dead, and he will raise us also (v. 14).

Question 7. Verse 13 states that our bodies are not meant for sexual immorality, but they are meant for the Lord. The very next verse speaks about the resurrection of Jesus Christ and states that we will be raised as well. What connection do you see between these two verses?

> [15]Do you not know that your bodies are members of Christ himself? Shall I then take the members of Christ and unite them with a prostitute? Never! [16]Do you not know that he who unites himself with a prostitute is one with her in body? For it is said, the two will become one flesh. [17]But he who unites himself with the Lord is one with him in spirit.

Question 8. What are your thoughts on verses 15-17 above?

> Flee from sexual immorality. All other sins a man commits are outside his body, but he who sins sexually sins against his own body (v. 18).

Question 9. Now let's think about this in regards to drugs. Do you see how the "lust" for substances parallels this teaching? We are to flee from this lust! Please think through times when you are specifically hit with heavy temptations, and how you will "flee." Write your thoughts here:

Question 10. Verse 18 contains an admonishment regarding sexual immorality. What are we to do to overcome it?

> Do you not know that your body is a temple of the Holy Spirit, who is in you, whom you have received from God? You are not your own (v. 19).

Question 11. Verse 19 describes the body as what?

> …you were bought at a price. Therefore honor God with your body (v. 20).

Question 12. According to the same verse, who owns the Temple of my body?

Question 13. Verse 20 tells us "we were bought at a price." What was the purchase price?

Friend, these verses tell us that our bodies are temples belonging to the Lord. The Temple of the Old Testament became "Ichabod" because the people of God were "lusting after idolatrous images" in their hearts and committing "detestable practices." God slowly left them, and they were dispersed into foreign lands where they became "captives."

We, too, have spent time lusting after idolatrous images (alcohol) and have been involved in detestable practices (drunkenness). And depending on how long we were involved we may have lost the presence and power of God. Our lives may have become "Ichabod." It may have happened slowly, over time, but now we are destitute of power, spiritual weaklings trying to fight "principalities and powers of darkness" without Christ. We have been handed over to the enemy and are now "captives" in exile. But there is hope.

Much like a pornographic picture or a large pile of money, I would "lust" after alcohol and cocaine. A picture in a magazine or even the thought of a bottle of liquor would almost cause me to salivate in anticipation. I knew that it was destroying me, yet I willfully chose to pursue my lust despite any consequence. Make no mistake about this—drunken behavior is the culmination of lust after an idol alcohol. We treat the temple of the Holy Spirit with contempt and we join with the "prostitute" of alcohol every time we indulge our lust in drunkenness.

Question 14. Please read and comment on our final portion of Scripture today:

Therefore say: "This is what the Sovereign LORD says: 'I will gather you from the nations and bring you back from the countries where you have been scattered, and I will give you back the land of Israel again. They will return to it and remove all its vile images and detestable idols. I will give them an undivided heart and put a new spirit in them; I will remove from them their heart of stone and give them a heart of flesh.

'Then they will follow my decrees and be careful to keep my laws. They will be my people, and I will be their God. But as for those whose hearts are devoted to their vile images and detestable idols, I will bring down on their own heads what they have done,'" declares the Sovereign LORD. Then the cherubim, with the wheels beside them, spread their wings, and the glory of the God of Israel was above them (Ezekiel 11:17-22).

Notice the "removal of the detestable idols" brought the captives back to the land and the glory of God returned to the people. Ichabod no more! The glory returned. Friend, are you wondering if, since you have devoted yourself to detestable drunkenness, you will ever enjoy the presence of God again? Remove those detestable practices, and the presence and power and purity of God will return. Your body is a temple.

One of the objections we hear from course members quite often is that they feel that God will not return to them; that they will not experience His presence again. This passage of Scripture should confirm to the questioning soul that God returns to those who repent and return to Him.

Question 15. What are your thoughts and insights on today's teaching? Specifically, how will you apply what you are learning?

Questions

Friend, I lost the presence and power of God through my involvement in drunkenness and drugs, and I didn't even know it. Samson lost the presence of God through his lust, but was not aware of it: "Then she called, 'Samson, the Philistines are upon you!' He awoke from his sleep and thought, 'I'll go out as before and shake myself free.' But he did not know that the LORD had left him" (Judges 16:20). But since God has granted me repentance and I've been away from alcohol and all forms of impurity for several years, I can attest to the presence of God returning to me. I sense closeness with Him, unity with Him, and love from and to Him. But this has been a slow process. Slowly savor the following precious promises from the Lord in the Scripture to Consider.

Course member Teresa writes, "I am enjoying the presence of God again in my life. Each day I am aware of the blinders being taken off and 'see' His work in my life. Everything looks different to me now. I find that I freely speak of the mercy and forgiveness of Christ to others (more than I had in the past). It has become a real, living thing to me. There is a 'quietness' to my life (not sure that makes sense). I am less anxious and tense. I have a real sense of 'cleanness' and peace. Alcohol has become much less of a temptation to me. My husband and I were traveling this weekend and stopped at a restaurant along the way for dinner Friday night. I noticed a woman drinking a glass of wine across the way and could 'see' the intoxication settle down upon her. It was interesting to me that I didn't desire the wine. Rather, I had the sense that the Lord was giving me a picture of the slow transformation that would take place in my own life as I became intoxicated. I felt as though I was looking at myself and that he had given me a clear picture of what I had become. It was humbling."

Scripture to Consider

"Ever since the time of your forefathers you have turned away from my decrees and have not kept them. Return to me, and I will return to you," says the LORD Almighty (Malachi 3:7).

"…and call upon me in the day of trouble; I will deliver you, and you will honor me" (Psalm 50:15).

Arise, shine, for your light has come, and the glory of the LORD rises upon you. See, darkness covers the earth and thick darkness is over the peoples, but the LORD rises upon you and his glory appears over you. Nations will come to your light, and kings to the brightness of your dawn" (Isaiah 60:1-3).

This is what the LORD Almighty says: "Return to me," declares the LORD Almighty, "and I will return to you," says the LORD Almighty. "Do not be like your forefathers, to whom the earlier prophets proclaimed: 'This is what the LORD Almighty says: "Turn from your evil ways and your evil practices."' "But they would not listen or pay attention to me," declares the LORD (Zechariah 1:3-4).

"Come to me, all you who are weary and burdened, and I will give you rest. Take my yoke upon you and learn from me, for I am gentle and humble in heart, and you will find rest for your souls. For my yoke is easy and my burden is light" (Matthew 11:28-30).

Did you feast on God's Word in the last 24 hours?

     Yes   No

If so, how did you feast? In other words, circle the ways you enjoyed God today. Reading? Prayer? Worship? Fellowship? Witnessing?

Were you free from drug and alcohol abuse since you did the last lesson?

     Yes   No

Did you spend personal time with the Lord since you did the last lesson?

     Yes   No

If you answered "no" to any of the above questions, describe what led to your fall.

If you answered "yes" to the above questions, you may use this area for additional comments.

DAY 22 - EXCLUSIVE DRINKING

Dear Friend,

The first few days of this course were about satisfying ourselves in the Living Water of Jesus Christ. Today we want to be very practical in providing help in overcoming drunkenness. What does it mean to "drink the Living Water?" What does it look like in daily living to be satisfied in Christ? And how does drinking Living Water actually enable us to leave our water pots of sin behind? These are the questions we will seek to answer today.

Let us begin with the first question: what does it mean to drink the Living Water? At the risk of sounding simplistic, it is as basic as reading the Bible. However, it is possible to read the Bible and not drink of the Living Water. So what is the difference?

Drinking implies taking something into your system, and receiving nourishment and sustenance from it. I can read that Jesus is Living Water all day long and not drink of Him. Drinking is directly related to the application of Scripture in my life, and it is much more than mere reading. When you read Scripture, ask God to apply it to your heart and to change your life by the reading of it. This is what it means to drink the Living Water.

The next question is what does it look like in daily living to be satisfied in Christ? It means rejoicing in the love, forgiveness and grace of God on a daily basis. It is discovering Christ fresh every day and being irresistibly drawn to him by what we discover. When we become happy in Him, we need not look for happiness in alcohol, food, or other substances. So then, as one of the Puritans of long ago said, "our first duty as Christians is to get ourselves happy in God." This is the only sure means of avoiding drunkenness. This is what Jesus taught the Samaritan woman in John chapter 4 which we studied in our first lesson.

And how does this drinking actually enable us to leave drugs behind? Simply put, if we are full and satisfied in Jesus Christ, we don't need anything else. Our heart has found its rejoicing in Him and needs nothing else.

The problem is that today's society offers so many other "water fountains" from which to drink; each one promising joyful satisfaction and delight. Alcohol, in its basic intent, promises to satisfy. It is an invitation to drink of happiness. These same promises are subtly conveyed through the allurement of pornography, smoking, TV, card playing, money chasing, relationships, gambling, drugs, etc. Even relationships with family and seemingly innocent activities, such as religion, sports, theme parks, the Internet, vacations, newspaper reading, or work, etc., may be an attempt to satisfy the heart apart from Christ. How do we live in today's society that offers so many fountains from which to drink? The answer is to be "exclusive drinkers." What do we mean by this? Notice the following verse:

> "As they make music they will say, 'All my fountains are in you'" (Psalm 87:7).

The context of this passage is that God is gracious to outsiders. He brings pagan gentiles into his family and calls them his own. And it is those heathen outsiders who, by the grace of God, have been brought into God's family who sing of their enjoyment of God: "all my fountains are in you." This is an affirmation of the truth that we have been studying from the beginning of the course; Jesus alone can satisfy. And it is a commitment to have no other source of life, refreshment, or satisfaction than what can be found in Jesus. It is a statement of fact, that they would be "exclusive drinkers."

Now we will examine some very practical ways to ensure that all our fountains are only in Jesus Christ. Please read the following passage and answer the questions below.

> The whole Israelite community set out from the Desert of Sin, traveling from place to place as the LORD commanded. They camped at Rephidim, but there was no water for the people to drink. So they quarreled with Moses and said, "Give us water to drink."
>
> Moses replied, "Why do you quarrel with me? Why do you put the LORD to the test?"
>
> But the people were thirsty for water there, and they grumbled against Moses. They said, "Why did you bring us up out of Egypt to make us and our children and livestock die of thirst?"
>
> Then Moses cried out to the LORD, "What am I to do with these people? They are almost ready to stone me."
>
> The LORD answered Moses, "Walk on ahead of the people. Take with you some of the elders of Israel and take in your hand the staff with which you struck the Nile, and go. I will stand there before you by the rock at Horeb. Strike the rock, and water will come out of it for the people to drink." So Moses did this in the sight of the elders of Israel (Exodus 17:1-6).

Questions

Question 1. Where were these people during this event?

Question 2. Why were they complaining?

Question 3. What did God tell them to do about their thirst?

Compare the following passage: "They all ate the same spiritual food and drank the same spiritual drink; for they drank from the spiritual rock that accompanied them, and that rock was Christ" (1 Corinthians 10:3-4).

Question 4. According to the above verses, who did the rock represent?

Question 5. What did Moses have to do to the rock before the people could drink from it?

Notice the teaching from this passage of Scripture. The rock that was struck poured forth water for the people to drink. This rock represents Jesus Christ. Oh friend, here is lasting satisfaction; Jesus Christ, on the cross, was "struck," and he poured out his life that we may drink and live. But the rock that was struck in the wilderness was God's only provision at this time to quench their thirst. They had to drink from that rock.

Are you still thirsting? Are you looking to alcohol or prescription meds for your thirst to be quenched? It never will be. But come to the cross of Jesus Christ. He was pierced by a Roman soldier and his life gushed out. It is on the cross of Jesus Christ where the "Rock" was struck.

But Friend, we must drink only from the Rock. We must say "all my fountains are in You." We must be exclusive drinkers.

Time for reflection . . .

Question 6. Are there other "fountains" in your life from which you have been drinking? If so, what are they? List them here:

Question 7. Will you now make a conscious effort to rid your life of all other "drinking" sources? Will you, by the grace of God, say from now on "All my fountains are in you?"

Please comment on this quote from **Matthew Henry**:

> Nothing will supply the needs, and satisfy the desires of a soul, but water out of this rock Jesus Christ, this fountain opened. The pleasures of sense are puddle-water; spiritual delights are rock water, so pure, so clear, and so refreshing—rivers of pleasure.

Question 8. According to Matthew Henry's quote above, what would you say is a major difference between "drinking" from drunkenness and drinking from Jesus? Write your answer here:

Questions

How satisfying is Jesus? Will becoming an exclusive drinker really satisfy? I had become a suicidal, depressed shell of a man. All psychiatry could do for me was to medicate me and tell me to look for the source of the problem. That source was sin. The only prescription for sin is Jesus Christ. Friend, please take this teaching to heart because the satisfaction of being an exclusive drinker is lasting and it brings joy. The joy that God has placed in my heart is something that no medicine could ever produce. It comes from within, and it will change every part of our lives!

> Then the angel showed me the river of the water of life, as clear as crystal, flowing from the throne of God and of the Lamb down the middle of the great street of the city. On each side of the river stood the tree of life, bearing twelve crops of fruit, yielding its fruit every month. And the leaves of the tree are for the healing of the nations. No longer will there be any curse (Revelation 22:1-3).

Question 9. How do the above verses in Revelation coincide with the teaching in today's lesson?

Question 10. Please write out a paragraph that summarizes the teaching of today:

Question 11. How is your life going right now? Are you beginning to walk in victory by God's grace?

Scripture to Consider

On the last and greatest day of the Feast, Jesus stood and said in a loud voice, "If anyone is thirsty, let him come to me and drink. Whoever believes in me, as the Scripture has said, streams of living water will flow from within him." By this he meant the Spirit, whom those who believed in him were later to receive (John 7:37-39).

They are before the throne of God and serve him day and night in his temple; and he who sits on the throne will spread his tent over them. Never again will they hunger; never again will they thirst. The sun will not beat upon them, nor any scorching heat. For the Lamb at the center of the throne will be their shepherd; he will lead them to springs of living water. And God will wipe away every tear from their eyes (Revelation 7:15-17).

Did you feast on God's Word in the last 24 hours?

     Yes   No

If so, how did you feast? In other words, circle the ways you enjoyed God today. Reading? Prayer? Worship? Fellowship? Witnessing?

Were you free from drug and alcohol abuse since you did the last lesson?

     Yes   No

Did you spend personal time with the Lord since you did the last lesson?

     Yes   No

If you answered "no" to any of the above questions, describe what led to your fall.

If you answered "yes" to the above questions, you may use this area for additional comments.

DAY 23 - THE POWER OF THE WORD

There is a continual need to profit from Scripture, and utilize the power of God's Word in an individual's life. The antidote to self-deception is to listen to God through His Word and to mistrust one's own capacity to reason (Proverbs 3:5-6, 13:14, 14:15, 14:27). The propensity of the human heart to rationalize and justify sin is an active force in the tangled lives of those enslaved to sin. Only by fearing the Lord (yielding oneself to the Word of God) may one find life and freedom. The power of God through His Word is the source of my freedom from drunkenness! As God applied His Word to my heart and my life, a change took place in me. That change had nothing to do with any "work" I did, but it had everything to do with the grace and power of God. The following is written by Pastor Dave Wagner from Windsor Ontario, Canada, and can be the basis for personal growth in Christ. Please read this excellent article and answer the questions throughout today's lesson.

Learning To Enjoy Freedom In Christ

I would like to take a few minutes to speak to the course members of New Wine. This course has the ability to help shape the hearts, minds, souls and spirits of the students that come seeking freedom from addiction. On the whole, the majority of people who come to the website are Christians or have some church background. In spite of the "availability of Scripture and truth" many come to the site hopelessly addicted to the slavery of drunkenness.

Many who come have been reading the Bible for years, yet the truth has escaped them! They find no spiritual profit from their study of it. The evidence of "bad fruit" in their lives brings us rapidly to the conclusion that although their store of knowledge has increased, so also has their pride. Like a chemist engaged in making interesting experiments, the intellectual searcher of the Word is quite elated when he finds or makes some discovery in it. The joy they have holds no spiritual meaning for them. Their success, and their sense of self-importance only increases and causes them to look with distain upon others more ignorant than themselves.

We have found from working with course members that there is a type of person who in their answers makes frequent references to Scripture left, right and center, and yet when it comes to constant scriptural accountability they end up going through cycle after cycle of checking "no" to the accountability questions at the end of each lesson. Satan is constantly active to get this type of personality to quote much Scripture but never apply it. It is always meant for someone else.

Questions

Question 1. How should we read Scripture?

Some who come to the course are reading the Word of God for the wrong reasons, such as curiosity or pride (in the sense that they can tell others how often they read it) and others read to accumulate knowledge as a weapon of war, but not against Satan. They use it for the purpose of being able to argue successfully with those who would differ from them or have an opposing point of view. As a result of their wrongful reading there is no thought of God, no yearning for spiritual edification, no benefit to the soul, and most important no power in their lives to overcome the addictive lifestyle in which they find themselves even as Christians.

Our goal for you the student is to help you profit from the Word. 2 Timothy 3:16, 17 gives us clear guidance as to how the Word can influence our lives:

> All Scripture is given by inspiration of God is profitable for Doctrine, for reproof, for correction, in instruction and in righteousness that the man of God may be perfect thoroughly furnished unto all good works!

Question 2. Please write down for what things Scripture is profitable:

The Word within this New Wine course will accomplish many things!

1. First, the Word of God will convict of sin and reveal our depravity, expose our vileness and make known our wickedness. One of the ways you will know that you are profiting from the Word, and not merely gaining knowledge, is when you begin to see these things occurring in your life.

Question 3. Friend, is this happening in your life currently? If so, can you give an example?

Questions

2. The Word of God will make the captive Christian sorrow over sin. Many come to the course with a stony heart. As the Holy Spirit applies the Word, the student is able to see and feel their inward corruption and many discover the strongholds that Satan has set up in their lives. This discovery by the Word produces a broken heart and leads them to humble themselves before God.

> **Course member Teresa writes,** "As I have been in the Word I see clearly the warnings from God that He will not share His glory with anyone or anything. God has warned me of how my heart has been deceived and carried away because my first love was no longer for Him. I cannot claim ignorance in this regard. I have read many passages of Scripture that show me that as I have called out to Him, really called out to Him, He was willing to restore me in our relationship. I've experienced being soothed and tenderly loved by God through His Word. As the chains of bondage strangled my soul, I read those same passages believing that either the warnings were 'for someone else' (they didn't apply to me because after all, I was already a believer) or with fear because I was afraid I was beyond help or hope. The soothing words of restoration and love by God seemed far beyond my grasp. My heart was not penetrated because it was being strangled by pride, lust and unbelief."

Question 4. Has God been revealing your sinfulness and causing you to sorrow over it?

You will know that you are on the right track and heading down the right road when you see this humbling of spirit start to take place. It will be shown by the words you write. If God is working in your heart in this way, you will be brought to a daily repentance before Him. You will also experience the liberation from guilt and shame and you will be able with joy to answer the daily accountability questions at the end of each lesson. This "sorrow over sin" goes through a pre-defined process. God had a process for the sacrifice of the Pascal Lamb; it was to be eaten with "bitter herbs" (Exodus 12:8). As the Word does the work on your heart the Holy Spirit makes it "bitter" before it becomes sweet to your taste. So we see there must be mourning before comfort (Matthew 5:4), humbling before exalting (1 Peter 5:6).

The reading of the Word of God causes us to remember our sinful life that was a bitter experience for us. As God changes our hearts and lives, that bitterness is changed to sweetness. The cross of Jesus Christ brings us to a place of forgiveness, and the bitterness of our former sins is changed to sweetness. We have examples of this in Scripture.

3. The Word of God leads to confession of sin. The Scriptures are profitable for reproof (2 Timothy 3:16). When you come to God with an honest heart and soul, you start confessing and acknowledge your faults.

For every one that doeth evil hateth the light, neither cometh to the light, least his deed should be reproved (John 3:20).

This is a great battlefield for Christians coming to the New Wine course with habitual sin in their lives. They are like people who gather on the fringe of darkness around the campfire in a dark forest. They know that sooner or later they will have to choose: step forward and drag their sins out into the light where that sin will die or stay in the comfort of the shadows slipping in and out of the light and never fully committing to the light. The sin of captivity to substances is often a secret or covered sin.

> He that covereth his sins shall not prosper: but whosoever confesseth and forsaketh them shall have mercy (Proverbs 28:13).

> There can be no spiritual prosperity or fruitfulness while we conceal within our breasts our guilty secrets (Psalm 1:3).

There is no real peace for the conscience and no rest for the heart while there is the burden of unconfessed sin.

Question 5. Is there any unconfessed or secret sin in your life?

4. The Word of God within the course will also produce within you a deeper hatred of sin. It is when you start coming to the place where you really hate the sin and hate the captivity it brings that you will be taking the first steps towards freedom.

> … ye that love the Lord, hate evil (Psalm 97:10).

We cannot love God without hating that which he hates. Through Thy precepts I get understanding: therefore I hate every false way (Psalm 119:104). It is not merely "I abstain from" but "I hate" not some or many but every false way.

Question 6. Is God producing this hatred of sin in your life, Friend? If so, how is He doing it?

5. The Word of God will produce a forsaking of sin. It is very simple. Satan's job is to keep us from reading the Word. Like the parable of the sower with the seed, some will read it and it will take root. Others will read it and there will be no forsaking of sin.

> Let every one that nameth the name of Christ depart from iniquity (2 Timothy 2:19).

Questions

The reading and studying of God's Word produces a purging of my ways. If it is not doing this, we need to ask "Why Not?" When the Word of God is personally applied to our lives, the end results are dynamic. It causes us to "cleanse our ways." It causes us to "take heed" and it exhorts us to flee drunkenness. Sin needs to be not only confessed but forsaken (Proverbs 28:13).

6. The Word of God produces a fortification against sin.

> Thy Word have I hid in my heart that I might not sin against thee (Psalm 119:11).

The more that Christ's Word dwells in us richly (Colossians 3:16) the less room there will be for the exercise of sin in our hearts and lives. The Word of God fortifies us. Nothing preserves from the infections of this world, delivers from the temptations of Satan and is so effective a preservative against sin as the Word of God. As long as truth is active within us, stirring the conscience and really loved by us, we shall be kept from falling. You must be prepared and fortified ahead of time for Satan's attacks. We often call this having a "plan of action." By storing up the Word in our hearts we will be prepared for coming emergencies and the attacks of Satan.

Question 7. Please state, in your own words, what six things the Word of God is designed to do, and give any comments.

1.

2.

3.

4.

5.

6.

Question 8. How are you doing today?

Scripture to Consider

For the word of God is living and active. Sharper than any double-edged sword, it penetrates even to dividing soul and spirit, joints and marrow; it judges the thoughts and attitudes of the heart. Nothing in all creation is hidden from God's sight. Everything is uncovered and laid bare before the eyes of him to whom we must give account (Hebrews 4:12-13).

I write to you, fathers, because you have known him who is from the beginning. I write to you, young men, because you are strong, and the word of God lives in you, and you have overcome the evil one (1 John 2:14).

Did you feast on God's Word in the last 24 hours?

       Yes   No

If so, how did you feast? In other words, circle the ways you enjoyed God today. Reading? Prayer? Worship? Fellowship? Witnessing?

Were you free from drug and alcohol abuse since you did the last lesson?

       Yes   No

Did you spend personal time with the Lord since you did the last lesson?

       Yes   No

If you answered "no" to any of the above questions, describe what led to your fall.

If you answered "yes" to the above questions, you may use this area for additional comments.

DAY 24 - PURITY PRECEDES POWER

Read the following passage from Scripture and notice how serious these people were about radical amputation.

> Many of those who believed now came and openly confessed their evil deeds. A number who had practiced sorcery brought their scrolls together and burned them publicly. When they calculated the value of the scrolls, the total came to fifty thousand drachmas. In this way the word of the Lord spread widely and grew in power (Acts 19:18-20).

There! Did you notice it, Friend? Immediately after Scripture records the people "radically amputating" their books of sorcery, it records the power that came with it. Read it again: "In this way the word of the Lord spread widely and grew in power!" Purity precedes power.

But now, let us examine one of the ways that the devil keeps people enslaved to substances, such as heroin. He tries to turn things upside down and make us think that power precedes purity. Look at an email we received several months ago in The Way of Purity course:

From an anonymous writer: "I have not continued on in the course because I have been doing pornography. In response to your advice that I 'cut off and throw away the CDROM' that has the porn on it, I respond that it is not the CDROM that causes me to sin, it is my own heart. It would not be reasonable to cut off the CDROM and throw it away as I would just find something else to view. My idea of victory is to be able to have the CDROM nearby and say no to it. I will continue looking for another method of freedom."

This man will not find power to "say no" until he radically amputates his sin. This example is concerning pornography, but can you see how we do the same thing with drugs?

My life was a great example of this principle! I played music in bars an average of six nights a week. I resolved to stop drinking over and over but refused to give up my lifestyle. All my co-workers drank heavily and the patrons of the bars were coming to get drunk. The environment was terrible! Yet I was determined to continue going into that environment night after night and counting on my willpower to keep me from drinking. I resolved to do this many times and each time I failed miserably! This is the same as the person who continues to keep alcohol in the house. Radical amputation is needed here, and there is no substitute. Only after I amputated all the sources of alcohol from my life, including playing music in bars, did God's power release me.

We may think that power means being able to handle temptation by facing it. And there will be times when we have to face temptation because it is unavoidable. At those times we must rely on God to provide the strength. The best plan is to flee from temptation! Radical amputation actively removes any source of temptation before it can become a problem!

Radically amputating alcohol from our lives takes planning. Restaurants serve alcohol, grocery stores and convenience stores sell beer, wine and liquor. The world around us is full of opportunities to indulge in drunkenness, yet we must amputate all that we possibly can! This is a great moment to develop a plan: think out the normal steps you take in a day and then list those things that are areas of temptation. Share this plan with your mentor so he/she can help you in the planning as well as keep you accountable with it. This is a sample battle plan for one person:

- Smash every bottle and pour out every can of alcohol in the house.

- Carry no money or credit cards. Buying alcohol takes money!

- Avoid restaurants that sell alcohol.

- Take different routes home so as to not pass by places of temptation.

- Tell several others about your struggles and have them be accountability partners. Give these partners permission to regularly ask questions about whether your plan is being followed or not. They can be available for confession if there is a stumble and prayer support when tempted.

Warning: those who trifle with clear teaching of God's Word that we are to deal radically with sin will not achieve lasting purity, will not perceive spiritual matters correctly, and will not receive God's power in their lives.

"There must be a divorce! Within the egg of sin there sleeps the seed of damnation! Man, there must be a divorce between you and your sins. Not a mere separation for a season, but a clear divorce. Cut off the right arm; pluck out the right eye, and cast them from you, or else you cannot enter into eternal life" (**Charles Spurgeon**, *The Chief of Sinners*).

Why ask for trouble and cause your own downfall...? (2 Chronicles 25:19).

Questions

Question 1. What is the title of Day 24?

Question 3. What words did God use to tell the Israelites why they were defeated by Ai?

Now let us see a powerful demonstration of this truth taught in story form. Here is the background: The Israelites had just won a great victory over the very fortified city of Jericho and were preparing for battle against the small town of Ai. They were not too concerned about the outcome of this battle, due to the size of Ai. But they lost! And they were humiliated. Notice why they lost:

Question 4. What did the Israelites do to the man who was cherishing and hiding items of destruction?

> Israel has sinned; they have violated my covenant, which I commanded them to keep. They have taken some of the devoted things; they have stolen, they have lied, they have put them with their own possessions. That is why the Israelites cannot stand against their enemies...You cannot stand against your enemies until you remove it! (Joshua 7:11-13).

As it turns out, a man by the name of Achan took a "beautiful robe, two hundred shekels of silver and a wedge of gold..." (v. 21) from the victory at Jericho, and was cherishing and hiding them. But notice the words that God used to show why the Israelites lost the battle: "You cannot stand against your enemies until you remove it."

Note: They did not only eradicate Achan, but his entire family, cattle, donkey, sheep and "all that he had." They stoned him, stoned the rest, and then burned them all. Here is truth for us. To become pure and powerful in battle we need to thoroughly destroy everything remotely connected to our previous bondage to sin. Stone it, burn it, and bury all of its "relatives." Then watch God's power at work in us.

Question 5. What did it take for the Israelites to have power in battle?

This is highly instructive for us today. Until we remove that which has caused us to sin we cannot expect power over the enemy. Purity precedes power. Notice what happens next:

> Then Joshua, together with all Israel, took Achan son of Zerah, the silver, the robe, the gold wedge, his sons and daughters, his cattle, donkeys and sheep, his tent and all that he had, to the Valley of Achor. Then all Israel stoned him, and after they had stoned the rest, they burned them (Joshua 7:24,25).

Now that is radical amputation. It is removing that which has caused sin. Notice what happened next:

Friend, there is a spiritual principle taught in the above passage that has everything to do with our fight against sin. If we will radically amputate anything that can trip us up, God will fight for us. We will have power that results from purity. We cannot expect victory over sin while keeping an "Achan" in the camp. Get rid of it. Cut it off, and experience true power over temptation. Remember, "you cannot stand against your enemy until you remove it!"

> Twelve thousand men and women fell that day--all the people of Ai. So Joshua burned Ai and made it a permanent heap of ruins, a desolate place to this day (Joshua 8:25-28).

Question 6. Where are you right now with your level of understanding and commitment?

Friend, if we want to make drunkenness in our lives "a permanent heap of ruins—a desolate place" then we must cut off that which causes us to sin. Purity precedes power.

Question 2. Why did Israel lose the battle with Ai?

> Throw out your calf-idol, O Samaria! My anger burns against them. How long will they be incapable of purity? (Hosea 8:5).

Questions

Question 7. How are you doing? Did you learn anything new in this lesson today, and what will you put into practice?

Scripture to Consider

Blessed are the pure in heart, for they will see God (Matthew 5:8).

Did you feast on God's Word in the last 24 hours?

      Yes   No

If so, how did you feast? In other words, circle the ways you enjoyed God today. Reading? Prayer? Worship? Fellowship? Witnessing?

Were you free from drug and alcohol abuse since you did the last lesson?

      Yes   No

Did you spend personal time with the Lord since you did the last lesson?

      Yes   No

If you answered "no" to any of the above questions, describe what led to your fall.

If you answered "yes" to the above questions, you may use this area for additional comments.

DAY 25 - IDOLATRY

Friend, the abuse of prescription meds is deceitful, self-pleasing, rebellious idolatry. At times in the history of the nation of Israel, they were given over to sins of the same nature. Let's read this following passage, and then answer the questions below:

> These are rebellious people, deceitful children, children unwilling to listen to the LORD's instruction. They say to the seers, "See no more visions!" and to the prophets, "Give us no more visions of what is right! Tell us pleasant things, prophesy illusions. Leave this way, get off this path, and stop confronting us with the Holy One of Israel!" (Isaiah 30:9-11).

The above Scripture describes the life of one who habitually is involved in pill-popping. It mentions four specific things about them:

1. They are rebellious people.

2. They are deceitful.

3. They are unwilling to listen to godly instruction.

4. They do not wish to be confronted about their sin.

I remember how rebellious my heart was during my 17 years of enslavement to crack and alcohol. I was determined to follow my sin no matter what the consequences. I would lie to my family and to others about my sin. I would beg, borrow, or steal to get more crack. I grew up in a Christian home and was convicted in my heart that what I was doing was wrong. My family confronted me many times which only led me to anger. My heart was as hard as a rock and I would not listen to anyone, no matter how convincing their argument or how much their words pierced my conscience. The guilt only made me angrier in the end. Just like the passage above, I was a rebellious, deceitful idolater!

Questions

Question 1. How has your life in the past resembled these four truths? Which one described you best? Rebellious, deceitful, unwilling to listen, or not wanting to be confronted? Write out a description of your life here:

> Therefore, this is what the Holy One of Israel says: "Because you have rejected this message, relied on oppression and depended on deceit, this sin will become for you like a high wall, cracked and bulging, that collapses suddenly, in an instant. It will break in pieces like pottery, shattered so mercilessly that among its pieces not a fragment will be found for taking coals from a hearth or scooping water out of a cistern" (Isaiah 30:12-14).

Questions

All who continue in substance abuse will find that their lives will come crashing down to the ground and be smashed to pieces. I stopped traveling in 1994 and found myself homeless and without any means to support myself. I had spent every dime that I made buying alcohol and crack, which left me penniless. I had also lost nearly everyone that I called a friend. My family took me in, but I continued to lie about my slavery to drugs. My depressed state was so severe that they took me to a psychiatrist who prescribed anti-depressants in the hope of relieving the pain I carried around inside of me. The drugs could not cure sin, however, and did little good. My world had come crashing down, and I felt as if I had nowhere to turn.

At Setting Captives Free, we have seen numerous stories of great devastation. Families split apart, jobs lost, pastors asked to resign, criminals taken into custody, etc. Possibly your life has come crashing down around you because of your sin. Possibly you are not at that stage yet; maybe you're just "having fun" with alcohol and have not experienced this "crash." Maybe you have gone for 10, 20 or even 30 years with seemingly minimal adverse side effects. But like the giant tree that finally topples after years of internal decay, Friend, if you continue on this path your life will fall to pieces, because God cannot be mocked.

Question 2. Please explain where you are with this teaching. Have you crashed yet?

Questions

This is what the Sovereign LORD, the Holy One of Israel, says: "In repentance and rest is your salvation, in quietness and trust is your strength, but you would have none of it.

You said, 'No, we will flee on horses.' Therefore you will flee! You said, 'We will ride off on swift horses.' Therefore your pursuers will be swift! A thousand will flee at the threat of one; at the threat of five you will all flee away, till you are left like a flagstaff on a mountaintop, like a banner on a hill" (Isaiah 30:15-17).

Some conditions caused by habitual sin are: Escapism and Paranoia

- Escapism is where a person knows he is guilty and he has a bad conscience, and seeks to escape his trouble by running away. This escapism is described above as "fleeing away on swift horses" and shows the desire of these people to get away from it all.

- Paranoia is where a person exhibits irrational fear of people, places, or things, and any of these can literally terrify them. When a person is in habitual sin there is a fear of getting caught, and they always wonder if they've covered their tracks sufficiently. They can become paranoid that someone will find out, or that God will strike them dead.

Question 3. Have you ever experienced this type of escapism or paranoia?

Yet the LORD longs to be gracious to you; he rises to show you compassion. For the LORD is a God of justice. Blessed are all who wait for him! (Isaiah 30:18).

Friend, if you find yourself described in the above scenario there is one thing that will fix it all: the grace of God! The solution to sin is the grace of God. And it is not as though God doesn't want to be gracious, for He "longs to be gracious to you." Another version of the above verse reads that God "waits to be gracious to you." The answer to a life reduced to rubble by the power of sin is the grace of God. It is not to turn to the psychologists and psychiatrists for that does not go to the root of the problem. It is not to learn behavior modification for that does not reach the heart of the problem. Only God's grace changes the heart and goes to the root.

[19]O people of Zion, who live in Jerusalem, you will weep no more. How gracious he will be when you cry for help! As soon as he hears, he will answer you. [20]Although the Lord gives you the bread of adversity and the water of affliction, your teachers will be hidden no more; with your own eyes you will see them. [21]Whether you turn to the right or to the left, your ears will hear a voice behind you, saying, "This is the way; walk in it." [22]Then you will defile your idols overlaid with silver and your images covered with gold; you will throw them away like a menstrual cloth and say to them, "Away with you!" (Isaiah 30:19-22).

The answer to sin is to cry out to God for help. When He hears, He will be gracious to you and answer you. He will send you "teachers" to help you learn and grow, and His Holy Spirit will help you to walk in purity, and provide you direction in life.

And the result of God showing you His grace will be that you begin to detest your drug of choice and you will rid your life of it: "Then (after God gives His grace) you will defile your idols . . . and images . . . you will throw them away like a menstrual cloth and say to them, 'Away with you!'" We can always tell when God is granting grace to someone, because they willingly rid their lives of their former idols, and it is not uncommon to hear them use strong language of hatred for their former idols such as "menstrual cloth."

Drunkenness is idolatry: We lust for substances and their numbing effects. "Put to death, therefore, whatever belongs to your earthly nature: sexual immorality, impurity, lust, evil desires and greed, which is idolatry" (Colossians 3:5). When God grants us grace we can't get rid of the idol fast enough!

Question 4. Time for personal reflection. Where are you in the above passage of Scripture? Are you yet rebellious, deceitful, unwilling to listen and trying to avoid confrontation? Or are you crying out to God for grace? Or are you ridding your life of idols and calling them names?

Questions

²³He will also send you rain for the seed you sow in the ground, and the food that comes from the land will be rich and plentiful. In that day your cattle will graze in broad meadows. ²⁴The oxen and donkeys that work the soil will eat fodder and mash, spread out with fork and shovel. ²⁵In the day of great slaughter, when the towers fall, streams of water will flow on every high mountain and every lofty hill. ²⁶The moon will shine like the sun, and the sunlight will be seven times brighter, like the light of seven full days, when the LORD binds up the bruises of his people and heals the wounds he inflicted (Isaiah 30:23-26).

When God gives His grace of forgiveness, He also restores fully. Sometimes sin causes such ruin that some relationships cannot be restored (divorce and remarriage), nor victims brought back (murder) but even so God gives grace to endure these difficulties. God's restoration can even make things "better" than before. Notice the above passage "the moon will shine like the sun, and the sunlight will be seven times brighter . . . when the Lord binds up the bruises of His people and heals the wounds he inflicted."

How does this look in the life of a man enslaved for 17 years and set free by God's wonderful grace? My wife and I have beautiful children and a marriage rooted in love given by our Lord. I have been called into full-time ministry by God and am currently serving in that capacity. God has removed the terrible, suicidal depression that plagued me for so many years and I have not taken any medications for it since being set free. Peace, joy, purpose, love—these are all part of the restoration given by God. Did I deserve it? No, but grace has nothing to do with what we deserve but rather what we are given. And now I have been given the opportunity to share this grace with you. You see, it does not matter where we have been—God's grace is bigger than all of that. I thank Him and Him only for what He has done in my life. This same healing and restoration will happen in your life by God's grace. This is hope, Friend, as He heals our hurts and our wounds!

Question 5. How are you doing today?

Course member Teresa writes, "I am enjoying a restored relationship with Christ. I believe it is not only restored but better than ever. My marriage has improved greatly. My husband and I spend a lot of time together now talking about the things of the Lord and the lessons we are learning through the correction we have gone through. My health is being restored. Many of the physical maladies I began experiencing from abusing alcohol appear to be gone. I have much more peace, joy and contentment. The Lord has granted 'spiritual eyes' to me in viewing life and myself. My friendships with other believers have improved greatly and new ones have been formed. The 'walls' I built around me are coming down. Spending time in the Word and in prayer has become a priority to me again."

Scripture to Consider

How great is the love the Father has lavished on us, that we should be called children of God! And that is what we are! The reason the world does not know us is that it did not know him. Dear friends, now we are children of God, and what we will be has not yet been made known. But we know that when he appears, we shall be like him, for we shall see him as he is. Everyone who has this hope in him purifies himself, just as he is pure (1 John 3:1-3).

Did you feast on God's Word in the last 24 hours?

     Yes   No

If so, how did you feast? In other words, circle the ways you enjoyed God today. Reading? Prayer? Worship? Fellowship? Witnessing?

Were you free from drug and alcohol abuse since you did the last lesson?

     Yes   No

Did you spend personal time with the Lord since you did the last lesson?

     Yes   No

If you answered "no" to any of the above questions, describe what led to your fall.

If you answered "yes" to the above questions, you may use this area for additional comments.

DAY 26 - VIGILANCE

We receive many emails from students who go through a portion of the course and feel as if they do not need any further instruction or help. They may have a period of freedom, but many times will fall and even end up deeper in sin than they were before they came to New Wine. It is very painful to watch a student leave the course full of pride, only to come back beaten down by sin.

Today we want to teach on a subject that Scripture speaks much about: the necessity to be vigilant against sin creeping back into our lives after a period of victory. Let's notice several passages:

> [7]Do not be idolaters, as some of them were; as it is written: "The people sat down to eat and drink and got up to indulge in pagan revelry." [8]We should not commit sexual immorality, as some of them did, and in one day twenty-three thousand of them died. [9]We should not test the Lord, as some of them did, and were killed by snakes. [10]And do not grumble, as some of them did, and were killed by the destroying angel.

> [11]These things happened to them as examples and were written down as warnings for us, on whom the fulfillment of the ages has come. [12]So, if you think you are standing firm, be careful that you don't fall! (1 Corinthians 10:7-12).

This passage traces the history of the nation of Israel after they had been released from their slavery in Egypt. They had come to the desert where they were involved in idolatry, and God's wrath broke out against them and He killed 23,000 of them by snakes. The Apostle Paul tells us that the experiences of the nation of Israel were given as examples and warnings for us. What are we to learn from the experience recorded above? To be vigilant! "So, if you think you are standing firm, be careful that you don't fall."

Questions

The above verses describe the scenario leading up to Judas' betrayal of Jesus. Jesus knew He would be betrayed and knew He needed strength from above to endure the coming events, so He was seeking His Father in prayer. And it is right here that Jesus instructs His disciples, and us, on how not to fall: "Watch and pray so that you will not fall into temptation." Be vigilant. Watch against a developing chain of events that lead to a fall into sin, and remove a link in the chain. Watch for familiar areas in which you are tempted, watch for the uprising of the flesh, watch out for when you are tired, and watch out for times when you have just had a high spiritual experience, WATCH. But don't watch only—watch and pray. Pray that God will keep you from falling. Pray that He would give you grace to endure temptation without giving in. Pray for power from above to extinguish the fiery darts of the devil.

Question 2. What are some specific areas of temptation in which you need to be watchful and how may we pray with you about them?

Questions

Question 1. Can you think of a time when you thought you had mastered sin, and were "standing" only to fall, Friend?

We have seen course members begin walking in victory over their past sins, and truly be overcomers for many days in a row, and then we notice some pride creeping in and their answers and their emails become more instructive as if they were the authority. It isn't long before they fall, and oftentimes we never see these people again. Their fall came because of pride, and pride keeps them in their fallen condition. There is much caution needed, especially when we begin to experience victory.

> [40]Then he returned to his disciples and found them sleeping. "Could you men not keep watch with me for one hour?" he asked Peter. [41]"Watch and pray so that you will not fall into temptation. The spirit is willing, but the body is weak" (Matthew 26:40-41).

Questions

Friend, no matter how many victories we have had or how long we have been walking in freedom, we always have a need to be vigilant. The reason for this is because "the flesh is weak." The flesh is always weak, no matter how long we've been pure or how strong we are in faith. There is no saint alive who does not have weak flesh, hence the need to watch and pray against falling. Many a Christian has fallen to the lies of the devil in the last hour of his life, and we must pray to guard against this.

> Be self-controlled and alert. Your enemy the devil prowls around like a roaring lion looking for someone to devour. Resist him, standing firm in the faith, because you know that your brothers throughout the world are undergoing the same kind of sufferings (1 Peter 5:8-9).

The above passage instructs us to "be self-controlled and alert" which is translated in the KJV as "be vigilant." We not only must be vigilant because our flesh is weak, but because our enemy is strong—like a lion. He prowls around looking to devour us. Should he find us not watching and not praying, we are easy prey to devour.

Question 3. Are you aware of the strength of your enemy? What experiences have you had with the enemy where you've felt his strength?

In **John Bunyan's** book, *Pilgrim's Progress*, Christian is often assaulted by numerous enemies, and in time comes to watch for them and pray against them. He writes this poem based upon his experiences of surprise attacks from his enemies:

> The trials that those men do meet withal,
> That are obedient to the heavenly call,
> Are manifold, and suited to the flesh,
> And come, and come, and come again afresh;
> That now, or some time else, we by them may
> Be taken, overcome, and cast away.
> O let the pilgrims, let the pilgrims then,
> Be vigilant, and quit themselves like men.

Notice that the purposes of the trials and temptations, and assaults of the enemy, are that we might be "taken, over-come, and cast away." That is what our prowling enemy seeks to do to us, is cast us away from the faith. We must be watchful unto prayer, being ever vigilant.

> ⁵ You are all sons of the light and sons of the day. We do not belong to the night or to the darkness. ⁶So then, let us not be like others, who are asleep, but let us be alert and self-controlled. ⁷For those who sleep, sleep at night, and those who get drunk, get drunk at night. ⁸But since we belong to the day, let us be self-controlled, putting on faith and love as a breastplate, and the hope of salvation as a helmet (1 Thessalonians 5:5-8).

In the above passage we are admonished not to "sleep," which obviously does not refer to refusing the nightly rest that the body needs, but rather to not being vigilant against temptation. The disciples in the garden were sleeping when they should have been watching and praying. Likewise, we sleep when we go about our day ignorant of the power of our enemy, and ignorant of the weakness of our flesh, which work together to cast us down and destroy our faith and make us reprobates.

Question 4. Please state what circumstances in the future may cause you to "sleep" when you should be watching and praying.

This is a good moment to remind us of something. Many deceive themselves by saying, "I just want to get to the point where I can drink socially like everyone else." The devil would love to get us to believe we can "try a drink" and test the waters. We must not fall victim to that lie but rather be vigilant and watchful. We must amputate alcohol from our lives for good, remembering that "one drink" could send us back into a worse spot than we were in before!

Finally, notice these words of Jesus that illustrate the need to be vigilant and not sleep:

> But concerning that day or that hour, no one knows, not even the angels in heaven, nor the Son, but only the Father. Be on guard, keep awake. For you do not know when the time will come. It is like a man going on a journey, when he leaves home and puts his servants in charge, each with his work, and commands the doorkeeper to stay awake. Therefore stay awake--for you do not know when the master of the house will come, in the evening, or at midnight, or when the cock crows, or in the morning lest he come suddenly and find you asleep. And what I say to you I say to all: Stay awake (Mark 13:32-37, ESV).

Question 5. How does this parable illustrate the truth in today's lesson? Write your thoughts here.

Questions

Friend, Jesus Christ declared that He who the Son sets free will be free indeed (John 8:36). And part of His work of making us free is to help us be vigilant. May we not be like those who walk many years in victory, only to fall through lack of vigilance. Watch and pray. Here are some specific ways you can do this:

1. **Make sure to attend a Bible-believing church (Hebrews 10:25).** The importance of this cannot be over-emphasized. Have daily accountability (Ecclesiastes 4:9-12; Hebrews 3:13).

2. **Seek the Lord daily (Proverbs 2:1-5; Hebrews 11:6)**

3. **Drag every known sin, and even temptation into the light.** If you struggle with something, humble yourself and talk to someone about it (John 3:19-21).

> **Course member Teresa writes,** "I need to have the discernment to not allow the tares of pride to take hold in my life. The tares that come in the form of believing I could drink socially or have a glass of wine occasionally or believing that alcohol will never pose a problem for me again. I remember clearly how after drinking one glass I was drawn back for another and another and another. And after that bottle was gone, buying another and emptying it only to want more. It was never enough."

Question 6. What are some other things you can do to be vigilant against sin? Write them here:

Scripture to Consider

I will set before my eyes no vile thing (Psalm 101:3).

Therefore, prepare your minds for action; be self-controlled; set your hope fully on the grace to be given you when Jesus Christ is revealed (1 Peter 1:13).

You will be like one sleeping on the high seas, lying on top of the rigging. "They hit me," you will say, "but I'm not hurt! They beat me, but I don't feel it! When will I wake up so I can find another drink?" (Proverbs 23: 34-35).

But you, brothers, are not in darkness so that this day should surprise you like a thief. You are all sons of the light and sons of the day. We do not belong to the night or to the darkness. So then, let us not be like others, who are asleep, but let us be alert and self-controlled. For those who sleep, sleep at night, and those who get drunk, get drunk at night. But since we belong to the day, let us be self-controlled, putting on faith and love as a breastplate, and the hope of salvation as a helmet. For God did not appoint us to suffer wrath but to receive salvation through our Lord Jesus Christ (1 Thessalonians 5:4-9).

Did you feast on God's Word in the last 24 hours?

     Yes   No

If so, how did you feast? In other words, circle the ways you enjoyed God today. Reading? Prayer? Worship? Fellowship? Witnessing?

Were you free from drug and alcohol abuse since you did the last lesson?

     Yes   No

Did you spend personal time with the Lord since you did the last lesson?

     Yes   No

If you answered "no" to any of the above questions, describe what led to your fall.

If you answered "yes" to the above questions, you may use this area for additional comments.

DAY 27 - ENJOYING THE LIGHT

Dear Friend,

Earlier in this course we briefly touched on a subject that we would like to dwell on more thoroughly at this point. When I was enslaved to alcohol and cocaine, I had a secret and hidden sin. There was an area of my life that nobody knew about, that was off-limits and that was protected carefully so as not to be exposed. This hidden area is precisely where sin thrives as the darkness conceals the deeds done.

So part of gaining the victory over sin is to drag this secret life into the light and expose it. This is always a scary prospect, but in this lesson I hope to give you help to exposing the sin in the least painful way, and to assure you that God is always with the one who will begin this task. Please examine the following Scripture and answer the questions below . . . .

> [12]The night is nearly over; the day is almost here. So let us put aside the deeds of darkness and put on the armor of light. [13]Let us behave decently, as in the daytime, not in orgies and drunkenness, not in sexual immorality and debauchery, not in dissension and jealousy. [14]Rather, clothe yourselves with the Lord Jesus Christ, and do not think about how to gratify the desires of the sinful nature (Romans 13:12-14).

Questions

Question 3. What are we instructed to do with these deeds of darkness?

Question 4. Getting specific now, in what exact way can you "lay aside" those deeds of darkness?

Question 5. To what is light compared?

Questions

Question 1. What are the "deeds of darkness" listed in verse 13 above? Write them here:

Question 2. What are the "deeds of darkness" that you have been doing in the past?

Friend, the above verses tell us that the light is armor, and armor protects a soldier from the attacks of the enemy. This is an important understanding to have: light, in the spiritual realm, is armor. The enemy always shoots at us in the darkness, and if we expose our sin to the light we have protection from his assaults. So, I can tell you, based on the authority of Scripture, if you will expose your sin to the light you will have protection from ongoing attacks of the devil.

After we "lay aside" the deeds of darkness, we are to clothe ourselves with the Lord Jesus Christ. We are to put Him on, to wear Him as our protection against the enemy, and to find our life in Him. I remember that after I exposed my sin to the light, not only did I have the protection that the light offers, but I also began to find my life in Christ. I loved studying God's Word, singing songs to Jesus in private, praying often and long, going to church to receive God's Word and fellowship with other believers, etc. Though I didn't know it at the time, I was learning to do what the above verses speak of: lay aside the deeds of darkness, and clothe yourself with Jesus Christ.

Questions

Question 6. How will you specifically begin clothing yourself with Jesus Christ?

So, the above verse tells us to lay aside things done in darkness, and to clothe ourselves with the Light of Jesus Christ. Part of clothing ourselves in Jesus is coming into the light, and exposing our sins.

We can't emphasize enough, that though it can be frightening to come into the light, the results will be immediate purity. A fungus that is exposed to the light is sapped of its strength and eventually withers away and dies. Sin that is exposed to the light loses all its power and eventually is no more. So, despite the initial difficulty of doing this, it is well worth the trouble to do it. It will indeed provide freedom.

Let's read additional verses on this subject:

> [17]When this became known to the Jews and Greeks living in Ephesus, they were all seized with fear, and the name of the Lord Jesus was held in high honor. [18]Many of those who believed now came and openly confessed their evil deeds. [19]A number who had practiced sorcery brought their scrolls together and burned them publicly. When they calculated the value of the scrolls, the total came to fifty thousand drachmas. [20]In this way the word of the Lord spread widely and grew in power (Acts 19:17-20).

The verses that precede this passage show the healing power of Jesus as He cast out unclean spirits. It is when this power of God was displayed that people were seized with fear and were in awe of Jesus' Name.

Question 7. Verses 18 and 19 show that those who were now reverencing the Name of Christ did two specific things. What two things did they do?

    1.

    2.

First, notice that they **"openly confessed their evil deeds."** They dragged their sin into the light, exposed and confessed it. Friends, let us be clear about this: there will be no true victory over drunkenness, abuse of prescription meds, or any type of substance abuse without an "open confession." I know that's scary, I've been there, remember? I had many hidden areas in my life and I had concealed my sin from many people. My family, my pastor, my accountability partner—all of these confessions have been made and the sin has been dragged out in the light to die. The freedom of having all that weight come off of my shoulders was tremendous.

Now here is something that will help you. I want you to write down a proposed plan of how you can "openly confess" your evil deeds. Now understand that you do not have to do all that is on your plan right now, this can be done over time. But please develop a plan that includes the person to whom you will openly confess, and in what order. Again, developing this plan does not mean you will do this right away, it is only a "seed plan" to begin working toward a goal. So, please write here to whom and what you will confess. Don't leave anything or anyone out.

Question 8. Please write out your plan of confession.

Second, notice that these people did not stop at public confession, they also "**radically amputated**" those things which had caused them to sin. They burned their scrolls publicly. Let me share with you that only confessing your sin will not be enough to keep you from sinning in the future. There must be a cutting off, a plucking out, a burning, or a total destruction of that which trips us up. This needs to be done with a vengeance or "with attitude" as we are destroying that which would have destroyed us.

Question 9. Have you "burned" (or somehow destroyed) every substance that has caused you to sin in the past? If not, now is the time, and today is the day. Please write down here if you have radically amputated everything that causes you to sin.

Questions

Now let us get some additional "light" on this subject:

> This is the verdict: Light has come into the world, but men loved darkness instead of light because their deeds were evil. Everyone who does evil hates the light, and will not come into the light for fear that his deeds will be exposed. But whoever lives by the truth comes into the light, so that it may be seen plainly that what he has done has been done through God (John 3:19-21).

Friend, are you aware of the extreme importance of the teaching we are considering? The above verses tell us that all who do evil hate the light, and will not come into the light for fear that their deeds will be exposed, while those who live by the truth will come into the light. Which are you?

And finally, notice something else that exposing sin does:

> "The visions of your prophets were false and worthless; they did not expose your sin to ward off your captivity. The oracles they gave you were false and misleading" (Lamentations 2:14).

Question 10. What does the above verse state would have happened if these false prophets would have exposed the sin of the people?

That's right! Exposing the sin would have warded off captivity. Let us be real clear on this: leaving sin covered by refusing to expose it leads to captivity. We become captives to the power of sin while it is hidden and kept secret. But, if we expose it we ward off captivity, and live as free men and women!

I can't tell you the relief I feel now that I am no longer sneaking around, trying to hide my sin, always looking over my shoulder to see if I will be caught. Confession and amputation (with accountability) will produce complete and total freedom from drugs, forever.

> For whatever is hidden is meant to be disclosed, and whatever is concealed is meant to be brought out into the open (Mark 4:22).

Friend, do you need help doing what you need to do? Contact your accountability partner and ask them to pray about your situation, and offer suggestions and counsel as to how to proceed. But please do not lose the value of the teaching in the Scriptures today, by continuing to hide your sin in the dark. Begin coming into the light. Confess openly, amputate radically, and by God's grace you will be free!

Scripture to Consider

"So there is hope for your future," declares the LORD. "Your children will return to their own land" (Jeremiah 31:17).

The visions of your prophets were false and worthless; they did not expose your sin to ward off your captivity. The oracles they gave you were false and misleading (Lamentations 2:14).

Did you feast on God's Word in the last 24 hours?

    Yes   No

If so, how did you feast? In other words, circle the ways you enjoyed God today. Reading? Prayer? Worship? Fellowship? Witnessing?

Were you free from drug and alcohol abuse since you did the last lesson?

    Yes   No

Did you spend personal time with the Lord since you did the last lesson?

    Yes   No

If you answered "no" to any of the above questions, describe what led to your fall.

If you answered "yes" to the above questions, you may use this area for additional comments.

DAY 28 - FLEEING TEMPTATION

Friend, today we will see a biblical story of victory! We will examine this story closely to see how the victory was won and how we can apply these truths to our own lives. Are you starting to enjoy victory over this deadly spiritual disease called sin? Me too! Please read the following story and answer the questions at the bottom.

> [6]Now Joseph was well-built and handsome, [7]and after awhile His master's wife took notice of Joseph and said, "Come to bed with me." [8]But he refused. "With me in charge," he told her, "my master does not concern himself with anything in the house; everything he owns he has entrusted to my care.
>
> [9]"No one is greater in this house than I am. My master has withheld nothing from me except you, because you are his wife. How then could I do such a wicked thing and sin against God?" [10]And though she spoke to Joseph day after day, he refused to go to bed with her or even be with her. [11]One day he went into the house to attend to his duties and none of the household servants was inside. [12]She caught him by his cloak and said, "Come to bed with me!" But he left his cloak in her hand and ran out of the house (Genesis 39:6-12).

Questions

Question 1. What did Joseph say to his master's wife when she wanted to sleep with him?

Question 2. Read verse 9 and answer who Joseph was thinking about when he said "no."

Question 3. Please write your thoughts about this story. Why did Joseph "win"? How did he win? How will you apply this to your own situation?

Being tempted in this way is very difficult to handle (as you no doubt know)! But Joseph was focused. Did you see who he was focused on in verse 9? It was God. To Joseph, God was very real and he was "aware" of God always being with him. Keep in close contact with God, and you will find strength against temptation, and saying "no" will be a lot easier. Next time you are tempted, act like Jesus is right there with you. He really is! Focus on Him. Enjoy His presence and you will run from sin!

Questions

Now let us notice something important from the previous story: Sin keeps coming after us. Notice that Joseph's master's wife kept after him. She kept pressing him, kept tempting him. She "spoke to Joseph day after day." Possibly you've experienced the same thing with your drug of choice, Friend. The thoughts and desires to indulge keep coming at you and you resist. They leave for a bit after you resist and seem to be gone. But they keep coming back, don't they? You may send them away again but soon, like Potiphar's wife, they are begging and pleading with you, tempting you again.

To illustrate the truth that sin keeps pressing you, please read Judges 16: 4-18:

> [4]Some time later, he fell in love with a woman in the Valley of Sorek whose name was Delilah. [5]The rulers of the Philistines went to her and said, "See if you can lure him into showing you the secret of his great strength and how we can overpower him so we may tie him up and subdue him. Each one of us will give you eleven hundred shekels of silver."
>
> [6]So Delilah said to Samson, "Tell me the secret of your great strength and how you can be tied up and subdued." [7]Samson answered her, "If anyone ties me with seven fresh thongs that have not been dried, I'll become as weak as any other man."
>
> [8]Then the rulers of the Philistines brought her seven fresh thongs that had not been dried, and she tied him with them. [9]With men hidden in the room, she called to him, "Samson, the Philistines are upon you!" But he snapped the thongs as easily as a piece of string snaps when it comes close to a flame. So the secret of his strength was not discovered.
>
> [10]Then Delilah said to Samson, "You have made a fool of me; you lied to me. Come now, tell me how you can be tied." [11]He said, "If anyone ties me securely with new ropes that have never been used, I'll become as weak as any other man."

Questions

¹²So Delilah took new ropes and tied him with them. Then, with men hidden in the room, she called to him, "Samson, the Philistines are upon you!" But he snapped the ropes off his arms as if they were threads.

Delilah then said to Samson, "Until now, you have been making a fool of me and lying to me. Tell me how you can be tied." He replied, "If you weave the seven braids of my head into the fabric on the loom and tighten it with the pin, I'll become as weak as any other man." So while he was sleeping, Delilah took the seven braids of his head, wove them into the fabric ¹⁴and tightened it with the pin.

Again she called to him, "Samson, the Philistines are upon you!" He awoke from his sleep and pulled up the pin and the loom, with the fabric.

¹⁵Then she said to him, "How can you say, 'I love you,' when you won't confide in me? This is the third time you have made a fool of me and haven't told me the secret of your great strength." ¹⁶With such nagging she prodded him day after day until he was tired to death.

¹⁷So he told her everything. "No razor has ever been used on my head," he said, "because I have been a Nazirite set apart to God since birth. If my head were shaved, my strength would leave me, and I would become as weak as any other man."

¹⁸When Delilah saw that he had told her everything, she sent word to the rulers of the Philistines, "Come back once more; he has told me everything." So the rulers of the Philistines returned with the silver in their hands.

Question 4. What did Delilah keep doing to Samson? How is that an illustration of how sin presses us?

This reminds me so much of my own struggle with drugs. Cocaine was my temptress, so sweet and so alluring yet so dangerous! I remember the white-knuckle days of facing that temptation head on, sweating and enduring pain both physically and emotionally. Eventually the siren song of crack would break down my resistance and I would succumb—defeated again.

Question 5. Share an experience you've had where temptation kept after you.

Course member Teresa writes, "Actually it was the night of my fall. I had promised my husband I would not drink while he was out of town. I became stressed during the day over a work matter. The problem became much larger in my mind than it actually was. My bondage to alcohol told me that the wine would help me feel better. It was overwhelming. I drove to the store and bought a bottle of wine and began drinking around 5:00. I was 'only having one glass'! The 'one glass' turned into the entire bottle. Now the guilt of breaking my promise to my husband settled in on me. To try and numb myself from feeling the guilt I drove (yes, drove!) to the store for another bottle. It was as though I were 'possessed'. I didn't enjoy it, there was no pleasure, I just didn't want to feel. I had begun losing track of just how much I had drunk and would be surprised at the quantity I had consumed. The strange thing is that even after two bottles, I was not 'numb'. My tolerance for alcohol had built up and required more and more to reach the state of numbness. The stores were closed and there was no way to buy more. I felt trapped! My husband and I had talked two days prior to this about my growing problem. I made vows to 'cut down' and broke them!"

If you study the temptation of Adam and Eve in the Garden of Eden (Genesis 3) you will see this same truth illustrated again: The devil kept after Adam and Eve, kept tempting them, kept arguing with them and weakening them with each word. So, guess what? We'll never win an argument with the devil. And, if we hang around long enough, we will develop enough excuses to just go ahead and sin. So, how in the world do we win against these pressing temptations?

RUN LIKE THE WIND!!

Flee the evil desires of youth . . ." (2 Timothy 2:22).

But you, man of God, flee from all this . . ." (1 Timothy 6:11).

Question 6. What did Joseph do when Potiphar's wife was tempting him?

a. He changed the subject, and began talking with her about the weather.

b. He decided to witness to her, so he sat down on the bed with her and explained the way of salvation!

c. He left his coat and ran!

Do you long to be able to look temptation square in the face and say, "NO!?" Chances are we may never be able to do it. Temptation is more powerful than we are, it is more persistent than we are, it is more persuasive than we are. Our only hope is to RUN, RUN, RUN. Flee away from it like it is a burning house. Run from it no matter what the cost. Joseph would rather lose a good coat than a good conscience.

Questions

Question 7. What can we learn from the way Joseph handled this temptation?

Specifically, in regards to drunkenness, the hardest part is remembering the numbing effects of alcohol while facing difficulties and pain in our lives. There were times when I have fallen and immediately afterward vowed to never do it again. I would pray constantly for strength and I found that as I prayed there were the memories and the temptation again. I would pray to not give in to the temptation but the desire to feel the numbing effects would come again and again. Soon I almost didn't want to pray about it anymore . . . .

Scripture to Consider

And it will be said: "Build up, build up, prepare the road! Remove the obstacles out of the way of my people" (Isaiah 57:14).

May the God of hope fill you with all joy and peace as you trust in him, so that you may overflow with hope by the power of the Holy Spirit (Romans 15:13).

Did you feast on God's Word in the last 24 hours?

     Yes   No

If so, how did you feast? In other words, circle the ways you enjoyed God today. Reading? Prayer? Worship? Fellowship? Witnessing?

Were you free from drug and alcohol abuse since you did the last lesson?

     Yes   No

Did you spend personal time with the Lord since you did the last lesson?

     Yes   No

If you answered "no" to any of the above questions, describe what led to your fall.

If you answered "yes" to the above questions, you may use this area for additional comments.

DAY 29 - FLEE, ABSTAIN, RESIST

Today, we are going to study various passages of Scripture that relate to our battle against drunkenness and substance abuse. Our purpose is to gain understanding and practical assistance in how to win this battle, by God's grace. Please think through the following passages, specifically asking yourself how you can apply them to your own life, and then answer the questions below:

> Flee the evil desires of youth, and pursue righteousness, faith, love and peace, along with those who call on the Lord out of a pure heart (2 Timothy 2:22).

Question 1. The above verse has two commands in it, what are they?

Question 2. Please think through how to apply these two commands in your own life. The first one is to "flee the evil desires of youth." In your specific situation, how can you do this? What wrong desires do you have and how can you flee from them?

Question 3. We are not only to flee evil desires, but we are to pursue righteousness. Again, in your situation, how can you do this? Please list some specific things you can do to pursue righteousness.

Now, Friend, will you please share these specific steps with your accountability partner, and ask him/her to hold you accountable to these things?

Here are some things that I did to "pursue righteousness" coming out of drunkenness:

1. I maintained weekly accountability with my pastor as well as a close friend in regards to my struggle.

2. I arose early in the mornings and sought the face of God, asking Him to break the power of sin in my life.

3. My wife and I maintained daily accountability with regard to alcohol and cocaine. I knew I must report to her daily in this area until the power of sin was broken.

4. I studied many of the writings of the Puritans and sought to learn from their practical and godly wisdom.

5. I attended every service that our church had, and sought the Lord during them.

6. My wife and I had daily devotionals where I washed her in the Word and we sought the Lord as a couple.

Question 4. We are to pursue righteousness "along with those who call on the Lord out of a pure heart." Are you calling to the Lord?

> "I will lift up the cup of salvation and call on the name of the LORD" (Psalm 116:13).

> [9]Then will I purify the lips of the peoples, that all of them may call on the name of the LORD and serve him shoulder to shoulder. [10]From beyond the rivers of Cush my worshipers, my scattered people, will bring me offerings. [11]On that day you will not be put to shame for all the wrongs you have done to me" (Zephaniah 3:9-11).

Questions

Course member Teresa writes, "Yes, I am. The Lord is answering in a mighty way. He is softening my heart, restoring my love for Him, giving me an appetite for the Word, giving me a new perspective to 'clearly' view things, the desire to be with believers once again, joy, peace, contentment, and strength to face my enemy and resist his temptations."

I remember when I first came out of drunkenness, I was pleading with the Lord to release me from the chains of sin. I was "calling on the Lord" in sincerity. I was calling out to Him often, begging for mercy, asking for Him to set me free, and pleading with Him to make me whole. Friend, don't hesitate to beg God's help, to plead and cry to Him, to latch onto Him as your only hope in life.

This type of crying out to God and begging Him for freedom is not a pleasant thing to watch, as people will plead with God out of desperation, and being nearly frantic for His help they cry and wail, and prostrate themselves before Him, seeking to be released from the trap in which they find themselves. Now I'm not suggesting that it is our tears, or bodily contortions that help our prayers to be heard, but I am saying that a heart that is **desperate for God will call on Him in reckless abandon, until He hears and answers.**

> [12]For there is no difference between Jew and Gentile; the same Lord is Lord of all and richly blesses all who call on him, [13]for, "Everyone who calls on the name of the Lord will be saved" (Romans 10:12-13).

> [11]Dear friends, I urge you, as aliens and strangers in the world, to abstain from sinful desires, which war against your soul. [12]Live such good lives among the pagans that, though they accuse you of doing wrong, they may see your good deeds and glorify God on the day he visits us" (1 Peter 2:11,12).

Question 5. Verse 11 above tells us that we are in a war. Evil desires war against our soul, and we fight internal battles every day. The goal that the enemy has is to drag our soul into hell, and he uses "evil desires" to do it. According to verse 11 above, what are we to do with these evil desires?

Abstaining is the scriptural method of winning the battle against evil desires. We are not to give in, or to vent, or act out in other ways; we are to abstain from evil desires. In some ways, this is like the "just say no" philosophy that the world promotes, but it is different, because the world only teaches half the truth. Yes, we are to "just say no" or rather to "abstain," but according to the next verse we are to "live such good lives among the pagans that, though they accuse

us of doing wrong, they may see our good deeds . . ." So, we are not only to abstain, we are to live such godly lives that others see our good deeds. This is much like the first verse we studied (2 Timothy 2:22) which taught us not only to flee evil desires, but to pursue righteousness, and both of these concepts must be embraced, not just one.

> [8]Be self-controlled and alert. Your enemy the devil prowls around like a roaring lion looking for someone to devour. [9]Resist him, standing firm in the faith, because you know that your brothers throughout the world are undergoing the same kind of sufferings" (1 Peter 5:8-9).

Many places in Scripture the devil and sin are pictured as a lion seeking to devour us. This concept is important to understand because it speaks of the strength of the enemy. He is a lion. Man is no match for a lion, as many martyrs in early church history show. And the evil one and sin are as a lion. They are very strong, and their purpose is to "devour us." Note this passage in Genesis 4:7: "If you do what is right, will you not be accepted? But if you do not do what is right, sin is crouching at your door; it desires to have you, but you must master it." Sin here is "crouching" at Cain's door, desiring to "have" and devour him, as a lion kills its prey.

We have a strong enemy, and we have weak flesh. This combination works powerfully together, and can drag us into sin and maul us, chewing us up and leaving us half dead. I remember resolving and "making deals" with God to release me. I would pray, "God if you will release me from this I will quit this or that" but those words were empty and God knew my heart. There were also times when things were so bad that I would cry out in brokenness and come away feeling better. My flesh, however, would soon begin to crave another drink and soon I was walking back down the path to destruction. It was just like fighting a powerful animal and my weak attempts at defense were futile while fighting alone.

Question 6. According to verse 9 above, what are we to do with this lion?

Question 7. In your own situation, Friend, how can you resist? Think through specifics of your situation, and write out how you will resist the enemy.

Questions

When I was first coming out of drunkenness and cocaine addiction, my plan to resist was actually a radical amputation. I quit playing in bars and threw out all alcohol and crack in my home. I resisted by not allowing any access to the temptation. The key to knowing whether you need to resist or to amputate is if you are getting the victory or not.

According to verse 9 above, we are not only to resist the devil; we are to stand firm in the faith. Now here is a key to doing this. The Bible says that "faith comes by hearing, and hearing by the Word of God" (Romans 10:17). Notice it does not say, "faith comes by what you heard," but rather "faith comes by hearing." There must be an ongoing "hearing" of God's Word in order for faith to remain active. So, how can we "stand firm in the faith"? One way is we can involve ourselves in God's Word often, and as we hear anew and afresh, faith is kindled again and remains active.

Question 8. Finally, verse 9 above says that our brothers throughout the world are undergoing the same trials and temptations. Have you ever thought that you were the only one who was sinning in such a horrible manner? Have you ever felt isolated, like nobody else would understand?

Course member Teresa writes, "Absolutely. Who did I know in the Christian community that was enslaved to alcohol? No one. Who would understand? How could I have allowed this to happen? I had been in leadership positions, taught classes, sat under the teaching of very godly men, my husband was a respected elder and teacher, I had what most would call a 'perfect life'. There were times that I wanted to stand up in church and tell everyone what I was doing. But I was so afraid of rejection. Felt isolated? Yes. It was just me and my glass (many, many, many glasses) of wine."

You are not alone! All our brothers and sisters get assaulted by the enemy; we are all under attack by evil desires. Our temptations, whatever they may be, no matter how severe or perverted they may be, are "common to man" (1 Corinthians 10:13).

So, today we learned to flee, abstain and resist. But we also learned to pursue righteousness, live good and godly lives, and stand firm in the faith. We have learned of the strength of our enemy, and we have thought through certain steps that we will take to ensure that we are pursuing righteousness. May our God enable us to do these things, by His grace.

Scripture to Consider

I have been crucified with Christ and I no longer live, but Christ lives in me. The life I live in the body, I live by faith in the Son of God, who loved me and gave himself for me. [21]I do not set aside the grace of God, for if righteousness could be gained through the law, Christ died for nothing! (Galatians 2:20-21).

A cry is heard on the barren heights, the weeping and pleading of the people of Israel, because they have perverted their ways and have forgotten the LORD their God."

"Return, faithless people; I will cure you of backsliding. Yes, we will come to you, for you are the LORD our God. [23]Surely the idolatrous commotion on the hills and mountains is a deception; surely in the LORD our God is the salvation of Israel. [24]From our youth shameful gods have consumed the fruits of our fathers' labor- their flocks and herds, their sons and daughters. [25]Let us lie down in our shame, and let our disgrace cover us. We have sinned against the LORD our God, both we and our fathers; from our youth till this day we have not obeyed the LORD our God" (Jeremiah 3:21-25).

Did you feast on God's Word in the last 24 hours?

Yes   No

If so, how did you feast? In other words, circle the ways you enjoyed God today. Reading? Prayer? Worship? Fellowship? Witnessing?

Were you free from drug and alcohol abuse since you did the last lesson?

Yes   No

Did you spend personal time with the Lord since you did the last lesson?

Yes   No

If you answered "no" to any of the above questions, describe what led to your fall.

If you answered "yes" to the above questions, you may use this area for additional comments.

DAY 30 – DON'T GO NEAR

In July of 1972, a McDonnell Douglas DC-9, loaded with 85 passengers and 5 crewmembers, was traveling from St. Louis, Missouri to Minneapolis, Minnesota. The time of departure was 2:30 p.m. and the aircraft had been airborne approximately 25 minutes. It was a typically hot and humid summer afternoon in the Midwest, with numerous thunderstorms building along the route of flight.

The Air Traffic Control monitor noticed the aircraft approaching the vicinity of several heavy thunderstorm buildups, and radioed this information: "___ ____ (airline name) flight 2164, weather radar indicates you are approaching an area of level 5 buildups with tops above Flight Level 410. Suggest an Easterly Deviation to heading 105 degrees within the next 10 miles."

The response from the pilots came back. "Uh Roger, Kansas City Center, we see the thunderstorms. Onboard radar indicates a possible hole to penetrate through the buildups at our 12 O'clock position and 18 miles. Do you agree?"

Air Traffic Control replied, "Negative, flight 2164, our radar does not confirm the existence of a hole in the storm, suggest an Easterly Deviation to the right immediately."

This is the last transmission recorded from this aircraft on Air Traffic Control's tapes:

"Uh, roger, Kansas City Center, we will proceed straight ahead . . . it may be a little close, but we, uh, do see a hole to penetrate."

The aircraft penetrated the severest part of the storm, a level 5 thunderstorm, and was sent plummeting to the earth, killing all 91 people aboard. What happened?

Aircraft radar is susceptible to what is known as "attenuation" which is the blocking of any weather returns that are behind severe storms. Because there is so much moisture in severe thunderstorms, the radar is unable to penetrate through the moisture to be able to accurately present any weather information immediately behind the severe storms. In the above situation the radar, because of attenuation, falsely presented the appearance of a safe route of flight. Seasoned and well-trained pilots are aware of the problem of attenuation and know to remain well clear of all thunderstorms. The key to safety is to not go anywhere near a storm.

For us, alcohol is a thunderstorm, Friend. But it can present the appearance of being harmless; a little fun, something that doesn't hurt anyone, a release, a little celebration, or a quick buzz. And yet drunkenness is a trap of the devil that has devastated the lives of countless people. How do we deal with this thunderstorm?

Answer: Don't go near!

Today, we will notice scriptural teaching on the subject: Don't go near. Please read the following passage and answer the questions that follow. Can you discover the approaching "thunderstorm?"

> [6]At the window of my house I looked out through the lattice. [7]I saw among the simple, I noticed among the young men, a youth who lacked judgment. [8]He was going down the street near her corner, walking along in the direction of her house [9]at twilight, as the day was fading, as the dark of night set in. [10]Then out came a woman to meet him, dressed like a prostitute and with crafty intent. [11](She is loud and defiant, her feet never stay at home; [12]now in the street, now in the squares, at every corner she lurks.) [13]She took hold of him and kissed him and with a brazen face she said: [14]"I have fellowship offerings at home; today I fulfilled my vows. [15]So I came out to meet you; I looked for you and have found you! [16]I have covered my bed with colored linens from Egypt. [17]I have perfumed my bed with myrrh, aloes and cinnamon. [18]Come, let's drink deep of love till morning; lets enjoy ourselves with love! [19]My husband is not at home; he has gone on a long journey. [20]He took his purse filled with money and will not be home till full moon."[21]
>
> With persuasive words she led him astray; she seduced him with her smooth talk. [22]All at once he followed her like an ox going to the slaughter, like a deer stepping into a noose [23]till an arrow pierces his liver, like a bird darting into a snare, little knowing it will cost him his life. [24]Now then, my sons, listen to me; pay attention to what I say. [25]Do not let your heart turn to her ways or stray into her paths. [26]Many are the victims she has brought down; her slain are a mighty throng. [27]Her house is a highway to the grave, leading down to the chambers of death (Proverbs 7:6-27).

Questions

Question 1. In verse 8, the young man is doing something foolish. What is it?

Question 2. What words are used to describe this young man?

Question 3. Notice the personal nature of the temptation. How many times does the seductress use the word "you" in verse 15?

Question 4. To what is this "personal touch" designed to appeal in this young man?

Personal illustration: I remember many nights of sitting down with a bottle in my hand. It was an inanimate object, just glass and liquor inside, but it seemed to "speak" to me without words. It was like it was beckoning me saying, "I am your only real friend. I will not let you down, because I am always here for you. Come and drink and I will make the pain go away. I won't hurt you." Now I know that a bottle cannot talk, but the lust I had for what that bottle contained made it seem as if it were speaking to my heart and whispering lies in my ear!

Question 5. Why is this personal, intimate form of communication so hard to resist? What are your thoughts?

How bad can it be for the man or woman in bondage to alcohol? Think of all the marriages and children that have been cast aside for the bottle. If there is any doubt about the allurement or the lust involved in drunkenness, one must look no further than the choice of lust for alcohol over the love of a child or a spouse. Alcohol will never "love" back, it promises pleasure, but delivers pain and destruction. Just like the temptress in the passage above, alcohol whispers silent words of seduction that lead to the "piercing" of the liver and death. Ask anyone who suffers from the painful sickness of cirrhosis of the liver—the "arrow" of drunkenness knows no mercy.

Question 6. Verse 18 says, "Come let us drink deep of love until morning . . . ." Let's see how good your memory is. In the early days of this course we studied through John 4 about "the woman at the well." How does verse 18 above compare with the story in John 4?

Note: Verse 22 says, "All at once he followed her." Here is the problem with going "near" the temptation: The choice to sin is often made all of a sudden and without rational thought. If this young man were reasonable and rational, he could have weighed out the benefits versus the disadvantages. He could have said, "I will think about it and let you know," or he could have asked a friend for advice before acting. But powerful temptation removes one's ability to be rational and decisions are often made immediately. This is "impulse buying" at its worst. And the longer we stay involved in drunkenness, the more things we do simply by impulse.

Friend, it did not take long after I began drinking regularly that my impulses were beginning to master me. I would find myself doing inappropriate things almost by reflex, without thinking about it, and it left me wondering why later. I vandalized other's property and stole things—I would never have thought of doing such things before I became deeply involved in drunkenness. I now know that habitual giving in to sin leads to living by impulse. I would spend money at bars that was supposed to be used for rent or bills without even considering the consequences for my family. It still breaks my heart to think of this, and I am so thankful to be delivered from it now.

Question 7. Have you experienced this "all of a sudden" decision with a substance? What happened?

Course member Teresa writes, "Yes. I can't point out one incident in particular. But when drinking, I would make foolish choices, dangerous decisions, act in an uninhibited manner, behave in an ugly manner and say harsh things. I have been told that I 'became a different person' and that 'alcohol changes you.' This would happen regularly. I did and said things that I absolutely would not normally do. I hurt my family tremendously."

Question 8. Verses 22 and 23 use four analogies to describe what the end result of giving in to temptation is like. What are they? I will write the first one:

1. Like an ox going to the slaughter

2.

3.

4.

Questions

It helps to keep in mind what the final outcome of any sin will be. Sin inevitably leads to death. It may lead to physical death, as we have seen in the lives of numerous celebrities as well as friends of my own, or it may lead to death of your marriage, or death to your spiritual life, etc.

Question 9. The temptress promised an enjoyment of life. But according to the last couple of verses where did her paths actually lead?

Question 10. There is only one admonition in this entire passage on how to escape the "slaughter," the "noose," the "arrow," the "snare," meaning "death," and the "grave." It is found in verse 25. Please write out verse 25 here. It would be a good idea for you to memorize this verse:

Note: Don't go near! Sometimes this is extremely difficult as temptation is "now in the street, now in the squares, at every corner she lurks." Here are some of the things I do to avoid temptation. I do not go into bars or go to any party or gathering where alcohol or drugs are present. As I go through a grocery or convenience store, I make a "covenant with my eyes" and don't go near the aisles with alcohol in them or even look at the ads or displays. I don't even give them a chance to become a temptation!

Friend, a deadly air disaster could have been averted in 1972 had the pilots lived by the principle to "not go near." In flying, when faced with a radarscope showing thunderstorms, the one policy is avoidance—not to look for holes or try to find a shortcut. When dealing with heroin or amphetamines, like deadly thunderstorms, the only safe approach is avoidance. "In the paths of the wicked lie thorns and snares, but he who guards his soul stays far from them" (Proverbs 22:5).

Question 11. What have been your areas of temptation in the past? Please give us your avoidance plan. How will you apply this principle now to not go near?

Question 12. Please record how you are doing today, and what is happening in your life.

Scripture to Consider

Do not set foot on the path of the wicked or walk in the way of evil men. Avoid it, do not travel on it; turn from it and go on your way (Proverbs 4:14-15).

Rather, clothe yourselves with the Lord Jesus Christ, and do not think about how to gratify the desires of the sinful nature (Romans 13:14).

Avoid every kind of evil (1 Thessalonians 5:22).

Did you feast on God's Word in the last 24 hours?

       Yes   No

If so, how did you feast? In other words, circle the ways you enjoyed God today. Reading? Prayer? Worship? Fellowship? Witnessing?

Were you free from drug and alcohol abuse since you did the last lesson?

       Yes   No

Did you spend personal time with the Lord since you did the last lesson?

       Yes   No

If you answered "no" to any of the above questions, describe what led to your fall.

If you answered "yes" to the above questions, you may use this area for additional comments.

DAY 31 - GROWING IN CHRIST

It is good to see from Scripture that there are different stages of growth in the Christian life. The teaching today will bring encouragement to those who stumble, strengthen the faith of those who are beginning to overcome, and confirm the faith of those walking in habitual victory.

Please read the following passage, and answer the questions below:

> [12]I write to you, dear children, because your sins have been forgiven on account of his name. [13]I write to you, fathers, because you have known him who is from the beginning. I write to you, young men, because you have overcome the evil one. [14]I write to you, dear children, because you have known the Father. I write to you, fathers, because you have known him who is from the beginning. I write to you, young men, because you are strong, and the word of God lives in you, and you have overcome the evil one (1 John 2:12-14).

Notice the three different groups the Apostle John addresses above:

1. Children (vs. 12, 14)
2. Young men (vs. 13, 14)
3. Fathers (vs. 13, 14)

The Christian life is one of ongoing growth, development and maturity. We can learn much in our fight against drugs and alcohol by studying what John writes to each of the above groups.

Questions

Question 1. There are two things that the Apostle John writes about "little children" above. What are those two things?

1.

2.

The Apostle John writes to children: "Your sins have been forgiven on account of his name." And, "you have known the Father." We come into the Christian family by being born again, and through drinking the pure milk of God's Word can soon become little children. But little children fall a lot, Friend, and so John writes to little children "your sins have been forgiven on account of his name."

Question 2. Have you come into God's family through the forgiveness of your sins?

Yes   No

Little children stumble as they are learning to walk; it is part of the growing process. And initially little children do more falling than walking. This is the reason John speaks of little children as being forgiven. This should teach us caution when dealing with those who fall a lot; they may be unsaved and living in sin, or they might be saved, but are children who are just learning to walk. Be careful in judging those who fall often.

Question 3. Please provide your comments on the two following Scriptures:

> For though a righteous man falls seven times, he rises again, but the wicked are brought down by calamity (Proverbs 24:16).

> Then Peter came to Jesus and asked, "Lord, how many times shall I forgive my brother when he sins against me? Up to seven times?" Jesus answered, "I tell you, not seven times, but seventy-seven times" (Matthew 18:21-22).

The passage we are studying in 1 John 2 tells us how one becomes born again: through a relationship with God, "You have known the Father." Jesus said, "And this is eternal life, that they may know You, the only true God, and Jesus Christ whom You have sent" (John 17:3). And knowing God starts with receiving His forgiveness, "Your sins have been forgiven on account of His Name." So the little child in Christ has a relationship with God that is based on forgiveness. He may not have grown much beyond this initial relationship and as a little child stumbles as much as he walks. John emphasizes forgiveness for the little child. Some of us feel like all we are doing is stumbling and falling and are in constant need of forgiveness. If this is you, keep seeking the Lord for grace, because with growth comes strength.

The Apostle John writes to young men: "You have overcome the evil one," and "You are strong, and the word of God lives in you, and you have overcome the evil one."

How do we know we are progressing in the Christian life? We begin winning battles. The Word of God becomes our sword with which we defeat the evil one. The "young man" in the Lord is characterized as one who

Questions

walks in victory over the enemy by the indwelling Word of God. Relating this to our subject, we are no longer living in drunkenness, but we have acquired the tools from Scripture to be strong in the Lord and overcome the evil one.

For many years of my life I was a stumbling little child spiritually. I fell so often, and then repented only to fall again sometimes on the same day. This continued way too long, as I had nobody who could assist me into growing spiritually. I am not blaming anyone, just stating facts that there was no New Wine course back in the days when I was drinking and doing drugs, and nobody I knew wanted to talk about it. Even the Christians I knew did not have the spiritual insight necessary to help me, so I remained stunted in my growth, malnourished and failing to thrive.

But then, through God's Word, I learned the principles that make up this course, and I entered a spiritual growth spurt. Pastors, as well as godly teaching from other sources, have helped me understand how to apply the principles of radical amputation, accountability, dragging sin into the light, feeding on the Word, etc. and now I am walking in perpetual victory over sin. I'm not sinless, no! Sinless perfection does not happen in this life, but I am simply referring to living in victory over habitual sin by God's grace. What's more is that God is even using me to help others, and this has been a great delight, too.

So, I can see that there has been growth in grace in my life. I have gone from an unsaved man who lived in sin continually, to a little child who stumbled often, to a young man who knows how to fight sin using the principles in God's Word, to a father who is helping others. I do praise God for growth in grace.

Question 4. According to the passage we are studying in 1 John 2, what is the evidence that one has grown from a "little child" to a "young man?" Write your thoughts here:

Question 5. Next, please provide your thoughts about the next two passages of Scripture. Include whether or not the author was a "little child" or a "young man."

We know that the law is spiritual; but I am unspiritual, sold as a slave to sin. I do not understand what I do. For what I want to do I do not do, but what I hate I do. And if I do what I do not want to do, I agree that the law is good. As it is, it is no longer I myself who do it, but it is sin living in me. I know that nothing good lives in me, that is, in my sinful nature.

For I have the desire to do what is good, but I cannot carry it out. For what I do is not the good I want to do; no, the evil I do not want to do - this I keep on doing. Now if I do what I do not want to do, it is no longer I who do it, but it is sin living in me that does it.

So I find this law at work: When I want to do good, evil is right there with me. For in my inner being I delight in God's law; but I see another law at work in the members of my body, waging war against the law of my mind and making me a prisoner of the law of sin at work within my members (Romans 7:14-23).

Your thoughts here:

Now, please understand that many see this passage in Romans 7 in different ways. Some see Paul as an unsaved man here, for he seems to be enslaved to sin and somewhat hopeless. Others see this passage as the time in Paul's life when he was an immature Christian before he grew to maturity. Still others see this as an ongoing experience in Paul's life, as we always struggle with sin in this life. Either way, what is clear is that there is growth in the life of the Christian, where habitual sin does not have the power over us that it once did. Please write your own thoughts here:

Shouts of joy and victory resound in the tents of the righteous: "The Lord's right hand has done mighty things! The Lord's right hand is lifted high; the Lord's right hand has done mighty things!" (Psalm 118:15-16).

The Apostle John writes to fathers: "You have known Him Who is from the beginning." The mature father in the Lord is again characterized by relationship. He still has his dependence on the Word of God but His attention now is

on the God of the Word, and he is characterized by His relationship to the Lord.

He is a father, so he has children and for our purposes this mature man has not only overcome the evil one himself, but is assisting others out of drunkenness by the grace of God.

Question 6. Can you see the growth in the Lord that is taking place here in this passage?

Question 7. Please compare the following passage of Scripture to our struggle with drunkenness or abuse of prescription meds:

> When I was a child, I talked like a child, I thought like a child, I reasoned like a child. When I became a man, I put childish ways behind me (1 Corinthians 13:11).

Question 8. Dear children, young men, fathers. Which are you, Friend? Explain how you know which one you are currently:

No matter the level of maturity in which you find yourself, just know that there is growth ahead for all of us. The New Wine course is designed to assist in our growth, taking us from little children who fall much and are in need of forgiveness often (beginning the course), to young men who know how to fight and are characterized by winning battles (middle portions of the course), and to fathers who are helping to produce fruit in other "little children" (mentors).

Keep growing dear children, and know that victory is around the next corner. Fight hard, young men for your adversary is angry at you. Enjoy your intimacy with the Father, fathers, and encourage your little ones to grow in the Lord.

Question 9. How is everything in your life? What are your struggles, temptations, and frustrations? What are the things you are doing well in?

Course member Teresa writes, "Where do I begin? One thing that is more dramatic to me than anything is my desire to spend time in the Word, prayer and 'listening' to the voice of God. It has been a long time since I have felt this 'hunger.' I do sense my heart softening. I truly WANT to obey and glorify Christ. God is changing my priorities, desires, and habits. Each day He brings something new to my mind that needs attention. I feel peace, much, much peace."

Scripture to Consider

I will surely bless you and make your descendants as numerous as the stars in the sky and as the sand on the seashore. Your descendants will take possession of the cities of their enemies, and through your offspring all nations on earth will be blessed, because you have obeyed me (Genesis 22:17-18).

And I tell you that you are Peter, and on this rock I will build my church, and the gates of Hades will not overcome it. I will give you the keys of the kingdom of heaven; whatever you bind on earth will be bound in heaven, and whatever you loose on earth will be loosed in heaven (Matthew 16:18-19).

Did you feast on God's Word in the last 24 hours?

     Yes   No

If so, how did you feast? In other words, circle the ways you enjoyed God today. Reading? Prayer? Worship? Fellowship? Witnessing?

Were you free from drug and alcohol abuse since you did the last lesson?

     Yes   No

Did you spend personal time with the Lord since you did the last lesson?

     Yes   No

If you answered "no" to any of the above questions, describe what led to your fall.

If you answered "yes" to the above questions, you may use this area for additional comments.

DAY 32 - SANCTIFICATION

Have you ever wondered about God's will for your life? Well, today we are going to explore this topic. We will be considering the following questions: What is the will of God for our lives? How do we find it? How do we do it? And what does that have to do with drug abuse?

> [1]Finally, brothers, we instructed you how to live in order to please God, as in fact you are living. Now we ask you and urge you in the Lord Jesus to do this more and more. [2]For you know what instructions we gave you by the authority of the Lord Jesus.
>
> [3]It is God's will that you should be sanctified: that you should avoid sexual immorality; [4]that each of you should learn to control his own body in a way that is holy and honorable, [5]not in passionate lust like the heathen, who do not know God; [6]and that in this matter no one should wrong his brother or take advantage of him. The Lord will punish men for all such sins, as we have already told you and warned you. [7]For God did not call us to be impure, but to live a holy life. [8]Therefore, he who rejects this instruction does not reject man but God, who gives you his Holy Spirit" (1 Thessalonians 4:1-8).

Questions

Question 1. In this passage Paul talks about avoiding sexual immorality, controlling our bodies, and living a holy life. But before he mentions all this, in verse one he provides a motive. What is this motive?

Question 2. In your own words, please tell why you believe Paul provides this motive for holy living.

If we are ingesting harmful drugs, we are not controlling our bodies! Think about how uncontrolled we are when intoxicated. I did and said things that I would never do unless I had been drinking. I certainly did not act in a way that was "holy and honorable." I think that heathen and despicable would be a better description of what I was like while intoxicated. I ignored everything the Bible had to say about drunkenness and lived a life that was controlled by my lust for alcohol and cocaine.

There are many good reasons why we should control our bodies. However, if we are Christians, our primary motivation for pursuing purity should be that we might please the Lord. Before we knew Jesus Christ, we lived to please ourselves in ever-increasing wickedness, but God's grace has changed our hearts so that we now earnestly desire to please Him instead of ourselves. A sincere desire to please Him will drive us on to resist the devil, to die to our flesh daily, to forsake the pleasure of sin continually, to avoid drunkenness and control our bodies in a way that is holy and honorable.

Questions

Question 3. Take a second and compare your past motive with your present motives. Where were you when involved in substance abuse and where are you now?

When we offer ourselves to meth and other drugs, we soon find that the enslavement process begins to increase. We want more; we continually seek for something new and different. There is never any satisfaction and it is never enough. We always want "more and more."

Question 4. But when we present ourselves to the Lord and become slaves of Christ we enter a path of increasing righteousness. What instruction does Paul give in verse one above to teach this truth? Write your thoughts here:

Note: The Christian life is one of ongoing improvement; growing in purity, increasing in holiness, abounding in the work of the Lord "more and more."

Question 5. Verse 3 above tells us very clearly what God's will is. Please write out all of verse 3 here:

Questions

Question 6. According to verse 4 as Christians we must "learn something." What is it?

Question 7. Verse 5 above describes those who live in "passionate lust" in two different ways. What are they?

1.

2.

Note: Paul is instructing Christians to not live like their pagan neighbors who did not know God. The pagans lived their lives in lust, giving in to the cravings of the flesh in sexual immorality, and the degrading of their bodies in sexual perversion.

Like a lust for sex, alcohol is a "lust" of our flesh. We feed that lust over and over but it is never satisfied. Since man discovered the intoxicating effects that alcohol produces, drunkenness has been a part of our world. We only need to look around us every day to see how deep this lust has gripped society. Knowing God—that is—having an intimate relationship with Him is the key ingredient that will enable us to "escape the corruption in the world caused by evil desires" (2 Peter 1:4).

Question 8. According to verse 6, what will God do to people who live like this?

Question 9. Verse 7 states what the "calling" of the Christian is. What is it?

Question 10. How are you doing with your calling?

Friend, as we seek to live a pure life in Christ, and do so "more and more" we will also be given opportunities to encourage others toward a holy life. Some may listen and heed our warnings and instructions, embrace Christ and forsake their sin. Others will cling to sin and attempt to justify themselves. Here at Setting Captives Free, we have heard many different excuses from people who will not forsake their sin. Sadly, many of these people will use overtly spiritual language in their rejection of the truth. Here is an example we received the other day:

"When I was saved and regenerated by the Holy Ghost (as salvation precedes regeneration) God showed me that His grace, mercy and loving-kindness are there to forgive every sin I have ever committed and the sins I will continue to commit as a born-again, adopted, grace-bought child of God. He does not expect perfection from me, nor does He demand (under this dispensation of grace) that I forsake all sin in order for Him to love me. His grace increases with my sin, and is magnified every time I fall. No, I have not forsaken (my sin) but yet remain convinced that I know God, am known by God, and loved unconditionally. I will remain His child and do not need you to tell me to forsake sin. God knows I am a human being dwelling in flesh, and is sympathetic to the frailties of my flesh."

Notice the mixture of truth and error in his message. Despite all his religious language, this gentleman is unable to forsake his sin and is hostile to encouragement and warnings to do so. Sadly, this is a view shared by many "Christians" in our society today.

Question 11. According to verse 8 above, when people reject teaching about avoiding immorality and learning to control their bodies, and about future punishment of those who continue to live in sin, what are they really rejecting?

Question 12. What do the following verses have to do with the situation described above?

But I will come to you very soon, if the Lord is willing, and then I will find out not only how these arrogant people are talking, but what power they have. For the kingdom of God is not a matter of talk but of power (1 Corinthians 4:19-20).

Questions

> **Course member Teresa writes,** "When the content of my 'Christianity' was merely words I had a HUGE problem. My faith is to be 'lived' every day. Personally, I could teach the Scriptures to others, quote passages, debate doctrines, etc., but my life of bondage was a true picture of the bankrupt state of my soul. I had no power to overcome self because I was depending upon ME. I was described as 'With their lips they flatter me, but their hearts are far from me...' I was living on the 'memory' of a time in my life when Christ was the focal point of my life. The problem was that my day to day personal relationship with Christ was one-sided. He was there, I had slowly walked away. When I made the move away from the Holy Spirit the power to overcome sin was gone."

Do you not know that the wicked will not inherit the kingdom of God? Do not be deceived: Neither the sexually immoral nor idolaters nor adulterers nor male prostitutes nor homosexual offenders nor thieves nor the greedy nor drunkards nor slanderers nor swindlers will inherit the kingdom of God. And that is what some of you were. But you were washed, you were sanctified, you were justified in the name of the Lord Jesus Christ and by the Spirit of our God (1 Corinthians 6:9-10).

Those who belong to Christ Jesus have crucified the sinful nature with its passions and desires (Galatians 5:24).

Let us summarize the teaching of the above passage of Scripture:

What is God's will for our lives? That we should be sanctified, that we should avoid drunkenness, and that we should learn how to control our bodies in a way that honors the Lord. Our motive for doing this is to live in such a way as to please the Lord. Drunkenness is a sin, and if there is no repentance, it will result in punishment from the Lord. If anyone rejects this teaching they are rejecting God. If we were to continue in these sins it would evidence that we do not know God, and no amount of "spiritual language" can fool God, who calls us to live a holy life and to be pure. God gives us His Holy Spirit to call us out of slavery to sin, to make us pure and to enable us to live holy lives.

But, let us also add that all of us who have come to this New Wine course have lived in drunkenness, in one form or another, in the past. Personally, for years I rebelled against God while in drunkenness and I presumed upon the grace of God by not forsaking my sins. God was indeed patient with me, and granted me repentance in His time. There is grace for all who will turn from their sin to Christ, and grace will enable us to live a holy life now, regardless of where we have come from. Grace is an amazing thing. It does not simply forgive the penalty of our sins while leaving us under the power of sin. It forgives and enables. It pardons and empowers. And it does so "more and more" as we grow in grace.

Please heed the warnings in these words by **F. L. Eiland**

Too Late

Too late, t'will be for you to cry,
When mercy's day has passed you by!
When solemn night, of dark despair,
Shall come upon you halting there!

Too late, when death has barred the door,
Your wailings can be heard no more!
Rejected, there, thy soul will be
Shut out, through all eternity!

Will you not heed the voice today?
Inviting you Christ to obey?
And be prepared to enter there,
A pure and spotless robe to wear?

No longer, there in sin abide!
This all important step decide!
Come out, where Christ can touch thy soul,
And at this moment be made whole!

Chorus:
Too late, too late, poor trembling soul!
O will this be your fate?
Too late, too late to be made whole!
Too late, too late, too late!

Scripture to Consider

You will be secure, because there is hope; you will look about you and take your rest in safety. [19]You will lie down, with no one to make you afraid, and many will court your favor. [20]But the eyes of the wicked will fail, and escape will elude them; their hope will become a dying gasp (Job 11:18-20).

Did you feast on God's Word in the last 24 hours?

     Yes   No

If so, how did you feast? In other words, circle the ways you enjoyed God today. Reading? Prayer? Worship? Fellowship? Witnessing?

Were you free from drug and alcohol abuse since you did the last lesson?

     Yes   No

Did you spend personal time with the Lord since you did the last lesson?

     Yes   No

If you answered "no" to any of the above questions, describe what led to your fall.

If you answered "yes" to the above questions, you may use this area for additional comments.

DAY 33 - OUR IDENTITY IN CHRIST

Today we are going to look at several Scriptures in the book of Ephesians. You will want to have your Bible handy and maybe a pen and paper to take notes. One of our students wrote the majority of today's course material.

Our Glorious Inheritance as God's Children:
Our Identity in Christ

One of the lies that Satan tells us is that our faith in Christ really has no affect on our lives. We are still the same old sinners we always were. We haven't really changed a bit. But this is a lie. God says in His Word the truth about who we are now as His children.

The reason we need to understand our identity in Christ is that knowing who we are will affect the way we respond to various things in our lives. When you're trying to overcome the sin of drunkenness, for example, you need to know that you're not a drunken person in God's eyes. If you believed that you were a drunk and that you couldn't help yourself when tempted, you would very easily succumb to every temptation that comes your way. Knowing who we are in Christ will help us to be victorious over drunkenness. We won't go near the temptation because we are not the same people.

The Apostle Paul tells us in 2 Corinthians 5:17, "Therefore, if anyone is in Christ, he is a new creation; the old has gone, the new has come!" If we have accepted Jesus as our Savior, then God tells us that we are in Christ. What exactly does this mean? What is Paul saying when he says we are in Christ? My Bible has a side note that says:

"In Christ: United with Christ through faith in Him and commitment to Him."

God is telling us that we have, as believers, a spiritual union with Jesus (and hence with God Himself). The bond we have with the Lord is unseen, but it is nonetheless very real.

Jesus explains this truth in His prayer in John 14:20-21, "On that day you will realize that I am in my Father, and you are in me, and I am in you. Whoever has my commands and obeys them, he is the one who loves me. He who loves me will be loved by my Father, and I too will love him and show myself to him."

This describes our relationship with God very well. It is one of living in Him and He living in us. He gives to us His life, and we give to Him our lives. He gives to us His love; we give to Him our love.

We need to understand how God has changed our lives in order for us to enjoy our relationship with Him to the fullest. To do that we need to take time to read from Scripture what God says about us now that we are in Christ.

Friend, let's look at some Scripture from Paul's letter to the Ephesians and contrast who we WERE with who we ARE now. On this page we will examine who we USED to be. Then we will see who we ARE.

Note: We readily acknowledge that a Christian, who is indeed alive in Christ, can succumb to the temptation of alcohol or abuse of medications. The believer is alive, and though he may be disobedient at the time, he is not dead, devilish, depraved, or under the wrath of God. But the passage we have just studied is about unbelievers who live in sin. As it says in Ephesians 2:1: "As for you, you were dead in your transgressions and sins, in which you used to live.

Questions

Ephesians 2:1-10: (v. 1) As for you, you were dead in your transgressions and sins,

Question 1. According to verse 1, what were we?

Note: When we were living in drunkenness we were, in reality, dead! We did not need education, or behavioral modification, or mere admonition to stop doing what we were doing. We needed life! Not that we were dead physically, (though we may have been headed there) but we were dead spiritually; dead to God, dead to His Word, dead to the church, etc.

2. . . . in which you used to live when you followed the ways of this world and of the ruler of the kingdom of the air, the spirit who is now at work in those who are disobedient.

Question 2. What does verse 2 tell us we were?

Note: We were not only dead; we were devilish as well; just following along after the "carrot" that Satan offered to lead us into his trap.

Question 3. What else does verse 2 tell us we were?

3All of us also lived among them at one time, gratifying the cravings of our sinful nature and following its desires and thoughts. Like the rest, we were by nature objects of wrath.

Question 4. What does verse 3 tell us we were?

Questions

Question 5. What else does verse 3 tell us we were?

Note: Not only were we dead, devilish, and disobedient, but we were also depraved! This is the condition of all who follow their impulses and live to gratify their flesh. If we had an impulse to view porn, we did it. Then if we had a desire to drink, we did. And slowly, over time, we began to be controlled by our impulses, which were becoming stronger and stronger.

Question 6. And what does verse 3 tell us is the final description of us as we used to be?

Note: That's right; we were the destination for God's wrath! We were the bull's-eye for the arrows of God's hatred; the object of His anger. This ought to frighten us to the core of our very being, and if we have escaped the trap of drunkenness we ought to be grateful for the grace of God!

Question 7. Friend, please describe how your past life of sin illustrates the above teaching. How were you dead, devilish, disobedient, depraved, etc. Describe how your life verified the truth of Scripture.

Course member Teresa writes, "As I began turning to alcohol to meet my needs, I slowly stopped listening to the voice of the Holy Spirit. I gave myself more and more to the flesh. My heart grew hard, cold and deaf to God. I was living as a 'free agent' trying to do things in my own strength. With each drink I consumed, my flesh called for more. It was never satisfied. My sin became a noose around my neck - I couldn't move away from it. I was living as one who had no claim of having a relationship with Christ. My enemy was quickly leading me to spiritual and physical death. Each time I tried to stop drinking on my own strength I failed - I just could not stop!"

Next we will notice that a great transformation has taken place. We are not who we were! Our identity is different. Read the following passage, noticing who we are NOW.

⁴But because of his great love for us, God, who is rich in mercy,

Question 8. According to verse 4, what are we?

Note: It is God's love and grace that changes our identity.

Question 9. What else does verse 4 tell us we are?

⁵. . . made us alive with Christ even when we were dead in transgressions; it is by grace you have been saved.

Question 10. What does verse 5 tell us we are?

Question 11. What do verses 5 and 8 tell us we are?

Note: Salvation is by grace alone. Not grace, plus what we do; it is all of grace. God chose us to be saved in eternity past (Ephesians 1; 2 Thessalonians 2:13), and then gave us grace to believe (Acts 18:27), and it is God who will keep us saved throughout eternity (Jude).

⁶And God raised us up with Christ and seated us with him in the heavenly realms in Christ Jesus.

Question 12. What else are we in verse 6?

Note: This very principle, of being alive and raised up from sin, is why man's methods of helping those with addictions will not work. Man can give advice, suggestions, and counsel but man cannot impart life! Only God can raise the dead.

⁷. . . in order that in the coming ages he might show the incomparable riches of his grace, expressed in his kindness to us in Christ Jesus.

Question 13. According to verse 7 who are we?

⁸. . . or it is by grace you have been saved through faith, and this is not from yourselves, it is the gift of God.

Questions

⁹ . . . not by works, so that no one can boast.

Question 14. According to verses 8 and 9 what are we?

¹⁰ For we are God's workmanship, created in Christ Jesus to do good works, which God prepared in advance for us to do.

Question 15. What does verse 10 tell us we are?

Note: The Greek word for "workmanship" in verse 10 is the word poema, from where we get our word POEM. We are God's poem to the world, His art that displays His grace, His workmanship of love.

Next we will examine who we are NOW.

WE WERE:

1. Dead in transgressions and sins (vs. 1, 5)
2. Followers of the world and Satan (v. 2)
3. Disobedient to God (v. 2)
4. Gratifiers of our sinful lusts (v. 3)
5. Followers of our every desire and thought (v. 3)
6. Objects of God's wrath (v. 3)

NOW WE ARE:

1. Loved by God (v. 4)
2. Recipients of God's mercy (v. 4)
3. Alive with Christ (v. 5)
4. Saved by grace (vs. 5, 8)
5. Raised up with Christ (v. 6)
6. Seated with Christ in heaven (v. 6)
7. Recipients of God's grace and kindness in Christ (v. 7)
8. Saved through faith in Christ (not from ourselves, it is a gift of God, and not by our works) (vs. 8, 9)
9. God's workmanship (v. 10)
10. Created (this means re-created) in Christ Jesus to do good works pre-prepared for us (v. 10)

Wow! Friend, isn't it awesome to think of all that God has done for us? Take time right now to praise God in prayer for all the wonderful things He's done in our lives. We are not the same anymore!

Paul said in 2 Corinthians 3:18, "And we, who with unveiled faces all reflect the Lord's glory, are being transformed into his likeness with ever-increasing glory, which comes from the Lord, who is the Spirit."

Question 16. Practically speaking, what are some differences in your life, now that you have left your drug of choice behind? Can you tell a difference, does anyone else see the change?

Course member Teresa writes, "Yes, I can tell the difference in my life. I no longer live to please my flesh—I am living to please Christ. Because my heart is 'in love' with Christ I no longer 'give myself' to another (Satan or flesh). Christ is restoring godly discernment to me. When dangerous situations arise or temptation sets in, the Spirit triggers an alarm in me. NOW I run to the Lord for refuge and strength, asking for a way out of the temptation. My desire is to please Christ. Others have told me that they do see a change in me. I am excited about where the Lord is taking me—I have hope for the future."

Scripture to Consider

"I have been crucified with Christ and I no longer live, but Christ lives in me. The life I live in the body, I live by faith in the Son of God, who loved me and gave himself for me" (Galatians 2:20).

Did you feast on God's Word in the last 24 hours?

    Yes   No

If so, how did you feast? In other words, circle the ways you enjoyed God today. Reading? Prayer? Worship? Fellowship? Witnessing?

Were you free from drug and alcohol abuse since you did the last lesson?

    Yes   No

Did you spend personal time with the Lord since you did the last lesson?

    Yes   No

If you answered "no" to any of the above questions, describe what led to your fall.

If you answered "yes" to the above questions, you may use this area for additional comments.

DAY 34 - NEW CREATIONS IN CHRIST (SALVATION ILLUSTRATED)

Today we will study a passage that encourages us toward a better understanding of how salvation works, and how it relates to our previous substance abuse. It follows on the heels of yesterday's lesson that taught us we are "new CREATIONS in Christ" (Galatians 5:17). I truly can't wait to share this with you! Let's get started.

> In the beginning God created the heavens and the earth. Now the earth was formless and empty, darkness was over the surface of the deep, and the Spirit of God was hovering over the waters. And God said, "Let there be light," and there was light (Genesis 1:1-2).

> Therefore, if anyone is in Christ, he is a new creation; the old has gone, the new has come (2 Corinthians 5:17).

Friend, we are new "creations" in Jesus. I am not a "refurbished" Jeff, I am totally new. God does not shave caterpillars to makes butterflies! And so it is profitable for us to study the biblical account of the creation of the earth, for in it we can see how God has saved us.

Notice there are three things said of the earth in the beginning. It was:

1. Formless

2. Empty

3. In darkness

If we look at Genesis 1 verse 9 we can see a fourth description of the earth:

4. Submerged underneath water.

Can you see how all of this relates to us as new creations in Christ? We, too, at one time were:

1. Formless: This same word is translated "confusion" in Deuteronomy 32:10.

2. Empty: Why did we turn to drugs anyway? Probably because we were trying to "fill the void." Emptiness in heart and life is the condition of all who are trapped in drunkenness. Instead of being "filled with all the fullness of God," and having an overflowing cup like David did, we were inwardly empty, lonely, yearning people.

3. In Darkness: Oh friend, can you remember the darkness that pervaded your life in drunkenness? The absence of light, wisdom, direction, and illumination all characterized my 17-year addiction to cocaine and alcohol.

4. Submerged underneath the water. We were dead and buried under the water of our sin: lost, sunk, submerged, and dead.

And so we have a perfect description of how we were when trapped in sin. We were "formless," confused, empty, in darkness and buried under the water of our sin.

Next, we will see how God saves us, but for now please answer the following questions.

Question 1. Please write out the description of the earth in its initial stages, using the four words in the above verses:

Question 2. Does this describe your past? Can you recall any of the feelings you had when living in drunken sin?

Course member Teresa writes, "Yes, I felt spiritually empty because I knew that I had turned away from God. I was living each day in spiritual darkness as though I had no true knowledge of Christ (actually I was worse than one who does not know of God at all, I KNEW, yet turned away). I did feel as though I were 'drowning' in my sin with no life-line to grab onto. There were times of panic as I felt myself move further and further away from Christ and more into my sin. The physical and spiritual addiction alcohol had upon me was strong. It was suffocating and strangling at the same time."

Question 3. Specifically focusing on "empty" from above. Can you see how using medications may have been an attempt to be fulfilled? Satisfied? Explain.

Questions

Question 4. Referring to the word "submerged" above. Did you ever feel like you were sunk down deep in it? Ever feel submerged? How so?

> **Course member Teresa writes,** "Absolutely. Years ago my older brother drowned and now I have fear of deep water. I have thought many times of how his last moments must have been, did he know he was dying? Did he feel panic? Or did he give in so that death would come quickly? In my bondage I felt as though my addiction was holding me under and I could not get air. At times I felt completely panic-stricken and would begin fighting. But I had come to the point of surrendering completely to alcohol. I remember many days that I just did not care anymore. I felt abandoned by people and God. I had 'given in' to death. I felt powerless to fight and knew that my own death was inevitable."

Next, God "said" let there be light. Please don't miss this: It is the Word of God that brings light. Notice this verse: "The unfolding of your words gives light; it gives understanding to the simple" (Psalm 119:130).

Friend, if you are saved, there was a time in your life that you were in darkness. Possibly this was when you were in drunken slavery. But then you began having an interest in Scripture and you were drawn to Jesus Christ. He spoke light into your heart through His Word, dispelling your sin and darkness. And now you are becoming, for lack of a better word, "addicted" to God's Word and you are receiving illumination, understanding, and wisdom (light).

The Apostle Paul, under the inspiration of the Holy Spirit applied Genesis 1:1-3 in this fashion. Paul says in 2 Corinthians 4:6 "For God, who said, 'Let light shine out of darkness,' made His light shine in our hearts to give us the light of the knowledge of the glory of God in the face of Christ." It is the same God who spoke light into darkness in creation that illuminates our hearts with Jesus Christ in salvation. Do you see it?

So, we were indeed confused, empty, in darkness, and buried in sin. But the Holy Spirit was "hovering" over us and God said, "let there be light." And the Word brought light into our hearts. Let us continue in our study:

> And God said, "Let the water under the sky be gathered to one place, and let dry ground appear." And it was so (Genesis 1:9).

Now, this is where it begins to get truly exciting. Do you see what is happening here? The earth, which was submerged beneath the water, has now come bursting up through the water, sort of like a resurrection. What was once buried is now alive, and is about to begin producing fruit!

Oh Friend, this is YOU if you are in Christ. Once empty, in darkness, buried in sin; now raised from the dead, full of the glory of God, enjoying the light of Jesus Christ. And watch this...

> Then God said, "Let the land produce vegetation: seed-bearing plants and trees on the land that bear fruit with seed in it, according to their various kinds." And it was so (Genesis 1:11).

This gets better and better. Now the earth is alive and producing fruit. Oh, how I wish you and I were sharing this Scripture together in person right now, feeding on the truth of it. Do you see what is happening? Now I am not going to comment on this verse, instead I'm going to ask you to do so.

Question 5. Write out how the above verse applies to you and salvation.

Question 6. John 15:5 says, "I am the Vine, you are the branches. If a man remains in Me and I in Him, He will bear much fruit." How does that verse apply to what we are studying?

Oh, Friend, it is truly quite wonderful to know God as Creator; not so much that He created the world (incredible as that is!) but that He can create good out of bad, light out of darkness, order out of chaos in our lives.

And now you can tell your testimony to others in a very short and simple manner: "I was empty, in darkness, and buried under the waters of sin; but God spoke light into my heart, raised me from the dead, filled me with His Son, and is making me fruitful." Amen!

And one last point: Did you happen to notice that it was on the third day that the "resurrection" of the earth happened? This point is important. In creation there was initial chaos, darkness, emptiness and death. And then, on the third day, there was a resurrection unto life and fruitfulness! Do you understand? The Lord Jesus emptied Himself for us amidst the chaos of His crucifixion. Then He hung on the cross in darkness and died for our sins. But on the third day He arose from the dead; victorious over sin, death, hell and the grave. And now you and I are the fruit of His suffering. We are the living souls He died to produce, and we carry precious seed to give life to others. Please do not miss this precious picture of our Lord Jesus Christ here in the first chapter of Genesis.

Drunkenness is darkness, and the dark pit into which we walk can become so dark that there seems to be no hope of ever finding light again. Do you see that the same God who created everything out of nothing is the light that penetrates even the darkest corner of our lives? He can light the darkness, raise us from the dead with Christ, and make us fruitful even though no one else would ever believe it to be possible.

Question 7. How are things in your life right now? Are you struggling with anything?

Scripture to Consider

[1]Therefore, there is now no condemnation for those who are in Christ Jesus, [2]because through Christ Jesus the law of the Spirit of life set me free from the law of sin and death. [3]For what the law was powerless to do in that it was weakened by the sinful nature, God did by sending his own Son in the likeness of sinful man to be a sin offering. And so he condemned sin in sinful man, [4]in order that the righteous requirements of the law might be fully met in us, who do not live according to the sinful nature but according to the Spirit" (Romans 8:1-4).

Did you feast on God's Word in the last 24 hours?

  Yes No

If so, how did you feast? In other words, circle the ways you enjoyed God today. Reading? Prayer? Worship? Fellowship? Witnessing?

Were you free from drug and alcohol abuse since you did the last lesson?

  Yes No

Did you spend personal time with the Lord since you did the last lesson?

  Yes No

If you answered "no" to any of the above questions, describe what led to your fall.

If you answered "yes" to the above questions, you may use this area for additional comments.

DAY 35 – THE GREATNESS, MAJESTY, POWER AND GRACE OF GOD

This course is not just a "how to" guide for overcoming drunkenness or addiction to prescription meds. The real purpose of this course is to assist us in viewing God as He really is, and loving Him supremely. For if the Holy Spirit opens our eyes to see majesty and glory of God, and we are brought to see His power and grace, then the natural response is worship and love of God. In other words, this course is not just about ceasing sinful behavior; it is about helping us to love God. It is not just about morality, it is about holiness.

So today we will examine a passage of Scripture that shows the glory, majesty and power of God, as well as His grace and compassion. May Scripture expand our view of Who God is, and cause us to be in awe of Him, for surely we cannot be viewing the greatness and glory of God and still be involved in habitual sin. Please read the following and answer the questions.

> See, the Sovereign LORD comes with power, and his arm rules for him. See, his reward is with him, and his recompense accompanies him (Isaiah 40:10).

The above verse describes God as the "Sovereign Lord" who comes with power and strength. This teaches us that God is God over all, the supreme Potentate, and the ruling King. "His arm rules for Him" is a metaphor for God being strong enough to rule, doing as He pleases and being able to accomplish what He decrees.

> [11]He tends his flock like a shepherd: He gathers the lambs in his arms and carries them close to his heart; he gently leads those that have young.

Verse 10 described God as the Sovereign Lord displaying His power, but verse 11 describes Him as a loving Shepherd displaying His grace. This God is not only One Who is in control of the entire universe, Friend, but He is also the caring Shepherd who loves individual "sheep;" carrying them closely and leading them gently.

This combination of Lord and Shepherd, of Divine Power and Divine Love, of Majesty and Grace is what makes our God so amazing.

> [12]Who has measured the waters in the hollow of his hand, or with the breadth of his hand marked off the heavens? Who has held the dust of the earth in a basket, or weighed the mountains on the scales and the hills in a balance?

Scientists tell us that the entire existing universe is so vast and expansive that it cannot be measured, and yet God marks it off with His hand. The use of the word "hand" here is not to teach us that God has body parts, for He is a Spirit, but to show the supreme greatness of God over His created universe.

The vast universe, that baffles the scientific genius of man and leaves him speechless, is but a handbreadth to God. In verse 10 above we saw the power of God, in verse 11 we saw His grace, and now in verse 12 we see His glory. Who is like unto our God?

> [13]Who has understood the mind of the LORD, or instructed him as his counselor? [14]Whom did the LORD consult to enlighten him, and who taught him the right way? Who was it that taught him knowledge or showed him the path of understanding?

These questions, and the verses that follow, are designed to show the insignificance of man in light of the greatness of God. Is there anyone on earth who might suggest to God that He measure the universe differently, or that He should use a different basket in which to carry the entire dust of the earth, or that He weigh the mountains using different scales? Actress Shirley MacLaine may declare all she wants, "I Am God" but when has she measured the entire universe with her hand, or carried the dust of the earth in a basket or weighed mountains? Those who do not see the greatness of God become great in their own eyes.

> [15]Surely the nations are like a drop in a bucket; they are regarded as dust on the scales; he weighs the islands as though they were fine dust. [16]Lebanon is not sufficient for altar fires, nor its animals enough for burnt offerings. [17]Before him all the nations are as nothing; they are regarded by him as worthless and less than nothing."

What God can look at the teeming nations, such as China whose population is the highest in the world at **1,362,391,579** (as of October, 2013) or Russia whose population is **142,572,794** and call them "a drop in the bucket" and "dust on the scales?" What kind of a God can weigh an island? And in light of the greatness of God, these nations of man are considered by Him as "nothing," "worthless" and "less than nothing."

> [18]To whom, then, will you compare God? What image will you compare him to?

God is the incomparably great God, unable to be reduced to words, inexplicable in human terminology, and unlike anything that has been or ever could be made.

Questions

Question 1. Please examine what these verses have to say about who God is, and compare the view of God that you have had up to this point. Are you growing in comprehension of the greatness of God? What are your thoughts so far?

Question 2. How does understanding God's greatness change how we view ourselves?

Question 3. If people think themselves to be great, what are they missing?

²¹Do you not know? Have you not heard? Has it not been told you from the beginning? Have you not understood since the earth was founded? ²²He sits enthroned above the circle of the earth, and its people are like grasshoppers. He stretches out the heavens like a canopy, and spreads them out like a tent to live in. ²³He brings princes to naught and reduces the rulers of this world to nothing. ²⁴No sooner are they planted, no sooner are they sown, no sooner do they take root in the ground, than he blows on them and they wither, and a whirlwind sweeps them away like chaff.

The questions in verse 21 are almost a mimic of man's inability to perceive the greatness of God. What, can't you understand? Can't you perceive that God is the God of the entire universe, the great King of all creation, who uses the entire heavens for His tent, who does as He pleases with all of mankind? Isn't this obvious to you? Paul says, ¹⁹"...since what may be known about God is plain to them, because God has made it plain to them. ²⁰ For since the creation of the world God's invisible qualities—his eternal power and divine nature—have been clearly seen, being understood from what has been made, so that men are without excuse" (Romans 1:19-20).

²⁵To whom will you compare me? Or who is my equal?" says the Holy One. ²⁶Lift your eyes and look to the heavens: Who created all these? He who brings out the starry host one by one, and calls them each by name. Because of his great power and mighty strength, not one of them is missing.

Though this passage compares mankind to "grasshoppers" yet God cannot be compared, for He is too great. God is awesome in splendor, powerful in majesty, beautiful in grace, and He has no equal. Can the great gurus of other religions create the heavens? Can all the prophets of all the religions down through the ages bring out each star and give it a name?

²⁷Why do you say, O Jacob, and complain, O Israel, "My way is hidden from the LORD; my cause is disregarded by my God"? ²⁸Do you not know? Have you not heard? The LORD is the everlasting God, the Creator of the ends of the earth. He will not grow tired or weary, and his understanding no one can fathom."

Since God is so great, and since He has created all things, and is ruling over all things, can we hide from Him? When we rush to the store to buy a bottle of alcohol or visit a dealer to get drugs does He miss us? Or when we are in a drunken stupor does He not see us staggering? "For a man's ways are in full view of the LORD, and he examines all his paths" (Proverbs 5:21). God sees everything we do, and though we think we are sinning in secret, the things done in darkness will be exposed by the light one day. Our way is not hidden from the Lord, and we can never sin in secret. As Moses was about to kill the Egyptian he "looked left and right" to see if anyone was looking, and having concluded that no one was watching he killed the Egyptian. Though he looked left and right, he forgot to look up.

²⁹He gives strength to the weary and increases the power of the weak. ³⁰Even youths grow tired and weary, and young men stumble and fall; ³¹but those who hope in the LORD will renew their strength. They will soar on wings like eagles; they will run and not grow weary, they will walk and not be faint" (Isaiah 40:29-31).

Here is what today's teaching on the greatness and awesome power of the Lord comes down to: All God's power is employed to strengthen the weary and to increase the power of the weak.

Question 4. Friend, verse 31 above is the "bridge" that enables us to cross over from stumbling and falling, to soaring and running. What is this bridge, and what does it mean?

Questions

Course member Teresa writes, "The 'bridge' is my hope in the Lord. My 'hope in the Lord' is the intimate, personal, ongoing relationship with Christ. His strength is imparted to me and provides the ability and desire to resist temptation and the enemy of my soul. Striving to resist in my own strength is futile. Without the solid ongoing relationship with Christ I now have, my strength was weak because the desire to honor and glorify Christ was missing. There was no 'driving force' behind my anemic efforts to resist my enemy."

Question 5. By way of review, please write down all the things that this passage teaches us about God. Please do not rush through this, but contemplate all that God is, and all that He can do.

Question 6. If God is showing you His own greatness and your own insignificance by comparison, how do you think this will affect your life?

Friend, when I was involved in the habitual sin of drunkenness, I thought that I was somebody. I had all the answers and was so smart. Even though my world was crashing down around me, I still thought that the answer was somehow inside of me. I was strong and able and I could figure it all out on my own. I didn't need God because I had all I needed in me. What a sad state of deception I was in as I hung suspended over a pit of destruction and couldn't even see my own inability. All of these great thoughts about myself were because my view of God was so small.

God gave me over to sin for a time, much like He gave King Nebuchadnezzar over to an insane mind for seven years, to live on the fields and eat grass like a cow. He showed me that my will was only free to sin, that He was in control of all things, and that He held my life (both physical and spiritual) in His hands. Through my sinning, and the subsequent loss of my marriage, my family, and

almost everything I had, God began bringing me low and reducing me to nothing. Finally, I had lost all self-respect, and thought God had thrown me away on the trash heap of sinful humanity. This is how I, as a young man "stumbled and fell."

But then God did an amazing thing. He began picking me back up, remaking me, giving me grace to forsake sin and embrace Christ, empowering me when I was so weak to "soar" and "run" and "walk," and now He is making me useful again. This is causing me to say, "Wow, look at who God is, and what He can do."

He not only created the heavens and the earth, but He has taken me out of the trap of the devil, is carrying me close to His heart, and giving me strength to overcome sin.

Scripture to Consider

[9]But you are a chosen people, a royal priesthood, a holy nation, a people belonging to God, that you may declare the praises of him who called you out of darkness into his wonderful light. [10]Once you were not a people, but now you are the people of God; once you had not received mercy, but now you have received mercy (1 Peter 2:9-10).

Did you feast on God's Word in the last 24 hours?

      Yes   No

If so, how did you feast? In other words, circle the ways you enjoyed God today. Reading? Prayer? Worship? Fellowship? Witnessing?

Were you free from drug and alcohol abuse since you did the last lesson?

      Yes   No

Did you spend personal time with the Lord since you did the last lesson?

      Yes   No

If you answered "no" to any of the above questions, describe what led to your fall.

If you answered "yes" to the above questions, you may use this area for additional comments.

DAY 36 - BATTLE STRATEGIES

YOU ARE AT WAR, SOLDIER. TIME TO LEARN HOW TO FIGHT!

During the next several days, we will examine the tactics of the enemy of our souls, as well as develop some battle strategy of our own to combat him. Please read the following verses, paying close attention to exactly where the enemy wages war on us.

> For though we live in the world, we do not wage war as the world does. The weapons we fight with are not the weapons of the world. On the contrary, they have divine power to demolish strongholds. We demolish arguments and every pretension that sets itself up against the knowledge of God, and we take captive every thought to make it obedient to Christ (2 Corinthians 10:3-5).

Questions

Question 1. Friend, from the above verses, where does the Devil attack us? In other words, where is the battle fought?

Question 2. What do the above verses call evil thoughts that can get lodged in our minds?

Soldiers, we are in a battle! The battlefield is the mind. The enemy desires to set up thought "strongholds" in our minds. These are thoughts that won't go away, that eventually must be acted upon. These "strongholds" are whatever is opposed to "the knowledge of God."

So, here is what happens: Everything is going just fine, and all of a sudden a thought about drinking alcohol comes into our thoughts. Maybe it is a memory of drinking or the "social" activity involved. Or perhaps it is a thought of how sweet or how soothing just one drink would be. The thought may be, "it would be so nice just to feel that numbness—what could one drink hurt?" Soldiers, THIS is the beginning of a thought-stronghold. This image that is lodging itself in our brain is in opposition to the knowledge of God. After all, the knowledge of God is whatever is true, noble, right, pure, lovely, and admirable (Philippians 4:8) and on such we are to constantly think. We can understand then that the evil one is setting that thought up in our minds to turn us away from God. This image, and the associated emotions that are conjured up in the heart, can become a stronghold of the Devil and lead us into drunkenness and/or other sins.

Or, if our particular downfall is going to a bar or party, we can be praying against going all day, but all of a sudden thoughts come into our heads: "Everybody loves you there! Somebody is just waiting to see you." A popular former television show centered in a bar invites us to go "where everybody knows your name." After all, the struggles of day to day life are so difficult, what would be wrong with a little reward, or a celebration of victory, or just a moment of escape from the pain? Though we try to push these thoughts away, and may be successful for the first or second time, eventually the thoughts get stuck in our minds and we are off to sin.

Question 3. What is your particular temptation scenario?

Questions

We need to make sure we understand that our minds are a battleground. And most importantly, we need to possess "divine weapons" and know how to fight using them. In today's study, it should become obvious that the enemy wages war on our minds. Notice the following verses:

> The mind of sinful man is death . . . (Romans 8:6).

The reason that the mind of sinful man is death is because Satan has numerous thought-strongholds there. Sinful man is fixated on sinful thoughts, and the wages of sin is death. In our case, thoughts about alcohol or drugs can totally overwhelm and control our minds.

> The sinful mind is hostile to God. It does not submit to God's law nor can it do so (Romans 8:7).

The sinful mind is saturated with sinful thoughts. When God's law requires it to think of pure, lovely, truthful thoughts it is totally unable to do so. The sinful mind is filled with sinful images and is bent on fulfilling the desires of the flesh.

> Many live as the enemies of the cross of Christ. Their destiny is destruction, their god is their stomach, and their glory is in their shame. Their mind is on earthly things (Philippians 3:19).

Friend, our minds are the battleground. If Satan can just get our minds fixed on "earthly things," he knows that we will be "enemies of the cross," and therefore enemies of God.

> Furthermore, since they did not think it worthwhile to retain the knowledge of God, he gave them over to a depraved mind, to do what ought not to be done. They have become filled with every kind of wickedness, evil, greed and depravity. They are full of envy, murder, strife, deceit and malice (Romans 1:28-29).

Questions

People who do not retain the knowledge of God are given over "to a depraved mind" to do what should not be done.

> But I see another law at work in the members of my body, waging war against the law of my mind and making me a prisoner of the law of sin at work within my members" (Romans 7:23).

In this verse we see that the war is waged against the mind, and when the enemy is successful we become prisoners of sin.

Question 4. Now it is time for personal reflection, Friend. What experiences have you had with your sin that verifies the truth that your mind is a battlefield? Have you felt at times that you were unable to control your mind? What "strongholds" have you experienced in the past?

Tomorrow, we will examine the resources with which we may fight. Meanwhile, we need to be aware of where the battlefield is—the thought life, and how the enemy gets access to our hearts—through thought strongholds. Friend, please be on guard. "Your enemy, the devil, prowls around like a roaring lion looking for someone to devour" (1 Peter 5:8). And one of the ways he "devours" is through these thought-strongholds.

Here are two things we can do to combat these thoughts that get lodged in our minds:

1. We can refuse to have access to any drug, which will cease the income of any additional experiences or 'visual' things that can drag us into sin. This point is key, and without allowing ourselves zero access, there really won't be any victory in this area. Please review Matthew 5:29-30, Romans 13:14 and Joshua 7:13.

2. We need to begin to immerse ourselves in Scripture, seeking God for grace to apply what we read. Taking in the Water of the Word has the effect of washing away the images that remain in the brain. Please review Joshua 1:8, Psalm 1:3.

As we continue to put these two things in place over time we will become free by the grace of God from all strongholds of the enemy.

Question 5. Please record the two things that are referred to above, that will rid the brain of sinful images:

1.

2.

None of us who have been enslaved to alcohol or prescription or other drugs can deny the difficulty involved in this war. I can remember how powerful this battle was at the beginning. I would see a commercial on TV or in a magazine and the image almost had a TASTE! The struggle began—beads of sweat would pop out on my forehead as I would attempt to white-knuckle it and resist. I think of how Pavlov's dog would salivate at the sound of a bell—I would literally be salivating at a thought or an image. Had I gone anywhere that served alcohol, I would have fallen in an instant! Over time, however, God's Word destroys this power as our minds are 'washed' clean of all the junk we have put in it over the years. I had put nothing but trash into my mind for 17 years, yet God's Word began to release me in an amazing way.

Best of all, we know who wins the war: GOD DOES!

Scripture to Consider

No one engaged in warfare entangles himself with the affairs of this life, that he may please him who enlisted him as a soldier (2 Timothy 2:4).

Did you feast on God's Word in the last 24 hours?

Yes   No

If so, how did you feast? In other words, circle the ways you enjoyed God today. Reading? Prayer? Worship? Fellowship? Witnessing?

Were you free from drug and alcohol abuse since you did the last lesson?

Yes   No

Did you spend personal time with the Lord since you did the last lesson?

Yes   No

If you answered "no" to any of the above questions, describe what led to your fall.

If you answered "yes" to the above questions, you may use this area for additional comments.

DAY 37 - DEMOLISHING STRONGHOLDS

Only Jesus Christ can give true and lasting victory.

Friend, there are many false saviors being offered today. If you were to do a search on the Internet for "help for addictions" you would discover 12-Step programs, psychological counseling programs, hypno-therapy, medication therapies, natural and alternative therapies, meditation . . . etc. I declare to you, on the authority of God's Word, that nothing can deliver us out of true substance addiction except Jesus Christ. "Salvation is found in no one else, for there is no other name under heaven given to men by which we must be saved" (Acts 4:12).

> For though we live in the world, we do not wage war as the world does. The weapons we fight with are not the weapons of the world. On the contrary, they have divine power to demolish strongholds. We demolish arguments and every pretension that sets itself up against the knowledge of God, and we take captive every thought to make it obedient to Christ (2 Corinthians 10:3-5).

We are continuing our study today in 2 Corinthians 10:3-5. Please fill in the blanks below.

literally be anything at all. This introduces a whole new form of idolatry into the mix and ignores the truth that only the one true God can set us free! New Wine, apart from Jesus Christ, is impotent to set anyone free. I have tried so many different "programs" that only left me frustrated and still in bondage. Only when I exhausted the programs of man and turned to God did freedom come—and it lasted!

Demolishing thought strongholds— by God's power!

Jesus Christ Himself is God's "divine power" and His "divine weapon." Without Him we have no way to permanently win the battle against addictions. So, let us examine how to demolish strongholds, and how to demolish every argument that sets itself up against the knowledge of God. Read the following verses and answer the questions.

> We demolish arguments and every pretension that sets itself up against the knowledge of God (2 Corinthians 10:5).

Question 5. According to the above verse, what are we to do when we are bombarded with thoughts or images that can become a stronghold?

Questions

Question 1. "For though we live in the world, we do not _____ _____ as the world does"

Question 2. "The weapons we _____ _____ are not the weapons of the world."

Question 3. "On the contrary, they have divine power to _____ _____."

Why do the programs mentioned above not work? They don't work because only "divine power" and divine weapons are effective against the demonic strongholds that Satan can set up in our minds. And only Jesus Christ, as God, is "divine."

Question 4. According to the above verses, what does it take to be able to demolish thought-strongholds?

Friend, no 12-step plan, no unbiblical counseling, no "_____" anonymous, no group therapy, no program of man (including this one) can deliver us from the clutches of drunkenness or drug addiction. It takes divine power and divine weapons. This teaching leaves us dependent upon God, who alone is divine.

I know that many may come to this point and say, "Hey, wait a minute! I am in a program called _____ and it really helps me!" What about my program?

I have been in several different programs and am also very familiar with psychiatric treatments (by experience) for addiction to alcohol and cocaine. Many times we are 'introduced' to accountability through these groups as we have a 'chip' or some token of our sobriety that we must break if we fall. This accountability is good, but it is only a STEP! You see, most programs leave out the only Person who can set us free—God. One popular program uses the name "God" in their "prayer" yet that god is only referred to as a "higher power" and can

Question 6. If you have ever tried to "demolish" these thought-strongholds in your own power, you've learned that it is impossible to do. It takes "divine power." Have you ever tried to just not dwell on your specific drug? What happened?

Questions

We are to "demolish" thought strongholds. We are to totally annihilate, exterminate, and eradicate sinful thoughts, so that our enemy does not gain a stronghold in our lives. Friends, if we begin to dwell on the object of our sin, we are rolling out the red carpet for Satan. We are not talking "mental warfare" here, but rather spiritual warfare. The difference is that in spiritual warfare we must possess Jesus Christ, and we must beg God for divine power in order to tear down the thoughts and images. In spiritual warfare, we lose the battle when a thought is able to lodge in our minds; and we win the battle when we demolish the thought. Do you see how we must become dependent on God in this battle?

Please write out your thoughts on the following verses and show how they teach us dependence on God:

> But thanks be to God Who gives us the victory through our Lord Jesus Christ (1 Corinthians 15:57).

Question 7. Please write your thoughts:

> No, in all these things we are more than conquerors through Him who loved us (Romans 8:37).

Question 8. Please write your thoughts:

> If the Son sets you free, you will be free indeed (John 8: 36).

Question 9. Please write your thoughts:

> For He has rescued us from the dominion of darkness and brought us into the kingdom of the Son He loves . . . (Colossians 1:13).

Question 10. Please write your thoughts:

For the grace of God that brings salvation has appeared to all men. It teaches us to say No to ungodliness and worldly passions, and to live self-controlled, upright and godly lives in this present age (Titus 2:11, 12).

Question 11. Please write your thoughts:

Again we see, from the above verse, that we must depend upon "divine power" in order to "take every thought captive." This is not easy to do. War is difficult. And yet with Jesus Christ we can indeed win. So, we are to make our thoughts prisoners of war. We are to notice when a particular thought is attempting to become a stronghold and we are to take it captive to Jesus.

So, this is what it may look like practically. I am cutting the grass on a hot summer day, tired and sweating and all of a sudden—WHAM!—the thought pops into my head: "It sure would be great to have a cold beer right now. Man, just think how refreshing and smooth it would be! One drink wouldn't hurt me . . . ." This starts to really make sense to me all of a sudden and it sounds like a REALLY good idea. Then I stop and cry out to God: "Oh, God, please Lord Jesus, rescue me. Satan is attempting to erect a stronghold in my mind to cause me to sin. Help! I see you, there, dying on the cross because you love me. I see you placed in the tomb so that my sins could be buried. I see you raised from the dead and know that your resurrection power is at work in me right now. Thank You, Lord Jesus, for dying for me, and forever living to intercede for me."

Tomorrow, we will take a look at some stories from the Bible that illustrate the truth that we've been studying. But, perhaps right now there is someone who is coming to understand why he/she is not having success over drunkenness. You might possibly be realizing for the first time that you do not have "divine power" and you simply are not able to "demolish strongholds." Maybe you realize that you need Jesus Christ. Please call to Him right now, won't you?

Read the following testimony from **Kathryn Wilson**:

"I also went to a 12-step program for _____ addiction. After a year, I quit. I found it very difficult to deal with a group of individuals who would admit their problems, but who wouldn't admit that God had the power to change them. The only support was supposed to come from being able to unload within a safe group of people who had similar problems. They talked about a 'higher power,' which could be anything, including a stuffed teddy bear. To this 'power' they gave the credit for their faithfulness, but then would have to admit failure again and again. It seemed to me they really had no hope and couldn't offer any. I know that system has benefits and works for some people but I was frustrated because I felt

God was missing from the formula." (*Stone Cold in a Warm Bed*, Kathryn Wilson with Paul Wilson, page 35, 36.)

John Bunyan, in *Pilgrim's Progress* described the battle that is fought with the enemy. In scene 4 he writes: "Apollyon, seeing an opportunity, came up close to Christian, and wrestled with him, giving him a dreadful fall; and with that Christian's sword flew out of his hand. Then Apollyon said, "I have won now," and nearly killed Christian. But, as God would have it, while Apollyon was about to strike the final blow, Christian nimbly reached out his hand for his sword, and grabbed a hold of it, saying, "Rejoice not against me, O mine enemy: when I fall, I shall arise," Micah 7:8; and with that he thrust his sword into Apollyon, which made him fall back, as one that had received a deadly wound. Christian seeing the devil retreat, rushed at him again, saying, "No, in all these things we are more than conquerors, through Him who loved us" Romans 8:37. And with that Apollyon spread forth his dragon wings, and hurried away, and Christian saw him no more. (James 4:7)

"He gives thanks for victory. Truly we are more than conquerors through Him that loved us; for we can give thanks before the fight is done. Yes, even in the thickest of the battle we can look up to Jesus, and cry, Thanks to God. The moment a soul groaning under corruption rests the eye on Jesus, that moment his groans are changed into songs of praise. In Jesus you discover a fountain to wash away the guilt of all your sin. In Jesus you discover grace sufficient for you, grace to hold you up to the end, and a sure promise that sin shall soon be rooted out altogether" (**Robert McCheyne**).

"The devil does not sleep, nor is the flesh yet dead; therefore, you must never cease your preparation for battle, because on the right and on the left are enemies who never rest" (**Thomas a Kempis**).

Question 12. Please record how you are doing now. Are you gaining the victory? Struggling?

I wanted to share a poem that one of our mentors wrote. This is shared by permission from John Stroud:

Setting Captives Free

Great and simple men alike have known the horrid chains
Of sin's enslavement and defeat of struggle without gain.

This battle common though it be takes daily casualties
And leaves the wounded living without hope of being free.

They walk in silent solitude behind their painted masks
And wallow in their private sins until somebody asks,

"Hey brother, how may I and these who know your plight
Walk side by side with you in grace to end your pain and strife?"

We've known defeat and sorrow in this battle you now see,

But now we spend our lives instead in Setting Captives Free.

Your battle scars and stories of entrapment and of blame, we know them all, we've lived them all, we understand the shame.

Step up and walk beside us now, we're going the same way
We're seeking life in Jesus Christ and trusting more each day

That He will change our hearts and minds so we might come to be
Ones who pass the truth along by Setting Captives Free.

Scripture to Consider

For the LORD your God is the one who goes with you to fight for you against your enemies to give you victory (Deuteronomy 20:4).

He put garrisons throughout Edom, and all the Edomites became subject to David. The LORD gave David victory wherever he went (2 Samuel 8:14).

You give me your shield of victory; you stoop down to make me great (2 Samuel 22:36).

The horse is made ready for the day of battle, but victory rests with the LORD (Proverbs 21:31).

Did you feast on God's Word in the last 24 hours?

     Yes   No

If so, how did you feast? In other words, circle the ways you enjoyed God today. Reading? Prayer? Worship? Fellowship? Witnessing?

Were you free from drug and alcohol abuse since you did the last lesson?

     Yes   No

Did you spend personal time with the Lord since you did the last lesson?

     Yes   No

If you answered "no" to any of the above questions, describe what led to your fall.

If you answered "yes" to the above questions, you may use this area for additional comments.

DAY 38 - DEMOLISHING STRONGHOLDS II

Okay, so we have been studying about how to demolish strongholds, and to take every thought captive using God's divine power. Now, we will look at how God illustrates these truths in His Word.

In the book of Joshua, we read of the many battles that the Israelites fought to conquer the land the Lord had given to them. Today, let us take note of one battle in particular, in Joshua chapter 11. It is the battle of the Israelites against the northern kings. These northern kings all bonded together to fight against the Israelites and the Bible says that they made "a huge army, as numerous as the sand on the seashore." They were a formidable foe to be sure; but God told Joshua, "Do not be afraid . . . I will hand them over to you." So Joshua and the Israelites went out in battle against the huge army of the northern kings. And Joshua 11:12 says that, "Joshua took all these royal cities (where those kings used to live) and put them to the sword. He totally destroyed them as he had been commanded." That's right; Joshua and his people totally annihilated that huge army. And the Bible says that they were victorious because the Lord fought for them!

Please answer the following questions.

Questions

Question 1. How large was the army of the northern kings?

Question 2. Joshua and the Israelites were to do what to the army of the northern kings?

Question 3. Please write, in your own words, how this story applies to our situation with drugs. Find as many parallels as you can.

Questions

Fellow soldiers, the desire for alcohol, prescription meds, or other substances, as I'm sure you know by now, is a formidable foe. It can, at times, be like a huge army that is much stronger than we are. And yet Scripture tells us that we are to demolish it. Destroy it. Annihilate it. Can you see how this does indeed take divine power?

> . . . And we take captive every thought to make it obedient to Christ (2 Corinthians 10:5)

Here is an illustration of taking our thoughts captive:

In the Old Testament, the nation of Israel was commanded to dislodge every nation that currently existed in the Promised Land. They had good success pulling down the strongholds of those nations, and dislodging most of them. However; a few nations were very powerful and very stubborn, and the Israelites were unable to demolish them. Notice what the Israelite nation did with those nations:

> "All the people left from the Amorites, Hittites, Perizzites, Hivites and Jebusites . . . all whom the Israelites could not exterminate—these Solomon conscripted for his slave labor force" (1 Kings 9:20-21).

Question 4. According to the above verses, what did King Solomon do with the nations that the Israelites were unable to exterminate?

Questions

Friend, there might be some thoughts so powerful that we may not be able to keep them from infiltrating our minds, especially in the first couple of months after we have turned from our sin. But if we stay away from those areas that might tempt us, and we seek the Lord, eventually we will no longer have thoughts that overtake us as they used to do. The Israelites were told to completely demolish the enemy . . . they wiped out enough of the enemy to inhabit the land, but then got tired of fighting and let some of them stay, even though they made them their slaves. They reasoned that, "hey, we don't need to wipe these guys out; we can use them as our slaves." They justified their disobedience by making them useful as slaves. But it was still disobedience, because God had told them to wipe them all out. The Israelites got tired of fighting and kept some of their enemies around. Those thoughts that we don't demolish or have victory over, and think we are making our slaves are still there. Question: Did those slaves stay slaves or did they eventually rise up and cause problems? Wouldn't it have been better and possible for the Israelites to completely wipe out the enemy? Total annihilation is the only answer!

Now, prepare yourself for this next power-packed verse:

> "If you do not drive out the inhabitants of the land from before you, then it shall come about that those whom you let remain of them will become as pricks in your eyes and as thorns in your sides and they shall trouble you in the land where you live" (Numbers 34:55).

You know what this means? You know those things that we let remain? Those things that we think aren't too bad? Those things that we justify and even say, "Hey, in comparison to where I was, this is nothing?" These are the areas where there is great potential for trouble in our lives. ". . . they shall trouble you in the land where you live." Annihilate!

Friend, before we move on we should remind ourselves that we are in a very serious battle. We are instructed to use God's power to demolish demonic strongholds, and we are to take captive every thought to Christ. This is serious business and cannot be taken lightly. If we truly want to win the battle, there must be a whole lot of crying out to God for victory, depending on God for power, and thanking God each time you win. If you have been winning battles for the past 37 days, then you can rejoice with Paul who said, "I thank Christ Jesus our Lord, who has given me strength . . ." (1 Timothy 1:12). Jesus Christ gave the strength to Paul, and Jesus must give us strength as well, in order for us to win the battle over sin. Will you pray right now that God would give you strength?

Please read the following quote from Thomas a Kempis and comment on it:

> "Above all, we must be especially alert against the beginnings of temptation, for the enemy is more easily conquered if he is refused admittance to the mind and is met beyond the threshold when he knocks.

> "Someone has said very aptly: Resist the beginnings; remedies come too late, when by long delay the evil has gained strength. First, a mere thought comes to mind, then strong imagination, followed by pleasure, evil delight, and consent. Thus, because he is not resisted in the beginning, Satan gains full entry.

> "And the longer a man delays in resisting, so much the weaker does he become each day, while the strength of the enemy grows against him" (**Thomas a Kempis**) *The Imitation of Christ.*

Question 5. Provide your comments about the quote from Thomas a Kempis here:

I have one particular friend who would always tell me that he was ready to quit drinking. He and I drank heavily together many times and he seemed to "have it all together" for quite a while. He even began to seek God to help him overcome his addiction. We both knew that we were enslaved to alcohol, but he seemed to really be on the right track. He continued, however, to hang out in bars with friends (including me) who would pressure him to drink.

After a while he began drinking again and settled right back into the lifestyle. One night, he left a bar where many of us had been drinking and drove himself home while intoxicated. The next morning I awoke to the news that he had struck a tree and was dead. It is still very painful at times to say this, but he did not put into practice what we have been learning today. I loved him dearly and I am pleading with you, Friend, to take this teaching to heart. He didn't totally annihilate the enemy and eventually he was overcome. The sad part is that the enemy annihilated him in the end. I pray that God has mercy on his soul.

Questions

Please read the following Scripture and consider it in relation to the 'battle' we have been looking at.

Question 6. Please record what you have learned today. How will you apply this teaching?

Scripture to Consider

When you go to war against your enemies, the Lord will help you defeat them so that you will take them captive (Deuteronomy 21:10).

Now the men of Judah approached Joshua at Gilgal, and Caleb son of Jephunneh the Kenizzite said to him, "You know what the LORD said to Moses the man of God at Kadesh Barnea about you and me. ⁷I was forty years old when Moses the servant of the LORD sent me from Kadesh Barnea to explore the land. And I brought him back a report according to my convictions, ⁸but my brothers who went up with me made the hearts of the people melt with fear. I, however, followed the LORD my God wholeheartedly. ⁹So on that day Moses swore to me, 'The land on which your feet have walked will be your inheritance and that of your children forever, because you have followed the LORD my God wholeheartedly.'

¹⁰Now then, just as the LORD promised, he has kept me alive for forty-five years since the time he said this to Moses, while Israel moved about in the desert. So here I am today, eighty-five years old! ¹¹I am still as strong today as the day Moses sent me out; I'm just as vigorous to go out to battle now as I was then" (Joshua 14:6-11).

Did you feast on God's Word in the last 24 hours?

     Yes   No

If so, how did you feast? In other words, circle the ways you enjoyed God today. Reading? Prayer? Worship? Fellowship? Witnessing?

Were you free from drug and alcohol abuse since you did the last lesson?

     Yes   No

Did you spend personal time with the Lord since you did the last lesson?

     Yes   No

If you answered "no" to any of the above questions, describe what led to your fall.

If you answered "yes" to the above questions, you may use this area for additional comments.

DAY 39 - THE LOVE OF GOD AND TEMPTATION

¹²Blessed is the man who perseveres under trial, because when he has stood the test, he will receive the crown of life that God has promised to those who love him. ¹³When tempted, no one should say, "God is tempting me." For God cannot be tempted by evil, nor does he tempt anyone; ¹⁴but each one is tempted when, by his own evil desire, he is dragged away and enticed. ¹⁵Then, after desire has conceived, it gives birth to sin; and sin, when it is full-grown, gives birth to death. ¹⁶Don't be deceived, my dear brothers (James 1:12-16).

Today we will see very clearly what it is that will get us through any temptation and trial we ever face. The teaching of God's Word in this area is powerful enough to help anyone who will embrace and apply the truths taught today to find freedom from slavery to alcohol, or any habitual sin. Jesus said, "If you hold to my teaching, you are really my disciples. Then you will know the truth, and the truth will set you free" (John 8:31-32). The inevitable result of embracing Truth is *freedom!*

In James 1:12 above we see a promise made to one who stands the test and "perseveres under trial" and we see the motive for persevering. The promise is "the crown of life" and the motive for standing and persevering is the love of God. The above verses make it clear that life will have its share of both trials and temptations, and this passage communicates God's way of victory through both. Let us see what we can learn, and may God help us to grasp His truth and enjoy the freedom that comes from it.

When I am faced with a severe trial, or an intense temptation I have a choice to either persevere in faith and stand up under the trial, or fall down in sin and deception. The passage we are studying in James promises me the "crown of life" if I stand and persevere, and shows me that death will be the end result if I follow the path of temptation, desire, and sin. So we are discussing life and death today. The critical question is this: What is the motive for choosing to stand and persevere?

Questions

Question 1. Please write out James 1:12 here:

Question 2. What motive do you see for persevering and standing under the trial?

Some may answer "the crown of life" to the question of motive, but when looking a little deeper we can see that the real motive for persevering through the trial, and standing up under temptation is the **love of God.** God promises the crown of life "to those who love Him."

Friend, any methodology of man for bringing freedom to those trapped in sin is doomed to fail, because it leaves out motive. For instance, worldly methodologies in the past have taught those given over to excessive drinking that they need help outside of themselves, and they are taught to ask for help from a "higher power." But this model falls short of helping people to have lasting heart-change because the program fails to address that man has a need to love and is created with the desire to worship. There is no true freedom in the heart that does not love God. But once this love for God is planted in the heart it will enable us to go through any trial, and to stand up under any temptation and not fall. If we are falling to sin, we do not have proper love for God. Notice how Paul's prayer for the Thessalonians reinforces the truth that it is the love of God that enables our perseverance:

> "May the Lord direct your hearts into God's love and Christ's perseverance" (2 Thessalonians 3:1).

So this brings up the next question which is, "How then do I acquire love for God?" This is a difficult question and does not come with a simple answer, but here are a few thoughts, along with some practical steps I've taken in my own life to grow in love for God.

1. The first step is to ask God to give you a heart that loves Him. "You may ask me for anything in my name, and I will do it" (John 14:14). "You do not have, because you do not ask God" (James 4:2). If this teaching is new to you, you may want to pause here and acknowledge to the Lord that your love for Him needs to be increased, and ask Him to do it. Feel free to pause in prayer, or to write out a request to God for Him to give you a heart that loves Him.

Questions

2. Dwell on the cross of Jesus Christ. "This is how we know what love is: Jesus Christ laid down his life for us" (1 John 3:16). There has never in all of human history been an act of love displayed to the world that demonstrates the love of God better than the cross of Christ. Meditate on this cross, asking God to give you love for the One who died in our place. Think often of His wounds in His hands and feet and side, which are really reminders of His love for us (Isaiah 49:15-16). Recall how He sweat drops of blood, how He offered His back to be smitten (Isaiah 50:6), how He was willingly beaten beyond recognition (Isaiah 52:14), all to pardon us from sin's penalty and free us from sin's power.

> But he was pierced for our transgressions,
> he was crushed for our iniquities;
> the punishment that brought us peace was upon him,
> and by his wounds we are healed.
> We all, like sheep, have gone astray,
> each of us has turned to his own way;
> and the LORD has laid on him
> the iniquity of us all" (Isaiah 53:5-6).

3. Obey God's Word. "But if anyone obeys his Word, God's love is truly made complete in him" (1 John 2:5). Of course we know that it takes the grace of God in order for us to obey the Word of God. It is an amazing thing to begin walking in obedience to God and to sense the love of God as we do. Do you want your heart flooded with the love of God? Walk in obedience and you will have it.

4. "Keep yourselves in the love of God, looking for the mercy of our Lord Jesus Christ unto eternal life"(Jude 21). Again, Friend, God alone can keep us from falling (Jude 24) but we are exhorted to keep ourselves in the love of God. This is similar to John 15 where we are told to "abide in the Vine" and in 1 John where we are told to "remain in Him" (1 John 2:27). This is a general statement that we are to do all we can to remain in God's love.

Question 3. Please write out the above 4 steps to God's love, and indicate whether you are currently doing them.

1.

2.

3.

4.

Next, let us look at James 1:12-16 again:

> [12]Blessed is the man who perseveres under trial, because when he has stood the test, he will receive the crown of life that God has promised to those who love him. [13]When tempted, no one should say, "God is tempting me." For God cannot be tempted by evil, nor does he tempt anyone; [14]but each one is tempted when, by his own evil desire, he is dragged away and enticed. [15]Then, after desire has conceived, it gives birth to sin; and sin, when it is full-grown, gives birth to death. [16]Don't be deceived, my dear brothers.

Verses 14 and 15 describe the nature of temptation, by using 2 analogies. Let us look at both of them:

1. Fishing. "But each one is tempted when, by his own evil desire, he is dragged away and enticed." The words "dragged away and enticed" have to do with bait. The bait is what the fisherman uses to lure the fish. When we are being tempted we only focus on the "bait" never on the hook. In the garden of Eden Eve saw that the fruit was "pleasing to the eye" but she did not focus on the death that would result from her eating it. For years I was enamored with alcohol and cocaine, along with the accompanying lifestyle, never considering what I was destroying in the process, including my marriage, family, and my own life.

Question 4. What has been the "bait" that you have been attracted to in the past?

Question 5. In what ways has the "bait" hooked you?

> Then, after desire has conceived, it gives birth to sin; and sin, when it is full-grown, gives birth to death.

2. Delivery: "Then, after desire has conceived, it gives birth to sin; and sin, when it is full-grown, gives birth to death." When desire and lust conceive, they give birth to sin, and when sin is full grown it gives birth to death. Again, when we are being tempted all we see is the conceiving, never the birth. Temptation not only obscures the "hook" but the "birth of death" as well. But Scripture teaches us to have a different perspective; that is, to view the consequences of our actions all the way from taking the bait to becoming hooked, and then to death. The wages of sin is death (Romans 3:23).

Question 6. You've described your "bait" and how it has "hooked" you above, now think through in what ways giving in to evil desires has given birth to death in your life. Some may describe how evil desires have taken them to such lengths that they have acquired liver disease, other health problems, or even sexually transmitted diseases from

Questions

promiscuous behavior, and now they are awaiting their own physical death. For others it will be that the mating of their evil desires with lust has conceived sin, and after sin grew their marriage died. Have you experienced a death from sin yet? If not, can you see how you were headed in that direction? What are your thoughts?

Friend, these verses end with a surprising remedy for this whole process of temptation and sin: "Don't be deceived, my dear brothers" (James 1:16). Sin is deception by its very nature. The fisherman is not offering the fish something good for it by displaying the bait; the fisherman means to kill the fish. Evil desires do not ultimately relieve tension, provide excitement, and spice up our lives—they bring death. Do not be deceived. How do we overcome drunkenness? We see it for what it is. Alcohol is the bait that is used to hook us and kill us, and the "excitement" of lust will bring about our death.

> Then, after desire has conceived, it gives birth to sin; and sin, when it is full-grown, gives birth to death. Don't be deceived, my dear brothers (James 1.15-16).

So, to summarize today's teaching: It is the love of God that enables us to endure trials and to stand up under temptation. It is the love of God that releases us from deception and frees us from sin's power. And it is the love of God that will bring us into glory as a spotless bride. Oh, for more love of God!

Question 7. What are your final thoughts on today's teaching? Did you learn anything new, or will you do anything different? How will you apply these Scriptures to the ongoing battle against drunkenness and all forms of substance abuse?

Scripture to Consider

Have nothing to do with the fruitless deeds of darkness, but rather expose them. For it is shameful even to mention what the disobedient do in secret. But everything exposed by the light becomes visible, for it is light that makes everything visible. This is why it is said: "Wake up, O sleeper, rise from the dead, and Christ will shine on you" (Ephesians 5:11-14).

Because of the LORD's great love we are not consumed, for his compassions never fail. They are new every morning; great is your faithfulness (Lamentations 3:22-23).

Did you feast on God's Word in the last 24 hours?

     Yes   No

If so, how did you feast? In other words, circle the ways you enjoyed God today. Reading? Prayer? Worship? Fellowship? Witnessing?

Were you free from drug and alcohol abuse since you did the last lesson?

     Yes   No

Did you spend personal time with the Lord since you did the last lesson?

     Yes   No

If you answered "no" to any of the above questions, describe what led to your fall.

If you answered "yes" to the above questions, you may use this area for additional comments.

DAY 40 – BREAK THE CHAIN

"Misloaded Douglas DC-8 Pitches Up Excessively On Takeoff, then Stalls and Strikes the Ground"

The cargo was not loaded aboard the airplane according to the airlines instructions. As a result, the flight crew inadvertently used a horizontal-stabilizer-trim setting that was not correct for the airplanes aft center of gravity.

FSF Editorial Staff

On Aug. 7, 1997, _____(airline name) Flight 101, a Douglas DC-8-61, stalled on takeoff and struck the ground approximately 3,000 feet (915 meters) from the end of Runway 27R at Miami (Florida, U.S.) International Airport. The three flight crewmembers, a security guard aboard the airplane and one person on the ground (a motorist) were killed. The U.S. National Transportation Safety Board (NTSB), in its final report said, "The accident resulted from the airplane being misloaded to produce a more aft center of gravity and a correspondingly incorrect stabilizer-trim setting that precipitated an extreme pitch-up at rotation."

NTSB said that the probable causes of the accident were: The failure of _____ (airline name) to exercise operational control over the cargo-loading process; [and,] the failure of [_____, a freight-forwarding company] to load the airplane as specified by _____ (airline name).

"Contributing to the accident was the failure of the [U.S.] Federal Aviation Administration (FAA) to adequately monitor (airline name) operational-control responsibilities for cargo loading and the failure of FAA to ensure that known cargo-related deficiencies were corrected at _____ (airline name)," said NTSB.

The captain, 42, was hired by _____ (airline name) in October 1993. He had 12,154 hours of flight time, including 2,522 hours as a (airline name) DC-8 captain. NTSB said that in 1995 the FAA "suspended the captain's airman certificate and medical certificate for 30 days because he had failed to report a revocation of his motor-vehicle driver's license." FAA records indicated that the captain was convicted for misdemeanor drunk driving in California in 1986 and convicted for driving under the influence in Arizona in 1994, said NTSB, Flight Safety Foundation.

As an airline pilot I often read up on the how's and why's of aircraft accidents. I do this to try to learn what happened and how I can prevent something similar from happening to myself, the crew, and passengers I carry. One of the greatest sites for studying aviation accidents is Flight Safety Foundation's Accident Prevention Website at http://www.flight-safety.org/ap_home.html One thing I have been noticing as I read through the accident reports is that there is usually an accident "chain" with many links that make up that chain.

In the above accident what "links" in the accident chain can you find? Here are some that I saw:

1. Improper loading of the aircraft by the company contracted to load.

2. The airline did not properly monitor the loading of the aircraft.

3. Failure of the FAA to properly monitor the loading operation of the airline.

4. Failure of the FAA to ensure previous known loading problems were corrected.

5. A possible 5th "link" in the accident chain could have been the Captain's known drinking problem.

All the above links in the chain caused the accident of this Cargo Flight 101, killing a total of 5 people. What if just one link in the accident chain had been broken? For instance, what if the FAA, citing known loading problems with the airline, had decided to shut it down until its problems could be corrected? That one break in the chain would have saved 5 people's lives.

Friend, you and I have had a problem with drunkenness and drug abuse. And if we examine times of failure we will always find a chain of events that lead up to the "crash." Here are some of mine:

1. I did not get up early and spend quiet time with the Lord.

2. I have had a long day at work and I am tired.

3. My wife and I are at odds over something.

4. I go to a restaurant where many people are around me drinking alcohol.

5. I saw a commercial on TV or in a magazine with an "image" of a bottle or drinking activity.

6. I go to a party or (worse) a bar and allow myself access to alcohol . . . .

Crash!

Now, I have learned to notice when links in an accident chain are developing and to break at least one link to prevent a drunken accident. So, now I rise early and spend time with the Lord, which sets me in a grateful and praying frame of mind throughout the day. I will communicate much with my wife and ensure we are loving each other. If my day is long I know I'm headed for trouble and I begin watching and praying. And finally, I might take a longer route to avoid any bar or restaurant I could stop at as well as letting my wife know when I am leaving and when I should arrive at home.

Next, let us notice how these "accident links" are all there in a particular incident in Scripture.

In the life of Lot, the nephew of Abraham, there was a terrible tragedy. He came to live in a city that was ultimately destroyed by God for its wickedness. Lot lost all his possessions, his wife was killed and he barely escaped with his own life and the lives of his two daughters. Notice the following passage of Scripture and see if you can spot the links in this developing "accident chain," then write in each "link" below:

> ⁸So Abram said to Lot, "Let's not have any quarreling between you and me, or between your herdsmen and mine, for we are brothers. ⁹Is not the whole land before you? Let's part company. If you go to the left, I'll go to the right; if you go to the right, I'll go to the left."
>
> ¹⁰Lot looked up and saw that the whole plain of the Jordan was well watered, like the garden of the LORD, like the land of Egypt, toward Zoar. (This was before the LORD destroyed Sodom and Gomorrah.) ¹¹So Lot chose for himself the whole plain of the Jordan and set out toward the east. The two men parted company: ¹²Abram lived in the land of Canaan, while Lot lived among the cities of the plain and pitched his tents near Sodom. ¹³Now the men of Sodom were wicked and were sinning greatly against the LORD (Genesis 13:8-13).
>
> ⁸Then the king of Sodom, the king of Gomorrah, the king of Admah, the king of Zeboiim and the king of Bela (that is, Zoar) marched out and drew up their battle lines in the Valley of Siddim ⁹against Kedorlaomer king of Elam, Tidal king of Goiim, Amraphel king of Shinar and Arioch king of Ellasar—four kings against five . . . . ¹¹The four kings seized all the goods of Sodom and Gomorrah and all their food; then they went away. ¹²They also carried off Abram's nephew Lot and his possessions, since he was living in Sodom (Genesis 14:8-12).

Note: Eventually Sodom was destroyed by the fire of God's wrath.

Did you spot the "links" that led to this disaster? Please write them here. I'll do the first one for you. (If you need help, see below.)

Questions

Question 1. First link: Lot and Abraham quarrel and separate (Genesis 13:8-11).

Question 2. Second link:

Question 3. Third link:

Question 4. Fourth link:

Question 5. Fifth link:

Questions

Break the Chain

Friend, to stop a drunken accident, and possibly save our souls, it is important for us to break the link in the chain. Remove one link and we don't crash. Had there been proper supervision in the loading of the cargo aircraft in Miami five people would not have lost their lives. What if Lot had broken chain link number one, or even number two? These are the links that I saw in the story of Lot:

1. Lot and Abraham quarrel and separate (Genesis 13:8-11). What if Lot and Abraham had worked out their differences instead of separating? (Note: watch out for separating from fellow believers for any reason, even if the reason seems legitimate as it did in Lot's case. There may come a time when separation is necessary, but weigh it carefully against the benefits derived from fellowship.)

2. Lot "looked up and saw" the valley of Sodom (Genesis 13:10). What if Lot had not focused on the valley but on the hill country instead? (Note: be careful what we focus on.)

3. Lot "set out toward" Sodom (Genesis 13:11). Would this "accident" have happened if Lot set out toward the great trees of Mamre instead of Sodom? (Note: Be careful of the general direction of your life. We are always moving, either more toward righteousness or more toward sin.)

4. Lot "pitched his tent near" Sodom (Genesis 13:12). Lot could have broken the "accident chain" even after he separated from Abraham, after he saw and set out toward Sodom, had he simply refused to pitch his tent so close to the filth and wretchedness of Sodom. (Note: To the extent possible, pitch your tent as far away from sinful traps as you can. We still must influence the world, but we have to watch ourselves, be discretionary, use wisdom and common sense as to how close we should get.)

5. Lot "was living in" Sodom (Genesis 14:12). Notice the progression: Lot separated from Abraham, saw Sodom, set out toward Sodom, pitched his tent near Sodom, and then was living in Sodom. And then we read of him being taken captive in battle. Friends, these can be our steps to destruction as well. We separate from fellowship, see something sinful and focus on it, set out toward it, pitch our tent near it, live in it, and are taken captive by it.

Question 6. Now please write out a quick summary of the above five points, just to reinforce the steps that lead to a fall.

Questions

Break the Chain!

Now, let us focus on your accident chains. What are the links? How can you remove one link (or more) and stop the accident? Please describe below your accident chains and your plan to "remove a link."

Question 7. What has been your accident chain in the past?

Question 8. Will you now conscientiously remove some links in the chain? What links will you remove and how will you do it?

Question 9. Will you share this plan with someone who can help you implement it and hold you accountable for it?

Question 10. Record how are you doing today?

Scripture to Consider

Be sober; be vigilant; because your adversary the devil walks about like a roaring lion, seeking whom he may devour. Resist him, steadfast in the faith, knowing that the same sufferings are experienced by your brotherhood in the world (1 Peter 5:8-9).

Did you feast on God's Word in the last 24 hours?

> Yes   No

If so, how did you feast? In other words, circle the ways you enjoyed God today. Reading? Prayer? Worship? Fellowship? Witnessing?

Were you free from drug and alcohol abuse since you did the last lesson?

> Yes   No

Did you spend personal time with the Lord since you did the last lesson?

> Yes   No

If you answered "no" to any of the above questions, describe what led to your fall.

If you answered "yes" to the above questions, you may use this area for additional comments.

DAY 41 - SEEK THE LORD

"But what if I've done horrible things? What if I've made a real mess of my life, I've hurt other people, I've broken promises and vows . . . etc. What if I've gone too far? Is it possible that what I've done is so bad that I'm unable to be forgiven?"

NO!

Read the following passage, and look for the words, "But if from there."

> After you have had children and grandchildren and have lived in the land a long time-if you then become corrupt and make any kind of idol, doing evil in the eyes of the LORD your God and provoking him to anger, I call heaven and earth as witnesses against you this day that you will quickly perish from the land that you are crossing the Jordan to possess. You will not live there long but will certainly be destroyed. The LORD will scatter you among the peoples, and only a few of you will survive among the nations to which the LORD will drive you. There you will worship man-made gods of wood and stone, which cannot see or hear or eat or smell. But if from there you seek the LORD your God, you will find him if you look for him with all your heart and with all your soul (Deuteronomy 4: 25-29).

Questions

Question 1. Please list all the ways that the Israelites would do wrong, according to the above passage:

Question 2. Note the things that would happen to them for their sins:

Question 3. But despite the horrendous sin in which these people were involved, was God willing to forgive them?

Questions

Question 4. How do we know that God would still forgive them? What does He say?

Note: This passage teaches us important things about the character of God: He forgives! Any sin! Any time! The Truth taught today is "But if from there...you seek the Lord" and your "there" may be anywhere. From wherever you are, Friend, if you will turn to God, seek Him, look for Him with all your heart and soul, you will find Him. He promises!

Question 5. How were the Israelites supposed to find God and be forgiven?

Question 6. How does Hebrews 11:6 compare with what we are studying?

> And without faith it is impossible to please God, because anyone who comes to him must believe that he exists and that he rewards those who earnestly seek him.

130

Questions

Question 7. What are your comments on Jeremiah 29:11-13:

> For I know the plans I have for you, declares the LORD, plans to prosper you and not to harm you, plans to give you hope and a future. Then you will call upon me and come and pray to me, and I will listen to you. You will seek me and find me when you seek me with all your heart.

Question 8. How does this verse compare? Psalm 10:4:

> In his pride the wicked does not seek him; in all his thoughts there is no room for God.

Question 9. What are your thoughts on 2 Samuel 14:14:

> But God does not take away life; instead, he devises ways so that a banished person may not remain estranged from him.

Question 10. Comments on Matthew 7:7:

> Ask and it will be given to you; seek and you will find; knock and the door will be opened to you.

Friend, there is no sin that God will not forgive if we will seek Him wholeheartedly about it. This is serious business—no half-hearted seeking of the Lord will do. Eternity is at stake. Hell is real. Let us seek Him while He may be found and we will rejoice in His forgiveness, love and acceptance.

Question 11. Write out your comments on 1 Kings 8:46-51:

> When they sin against you—for there is no one who does not sin—and you become angry with them and give them over to the enemy, who takes them captive to his own land, far away or near; and if they have a change of heart in the land where they are held captive, and repent and plead with you in the land of their conquerors and say, "We have sinned, we have done wrong, we have acted wickedly"; and if they turn back to you with all their heart and soul in the land of their enemies who took them captive, and pray to you toward the land you gave their fathers, toward the city you have chosen and the temple I have built for your Name; then from heaven, your dwelling place, hear their prayer and their plea, and uphold their cause. And forgive your people, who have sinned against you; forgive all the offenses they have committed against you, and cause their conquerors to show them mercy; for they are your people and your inheritance, whom you brought out of Egypt, out of that iron-smelting furnace (1 Kings 8:46-51).

Today I want to introduce you to some more writings of the Puritans. The first is from a Puritan pastor to one in his congregation. He is giving practical counsel. My prayer is that his counsel will sink right in to your heart and soul as you read. Once you get a taste of the medicinal value of these writings you will want more and more. We've got to replace the hours spent on alcohol or pot with something else; why not invaluable writings like these?

Memoirs of McCheyne:

> I DO NOT and cannot forget you; and though it is very late, I have to write you a few lines to say, Follow on to know Jesus. I do not know if you can read my crooked writing, but I will make it as plain as I can. I was reading this morning, Luke 2:29, what old Simeon said when he got the child Jesus into his arms: "Now lettest thou thy servant depart in peace, according to thy word: for mine eyes have seen thy salvation." If you get a firm hold of the Lord Jesus, you will be able to say the same.
>
> If you had died in your ignorance and sin, dear soul, where would you have been this night? Ah! How shall we sufficiently praise God if He really has brought you to the blood of the Lord Jesus Christ! If you all are re-

Questions

ally brought to Christ, it will be something like the case of the wise men of the East (Matthew 2). When they were in their own country, God attracted their attention by means of a star. They followed it, and came to Jerusalem, saying, "Where is he that is born King of the Jews? . . . for we are come to worship him." Herod and Jerusalem were troubled at the saying. No one was seeking Christ but the wise men. The world thought they were mad; but soon they saw the star again, and it led them to the house where the infant Savior lay, His robe of state a swaddling band, His cradle the manger. Yet they kneeled down and called Him, my Lord and my God, they got their own souls saved, and gave Him gifts, the best they had, and then departed into their own country with great joy in their hearts, and heaven in their eyes.

So it may be with you. The most around you care not for Jesus. But you are asking, Where is He? We are come to be saved by Him. None around you can tell. They think you are going out of your mind. But God is leading you to the very spot where the Redeemer is a lowly, despised, spit upon, crucified Savior. Can this be the Savior of the world? Yes, dear soul; kneel down and call Him your Redeemer. He died for such as you and me. And now you may go away into your own country again, but not as you came. You will carry with you joy unspeakable and full of glory.

More from Memoirs of McCheyne:

Some of you may have seen how short life is in those around you. Your fathers, where are they? And the prophets, do they live forever? How many friends have you lying in the grave! Some of you have more friends in the grave than in this world. They were carried away as with a flood, and we are fast hastening after them. In a little while the church where you sit will be filled with new worshipers, a new voice will lead the psalm, a new man of God fill the pulpit. It is an absolute certainty that, in a few years, all of you who read this will be lying in the grave. Oh, what need, then, to fly to Christ without delay! How great a work you have to do! How short the time you have to do it in! You have to flee from wrath, to come to Christ, to be born again, to receive the Holy Spirit, to be made meet for glory. It is high time that you seek the Lord. The longest lifetime is short enough. Seek conviction of sin and an interest in Christ. Oh, satisfy me early with thy mercy, that I may rejoice and be glad all my days.

Question 12. What are your thoughts on today's lesson? How are you doing today?

Scripture to Consider

Glory in His holy name; Let the hearts of those rejoice who seek the LORD! [4]Seek the LORD and His strength; Seek His face evermore! (Psalm 105:3-4).

Did you feast on God's Word in the last 24 hours?

      Yes   No

If so, how did you feast? In other words, circle the ways you enjoyed God today. Reading? Prayer? Worship? Fellowship? Witnessing?

Were you free from drug and alcohol abuse since you did the last lesson?

      Yes   No

Did you spend personal time with the Lord since you did the last lesson?

      Yes   No

If you answered "no" to any of the above questions, describe what led to your fall.

If you answered "yes" to the above questions, you may use this area for additional comments.

DAY 42 - RESTORATION AFTER LOSS

Friend, drunkenness is tremendously exciting—for a while. It promises to give fulfillment, stimulation and satisfaction. But if you have been doing it for any length of time you know that the promises are really lies; alcohol takes more than it ever gives! We will examine a story today of a young man whose heart was filled with the promise of excitement and satisfaction, and the gain of material wealth, lifelong friendships, ease and satisfaction. But he ended up losing everything. Let's read:

> [11]There was a man who had two sons. [12]The younger one said to his father, "Father, give me my share of the estate." So he divided his property between them. [13]Not long after that, the younger son got together all he had, set off for a distant country and there squandered his wealth in wild living. [14]After he had spent everything, there was a severe famine in that whole country, and he began to be in need. [15]So he went and hired himself out to a citizen of that country, who sent him to his fields to feed pigs. [16]He longed to fill his stomach with the pods that the pigs were eating, but no one gave him anything" (Luke 15:11-16).

This young man was not content with his life. So he asked his father to give him his inheritance. Then he went to a "distant country" and began living a "wild life" where he "spent everything."

Friend, drugs plant seeds of discontentment in a very powerful way. They can plant the seed of physical discontentment by the display of the seemingly problem free lives of the actors and actresses in ads. They can plant the seeds of emotional discontentment through the false promise of escape from our problems. We covet that "joy and contentment" portrayed in the ads which can never be attained through drugs. And following discontentment, depression comes and anger which can destroy our families and cause havoc that touches every corner of our lives. Drugs are an extremely powerful tool in the hands of the devil.

But if we were to follow the lives of people who have been involved in drunkenness for any length of time, we would discover lives of loss. Lives of need. Lives of emptiness. Walk down any street in any major city and the telltale trail of destruction is not hard to spot. I have talked with many of these people and it comes back to that first drink or needle and all the broken promises that followed. The results are stories of devastation and loss.

Questions

Question 2. There is a word in verse 16 that describes all who are not being satisfied in Jesus Christ. Fill in the blank. "He _____ to fill his stomach."

So, the young man initially longed to have his inheritance and longed to live the wild life; now he was longing for food. "Longing" is the characteristic of those who are not drinking the Living Water of Jesus Christ. Remember the woman at the well and her six relationships?

Question 3. When we were involved in drunkenness, we were longing for something. What were you longing for?

Question 4. Write down everything you can think of from the above story that this young man lost by going to the far country:

Question 5. Have you lost anything through involvement with your drug of choice?

Questions

Question 1. From verse 14 above, there are two things that caused this young man to "be in need." What are those two things?

Note: Regarding the famine, it can often be discovered that Providence is against us when we are sinning. And yet, in some cases, God is disciplining in order to restore. This famine, in the above story, was of Divine Providence, designed to increase the "need" of the young man, and was for his restoration.

And the God of all grace... will himself restore you and make you strong, firm and steadfast (1 Peter 5:10).

Friend, God is a restoring God. The devil prowls around like a roaring lion seeking for someone to devour. But God is able to forgive, save, heal, deliver, and restore us when we fall.

Questions

And then He is able to keep us from falling again. Notice the rest of the passage in Luke 15:

> 17"When he came to his senses, he said, 'How many of my father's hired men have food to spare, and here I am starving to death! 18I will set out and go back to my father and say to him: 'Father, I have sinned against heaven and against you. 19I am no longer worthy to be called your son; make me like one of your hired men.'
>
> 20So he got up and went to his father. But while he was still a long way off, his father saw him and was filled with compassion for him; he ran to his son, threw his arms around him and kissed him. 21The son said to him, 'Father, I have sinned against heaven and against you. I am no longer worthy to be called your son.'
>
> 22But the father said to his servants, 'Quick! Bring the best robe and put it on him. Put a ring on his finger and sandals on his feet. 23Bring the fattened calf and kill it. Let's have a feast and celebrate. 24For this son of mine was dead and is alive again; he was lost and is found.' So they began to celebrate.

Question 6. Verse 17 says that the young man "came to his senses." So what was this man's condition while in the far country?

Note: drunkenness is insanity! It puts us out of our right minds.

Question 7. What two words does the father use in verse 24 above to describe his son when he was in the far country?

Question 8. When he "came to his senses" where did he want to go?

The first indicator of true repentance is a desire for God. We know we are beginning to think correctly, after a time in the far country, when we want to go to our Heavenly Father.

Now let us review the picture we have been given of this young man. According to Jesus, this man was for a time not in his right mind, but did come back to his senses. According to his father, he was dead and lost. According to his own words, he had sinned and was unworthy.

Question 9. Do you see yourself and your involvement with drugs in the life of this prodigal? Write your thoughts here:

Like the prodigal, I was once discontent with what I had and alcohol and drugs stirred up lust in my heart. I was longing for contentment, and I attempted to satisfy it in the wrong way—a way that is far away from God. When involved with drugs, we are out of our minds; dead and lost spiritually, sinful and unworthy and we may lose much while in this condition. But, when we "come to our senses," and return to our Heavenly Father, He will accept, embrace, love and restore us.

> But while he was still a long way off, his father saw him and was filled with compassion for him; he ran to his son, threw his arms around him and kissed him (Luke 15:20).

Are there any sweeter words in all of Scripture? This verse reveals the heart of God the Father toward those who are leaving sin and coming to Him. If you are leaving drunkenness and coming back to God, you will be received warmly, no matter how far away you went, how long you have been gone, or how much you lost. Our God loves those who leave their sin and come to Him.

Notice that the father was "filled with compassion." If you are returning from drunkenness, our God has a heart wide open for you. His heart beats with love for those who are returning, and just the sight of us when we return fills our Father's heart with compassion.

> "As a father has compassion on his children, so the Lord has compassion on those who fear him" (Psalm 103:13).

> But the father said to his servants, 'Quick! Bring the best robe and put it on him. Put a ring on his finger and sandals on his feet. Bring the fattened calf and kill it. Let's have a feast and celebrate. For this son of mine was dead and is alive again; he was lost and is found.' So they began to celebrate.

The end of this story is all about loving and joyous restoration. He who had sinned, squandered the wealth, and had been living with pigs, was now reconciled to his father, given a robe, ring and sandals, and was feasting on the fatted calf.

Questions

How instructive this is for those of us who through drunkenness squandered away our spiritual inheritance, and possibly much more. But now we are reconciled to God, graced with the robe of righteousness, granted the ring of authority, and are wearing the sandals of readiness to tell the gospel. And most importantly, we are feasting on the Lord Jesus! Oh, friend, we were saved to celebrate! Reconciled to God to delight in His Son! Rescued from drugs to feast on Jesus!

Today's study was all about restoration after loss. Is someone reading this who has really lost a lot through involvement with heroin and other abusive substances? Oh my friend, if you come to God, or come back to God, you will see His heart of compassion for you. You will see your life restored, and made a blessing to others. You will look good in your new robe, and will enjoy a feast that will satisfy your longings. God will restore to you the years the locusts ate.

Question 10. What steps do you perceive in the young man's 180 degree turn-about?

Question 11. The young man wanted to come back and be a "servant." What did the father call him in verse 24?

Question 12. If you have "squandered," does this story give you hope of restoration? How so?

Question 13. Does this story move you to believe in the possibility of new or fresh changes in your relationship with God and/or others?

How do the following verses reinforce the truth we have been studying today? Please write your thoughts after each one:

> I will repay you for the years the locusts have eaten--the great locust and the young locust, the other locusts and the locust swarm my great army that I sent among you. You will have plenty to eat, until you are full, and you will praise the name of the LORD your God, who has worked wonders for you; never again will my people be shamed" (Joel 2:25-26).

Question 14. Please write your thoughts:

Note: This passage seems to be a promise of God that He would restore what the disobedience of the Israelites destroyed. The "locusts" here are used to picture sin, which devours and destroys everything in its path.

> Come, let us return to the LORD. He has torn us to pieces but he will heal us; he has injured us but he will bind up our wounds. After two days he will revive us; on the third day he will restore us, that we may live in his presence (Hosea 6:1-2).

Question 15. Please write your thoughts:

Questions

The Spirit of the Sovereign LORD is on me, because the LORD has anointed me to preach good news to the poor. He has sent me to bind up the broken-hearted, to proclaim freedom for the captives and release from darkness for the prisoners, to proclaim the year of the LORD's favor and the day of vengeance of our God, to comfort all who mourn, and provide for those who grieve in Zion to bestow on them a crown of beauty instead of ashes, the oil of gladness instead of mourning, and a garment of praise instead of a spirit of despair. They will be called oaks of righteousness, a planting of the LORD for the display of his splendor. They will rebuild the ancient ruins and restore the places long devastated; they will renew the ruined cities that have been devastated for generations (Isaiah 61:1-4).

Question 16. Please write your thoughts:

Scripture to Consider

Thus says the LORD: "Behold, I will bring back the captivity of Jacob's tents, And have mercy on his dwelling places; The city shall be built upon its own mound, And the palace shall remain according to its own plan. Then out of them shall proceed thanksgiving and the voice of those who make merry; I will multiply them, and they shall not diminish; I will also glorify them, and they shall not be small" (Jeremiah 30:18-19).

Did you feast on God's Word in the last 24 hours?

       Yes   No

If so, how did you feast? In other words, circle the ways you enjoyed God today. Reading? Prayer? Worship? Fellowship? Witnessing?

Were you free from drug and alcohol abuse since you did the last lesson?

       Yes   No

Did you spend personal time with the Lord since you did the last lesson?

       Yes   No

If you answered "no" to any of the above questions, describe what led to your fall.

If you answered "yes" to the above questions, you may use this area for additional comments.

DAY 43 - SPECIFIC STEPS TO FREEDOM FROM SIN

[7]"Submit yourselves, then, to God. Resist the devil, and he will flee from you. [8]Come near to God and he will come near to you. Wash your hands, you sinners, and purify your hearts, you double-minded. [9]Grieve, mourn and wail. Change your laughter to mourning and your joy to gloom. [10]Humble yourselves before the Lord, and he will lift you up" (James 4:7-10).

Today we will see from Scripture that we are to take specific steps to be free from sin. But first, let us notice from the above passage some characteristics of those who are in sin. Let us list them here:

1. They do not submit to God (v. 7).

2. They do not resist the devil (v. 7).

3. They remain at a distance from God (v. 8).

4. They have dirty hands and a defiled heart (v. 8).

5. They are double-minded (v. 8).

6. They are light and joking, and laugh much (v. 9).

7. They are prideful (v. 10).

Friend, I can think back into my time of drunkenness and see every one of these characteristics in my life:

1. My spirit was domineering and dictatorial, not submissive toward God or others.

2. I freely embraced drunkenness on many occasions, not realizing that in so doing I was worshiping at a demonic shrine (1 Corinthians 10:20-21).

3. I was far from God during this time, even though I claimed to be a servant of His. My life illustrated Proverbs 28:9, "If anyone turns a deaf ear to the law, even his prayers are detestable."

4. My hands were dirty from all my sin activity and my heart was defiled all the time. Oh, what a horrible condition to be in. Now I understand why Scripture compares sin to leprosy, for leprosy is a disease that defiles one entirely, and makes them unclean. Just as lepers had to remain isolated or in colonies of other lepers, so I came to feel that I should be banished from society because my guilt and shame were so great. Oh, how I thank God that He still cleanses lepers!

5. I was double-minded and unstable, because while I attempted to pray and meditate on Scripture, my thoughts often slid into drunken thoughts.

This occupied the majority of my time and I had no relationship with my family. It made me unstable for I could not keep my thoughts together on any one subject. "That man (who doubts God) should not think he will receive anything from the Lord; he is a double-minded man, unstable in all he does" (James 1:7-8).

6. I was never very serious, but was light and airy, joking all the time and laughing quite frequently. This was a cover up for my sinful ways, as I tried to hide all my pain with laughter.

7. I was very prideful and often put others down, hoping to lift myself up.

Questions

Question 1. Thinking through the above seven characteristics, which one (or several) describe your life when you were involved in substance abuse? Please give some instances where these characteristics showed themselves most clearly.

These verses also show us the remedy for our sin-sickness, and we are about to study specific steps on how to be free from habitual sin. But let us be careful to note that doing what Scripture commands requires the grace of God. This would be a good point to stop today's lesson and beseech God for grace to actually do each of these steps, Friend. I often pray, "God help me to apply what I learn today. I need your grace to actually do what your Word says to do, so please keep me from just gaining knowledge but help me to obey You." Feel free to write out a prayer here if you would like.

Step 1: "Submit yourselves, then, to God." (v. 7). Submission is a Greek military term meaning "to arrange [troop divisions] in a military fashion under the command of a leader." In non-military use, it was "a voluntary attitude of giving in, cooperating, assuming responsibility, and carrying a burden." Submission in Scripture is obeying God, whereas sinning is obeying the evil one. Job 22:21-27 contains much truth on how to be free from sin, and the first step is listed in verse 21: "Submit to God and be at peace with him;"

Questions

Question 2. Please write out in what areas you have failed to submit to God in the past, and then explain how you will submit to Him from now on.

Step 2: "Resist the devil, and he will flee from you" (v. 7). Resist means to set yourself against someone or something, or to stand in opposition to them. For me, this meant developing a "battle plan" of how to set myself against the evil one. Among other things, this meant throwing out all alcohol in my house as well as staying away from bars.

Question 3. How will you set yourself against the devil, and stand in opposition to him? What is your "Battle Plan"? Please be specific.

Step 3: "Come near to God and He will come near to you" (v. 8). Friend, let me speak a truth to your heart right now: there will be no real freedom, nor any lasting victory in a life that is not seeking closeness and union with Christ. Sure, we may be able to "white-knuckle" it, grit our teeth and use sheer "will power" for a short time, but we will not have freedom because that comes only through intimacy with Christ. We must not only resist the devil, but we must also draw near to God and experience His presence in order to overcome sin. For me, that meant spending much time in prayer and Bible study, attending church whenever possible, counseling with my pastor, etc.

Question 4. What will it look like for you to draw near to God? Again, please be specific.

Step 4: "Wash your hands, you sinners, and purify your hearts, you double-minded" (v. 8). There must be a cleansing of what we do (our hands) what we love (our hearts) and what we think (our minds). Scripture admonishes us to "wash" and "purify" and this requires diligence and effort, as well as using the proper tools with which to clean.

Question 5. Please list how you are planning on cleansing your hands, your heart and your mind.

Step 5: Become single minded (v. 8). Yes, it is entirely possible to rid our brains of those desires and images of drugs. It requires not allowing ourselves any access to additional images, and cleansing our minds of the images that are still there from the past. It also requires the ceasing of drinking alcohol and taking drugs, as each time we indulge the bondage becomes deeper and the desire stronger. This cleansing took me a few months to do, once I began the process of coming out of drunkenness, but I can tell you that I have not had a strong desire to drink in several years.

Question 6. Are you "double-minded" now? Or can you remember what it was like in the past?

Step 6: "Grieve, mourn and wail. Change your laughter to mourning and your joy to gloom" (v. 9). The basic instruction in this verse is to get serious, rid your life of flippancy, and begin to mourn over your sin. Now some will say that this is a life of morbid despair and gloom, and that it is contradictory to all the passages that refer to unspeakable joy (1 Peter 1:8) and being content in life (Hebrews 13:5). But this is not so. This passage in James refers to a person who is in need of repentance, whereas the other passages refer to the effects of repenting. Genuine repentance includes submitting to God, resisting the devil, gaining intimacy with Christ, purifying ourselves, changing our joy to gloom, and mourning over our sins.

Questions

Question 7. Have you sincerely mourned over your sin? Are you seeking to exchange light-hearted laughter for seriousness and sadness, at least for a time? Please explain.

Step 7: "Humble yourselves" (v. 10). During my years of drunkenness I thought I had it all figured out. I did not need anyone to tell me how to do things because I felt that I had all the knowledge and ability a person needed. I would get hostile with any authority figure and took great pleasure in debating "life" with others, especially those "narrow minded" people who thought every answer could be found in the Bible! Oh, how deceived I was! There came a point when all of my "world knowledge" had to be thrown out the door. I sat in a pew at the back of a church building listening to the instruction that would set me free from bondage, all in God's power and not in my own. I opened the pages of my Bible trembling like a child because I realized that the ONLY answers were found in between the covers of the book I had shunned for so long. THIS is what is required to get out of habitual sin, Friend. It requires humbling ourselves.

At this point in our mentoring program @www.setting-captivesfree.com we can tell when God is working in the heart of a course member because they find themselves not wanting to argue, or point out all the wrongs of the course, but simply to learn and ask for help. They recognize their need and so they humble themselves and ask God and us for help. We have noticed that the people who are serious about humbling themselves always find victory. Indeed, the last half of the verse that tells us to humble ourselves says, "and He will lift you up" (v. 10). Victory and freedom are the results for those who humble themselves!

Question 8. Finally, please share what you have learned today, or what you will put into practice. Have you seen yourself in this passage, and are you now aware of some things that will need to change in order to be truly free from habitual sin?

Scripture to Consider

Do you not know that your body is a temple of the Holy Spirit, who is in you, whom you have received from God? You are not your own; you were bought at a price. Therefore honor God with your body (1 Corinthians 6:19-20).

Submit to God and be at peace with him; in this way prosperity will come to you. Accept instruction from his mouth and lay up his words in your heart. If you return to the Almighty, you will be restored: If you remove wickedness far from your tent and assign your nuggets to the dust, your gold of Ophir to the rocks in the ravines, then the Almighty will be your gold, the choicest silver for you. Surely then you will find delight in the Almighty and will lift up your face to God. You will pray to him, and he will hear you, and you will fulfill your vows. What you decide on will be done, and light will shine on your ways" (Job 22:21-28).

There I will give her back her vineyards, and will make the Valley of Achor (valley of Trouble) a door of hope. There she will sing as in the days of her youth, as in the day she came up out of Egypt (Hosea 2:15).

Did you feast on God's Word in the last 24 hours?

     Yes   No

If so, how did you feast? In other words, circle the ways you enjoyed God today. Reading? Prayer? Worship? Fellowship? Witnessing?

Were you free from drug and alcohol abuse since you did the last lesson?

     Yes   No

Did you spend personal time with the Lord since you did the last lesson?

     Yes   No

If you answered "no" to any of the above questions, describe what led to your fall.

If you answered "yes" to the above questions, you may use this area for additional comments.

DAY 44 - THE HEART, THE MIND, AND THE ACTIONS

¹Since, then, you have been raised with Christ, set your hearts on things above, where Christ is seated at the right hand of God. ²Set your minds on things above, not on earthly things. ³For you died, and your life is now hidden with Christ in God. ⁴When Christ, who is your life, appears, then you also will appear with him in glory. ⁵Put to death, therefore, whatever belongs to your earthly nature: sexual immorality, impurity, lust, evil desires and greed, which is idolatry. ⁶Because of these, the wrath of God is coming. ⁷You used to walk in these ways, in the life you once lived. ⁸But now you must rid yourselves of all such things as these: anger, rage, malice, slander, and filthy language from your lips. ⁹Do not lie to each other, since you have taken off your old self with its practices ¹⁰and have put on the new self, which is being renewed in knowledge in the image of its Creator (Colossians 3:1-10).

When I was involved in drunkenness and drugs, my heart was set on impure things. I would walk around during the day with my heart racing, my hands sweating, my mind dwelling on alcohol and cocaine, just waiting to get to a dealer or a bar where I could indulge my flesh and appease my sinful appetite. That is how many of my days went.

Today we want to study how the heart and mind affect the actions, and we want to learn how to live in freedom from habitual sin.

Questions

Question 1. What does your heart love right now, Friend?

Question 2. List some practical ways that you will begin setting your heart on things above.

Questions

The above passage of Scripture talks about the "heart" (v. 1), the "mind" (v. 2), and the "actions" (vs. 5-10) and shows the relationship between them. The heart affects the mind, which in turn affects the actions. Let us look at each one of these:

1. <u>The Heart</u>: The heart loves and feels excitement. The heart longs, yearns, and lusts. The heart of one in bondage loves to sin, and feels excitement when sinning. It longs, yearns, and lusts after sin, and is kept in bondage to its cravings. In contrast, the heart of one who is being set free loves God and feels excitement about growing in righteousness. That heart longs, yearns, and lusts after the holiness of God and purity.

We are instructed in the above passage to "set our heart on things above, where Christ is seated at the right hand of God." In other words, we are to set our heart on loving Christ. Oh dear friend, here is freedom from substance abuse! Involve your heart with Jesus Christ. Make yourself be excited about Christ. Long to be with Him, yearn for intimacy with Him, lust after a closer walk with Him. Let the cry of the beloved be yours: "Take me away with you-let us hurry! Let the king bring me into his chambers" (Song of Solomon 1:4).

The heart that is set on Christ is the heart that is free from sin. The heart that is ravished by Christ refuses to let Him go, but instead embraces Him and clings to Him: "Scarcely had I passed them when I found the one my heart loves. I held him and would not let him go till I had brought him to my mother's house, to the room of the one who conceived me" (Song 3:4). This is what we are after in this course of **New Wine**!

We are after the heart being affected with Christ. Colossians 3:1 tells us to "set our hearts on things above, where Christ is seated..."

2. <u>The Mind</u>: The mind is obviously our thoughts. The mind that is in sin is continually thinking about sinful thoughts. Drunken and impure images consumed my mind while awake, and my dreams while sleeping. Those thoughts and images interrupted my work, my recreation, my family time, and all other areas of life. Romans 1:28 describes my previous condition: "Furthermore, since they did not think it worthwhile to retain the knowledge of God, he gave them over to a depraved mind, to do what ought not to be done."

Colossians 3:2 tells us "set your minds on things above, not on earthly things." When I was involved in drunkenness I was so earthly minded that I was no heavenly good. But now we are told to set our minds on Christ, and this will inevitably bring about a real battle, because for so long we have immersed ourselves in sinful images. Now we are to think heavenly thoughts, thoughts about Christ and God, thoughts about eternity and about heaven. We are to discern whatever is true, noble, right, pure, lovely, admirable, excellent or praiseworthy (in other words, Christ!) and we are to think on these things.

Questions

The reason that we are to do these things is listed in Colossians 3:3: "For you died, and your life is now hid with Christ in God." On the cross Jesus died for us, but we also died in Him. Our old sinful nature hung on that tree with Christ. My old heart that loved sin died 2,000 years ago. My mind that was consumed with sinful images was killed at the hands of Roman soldiers, and then my old sinful self was buried in a tomb.

Question 3. Notice that verse 2 does not tell us "Stop thinking about sinful things" but rather "set your minds on things above." Why is this so?

3. The Actions: What we do is tied in with what we love and what we think about. As Christians, we are not just about behavior modification without a heart change. We are about loving God passionately, about having our thoughts consumed in Christ, and then about walking in freedom from sin.

Colossians 3:5 tells us that we are to put to death whatever belongs to our flesh. Friends, here is where the Christian life turns violent, and where murder of our pet sins is encouraged. We are to put to death drunkenness, to crucify our lusts, and this requires spiritual acts of violence. It requires a battle plan, it uses spiritual weapons, and we won't be satisfied until there is complete annihilation of the sin. When I first started coming out of drunkenness, I smashed bottles, changed careers to get out of bars, and avoided certain places, as well as many other "radical" steps to be free from the power of sin.

So determine to destroy all that has been seducing you; smash the bottles, refuse to carry cash or credit cards so that you cannot buy drugs, ask the clerk at your local convenience store to not sell you alcohol and have your spouse or friends ASK where you are going and where you have been. And then set fences for yourself that will not allow you to go back to these sins. This may be embarrassing to you, but I have found that unless we are willing to be embarrassed we will never be free.

But not only are we to crucify drunkenness, but also all "sexual immorality" and "impurity, lust, evil desires and greed, which is idolatry." Everything has to go. Like the children of Israel when they were told to stone Achan, also stone his family, his sheep and cattle, and destroy everything connected with him, so we are to do violence to the entire realm of everything sinful. We are not only to destroy drunkenness, sexual immorality, impurity, evil desires, etc., but we are to rid our lives of anger, rage, malice, slander, and filthy language from our lips (v. 8). We will see this in upcoming lessons, as we study how to employ offensive, aggressive, violence in wiping out our sins.

Question 4. Read verse 5 above. What does it call drunkenness, sexual immorality, impurity, lust, evil desires, etc.?

Friend, drunkenness, lust and all other forms of self-pleasing is idolatry. Idolatry is the worship of false gods. Did you know you were worshiping false gods when you were giving in to evil desires? When I was drinking and doing drugs, I was kneeling down to a demonic god (1 Corinthians 10:19-20), and worshiping at the shrine of the devil. When I was indulging my desires I was adoring myself and living to please myself, which is self-idolatry.

I did not know this at the time, but the devil was deriving worship from me through drug abuse. No wonder the next sentence in Colossians 3 says "Because of these, the wrath of God is coming." God will destroy all idolaters, and as you read these words, this may be your last chance to repent of your idolatry before the wrath of God destroys you. So we must destroy sin in our lives before we are destroyed.

Question 5. How does Exodus 20:4-5 go with today's teaching?

> You shall not make for yourself an idol in the form of anything in heaven above or on the earth beneath or in the waters below. You shall not bow down to them or worship them; for I, the LORD your God, am a jealous God...

Today we have seen how the heart, the mind, and the actions are all tied in together, and we were given specific instructions about each. We are to set our hearts on things above, we are to set our minds on things above, and we are to put to death all sinful actions. This teaching really is a summary of the Christian life. We are to set our hearts toward loving God, we are to dwell on thoughts of Christ, and we are to destroy all sin in our lives.

Friend, I know people who are off-balance in these three areas. One person wants to focus only on his heart as he believes love for God is the only thing required to walk in victory. He is very much into emotionalism, praise songs, worshiping with His eyes closed, etc. But he practically ignores the teaching about the mind being engaged to dwell

Questions

on Christ, and he does not concentrate spiritual energy on putting to death the lusts of his flesh. Or there are others who are intellectuals, who have much information and learning, who know all the correct doctrine, but who have no passion for Christ, or for the destroying of sin in their lives. Still others focus all their efforts on stopping sinful behavior, of crucifying their flesh, of doing spiritual damage to their lusts, but where is their love for God?

Question 6. Think for a moment about what would happen if any one of these three things were missing in your life. Write out your thoughts as to what could happen if you did not set your heart on things above, yet you tried to do the other two things. Or what would happen if you did not set your mind on things above, or if you did not put to death drunkenness, sexual immorality, impurity, evil desires, etc.? Think through how these three spiritual truths all work together, and write out your thoughts here.

Question 7. What have you learned today, or have been reminded of, that will make a difference in your fight against sin? Please share your final thoughts here:

Scripture to Consider

No one whose hope is in you will ever be put to shame, but they will be put to shame who are treacherous without excuse (Psalm 25:3).

But you, man of God, flee from all this, and pursue righteousness, godliness, faith, love, endurance and gentleness. Fight the good fight of the faith. Take hold of the eternal life to which you were called when you made your good confession in the presence of many witnesses. In the sight of God, who gives life to everything, and of Christ Jesus, who while testifying before Pontius Pilate made the good confession, I charge you to keep this command without spot or blame until the appearing of our Lord Jesus Christ, which God will bring about in his own time-God, the blessed and only Ruler, the King of kings and Lord of lords, who alone is immortal and who lives in unapproachable light, whom no one has seen or can see. To him be honor and might forever. Amen (1 Timothy 6:11-16).

Did you feast on God's Word in the last 24 hours?

    Yes   No

If so, how did you feast? In other words, circle the ways you enjoyed God today. Reading? Prayer? Worship? Fellowship? Witnessing?

Were you free from drug and alcohol abuse since you did the last lesson?

    Yes   No

Did you spend personal time with the Lord since you did the last lesson?

    Yes   No

If you answered "no" to any of the above questions, describe what led to your fall.

If you answered "yes" to the above questions, you may use this area for additional comments.

DAY 45 - BATTLE STRATEGIES

Dear Friend,

In His Word, God tells us how to defeat the devil and overcome sin in our lives. Today's teaching will be a clear presentation of the truths of Scripture on how to eradicate bondage to any substance.

There is a primary thought expressed throughout Scripture that teaches us how to leave sin behind. It is to deal harshly with it, to be merciless in eradicating it, to annihilate every speck of it from our lives, and to seek God for grace to accomplish this. Notice the following Scripture, and its practical application to rid our lives of drunkenness:

> I pursued my enemies and overtook them; I did not turn back till they were destroyed. I crushed them so that they could not rise; they fell beneath my feet (Psalm 18:37-38).

Notice that the writer of this Psalm took the offensive in that he pursued and overtook his enemies. Notice that he was aggressive in his attack; he destroyed his enemies. And finally, notice that he was violent in the war; he crushed his enemies so they could not rise again. In our lesson today, let's apply the following principles to fight against our enemy of drugs.

Principle 1. We must take the offensive in our fight. For many years, I walked around in a defensive mode, just hoping to be able to dodge the next incoming fiery dart of the devil. I lived in fear that I would succumb to the lust of my flesh, and I lived in defeat: week after week, month after month and year after year. But now I see that type of a battle plan as all wrong, and instead I pursue the enemy for the purpose of annihilation. How do I do this?

The first step was smashing or tossing out any alcohol I had in my home and destroying all cocaine. I changed careers and stopped playing music in bars completely. This was hard, but it was absolutely necessary for freedom, as I would have never been able to win the fight in a bar! I found afterward that I did not miss it. In fact, freedom from bondage was more than worth the change! I also placed myself under the guidance and counsel of my pastor, who holds me accountable for my actions. I try to get involved in ministry to other people who want out of bondage whenever possible. This is our way to "get even" with the enemy for his devastation in our lives, as we use the grace of God to drag others from the jaws of the lion.

Some people say that the above is too "radical," and that it is not a "normal" life. My response is, "So?" God is enabling me to be free from the trap of the devil in drunkenness and drugs, and it does not bother me to be thought a little strange. I once had someone tell me I was becoming a "nut" because the changes I made were so radical. My answer to that is that my life in drunken bondage was chaos and the epitome of being "nuts" as he put it.

Freedom from this bondage is more than worth anything negative that might be said by others. Walking in purity, enjoying fellowship with Christ, and having effectiveness in ministry are more important. Be thinking about ways you are taking the offensive in your battle against the deception of alcohol/drugs? Can you do more?

It gets to be fun thinking of new offensive moves after awhile. My wife and I like to be creative as we plot our next offensive move against the devil.

Principle 2. We must pursue this enemy with a healthy dose of spiritual aggression. I drag every little temptation into the "light." Meaning, if I am tempted in some way I tell my wife right away or I'll email a friend to "expose" it. Substance abuse is like a fungus; it grows best in the dark. Learn to drag it into the light to sap it of its strength. Get in the habit of emailing your accountability partner and saying "I am tempted just now, can you help?"

I often run to the Word of God for help. "You, Oh Lord are a Strong Tower, a Sure Defense against my Foe." I seek to destroy the enemy when he first peeks his head around the corner. BAM! Hit him hard initially. By this, I mean, as soon as I sense an uprising of temptation, I open my Bible, or I begin singing a hymn or I call or email my wife or a friend. Be aggressive in the initial stages of temptation.

Principle 3. We must be spiritually violent with our "pet" sins:

> From the days of John the Baptist until now, the kingdom of heaven has been forcefully advancing, and forceful men lay hold of it (Matthew 11:12).

> If your hand causes you to sin, cut it off. It is better for you to enter life maimed than with two hands to go into hell, where the fire never goes out. And if your foot causes you to sin, cut it off. It is better for you to enter life crippled than to have two feet and be thrown into hell. And if your eye causes you to sin, pluck it out. It is better for you to enter the kingdom of God with one eye than to have two eyes and be thrown into hell... (Mark 9:43-47).

Treat alcohol as if it were your worst enemy trying to drag your soul into hell, and "hack," "chop," and "pluck out" your way to freedom from it.

Look for ways that you can expose the deeds done in darkness. Crush drunkenness, and grind it to powder, or it will rise again and you will be defeated in a weak moment.

Principle 4. Finally, we must pray for God's grace to accomplish this aggressive battle plan against the enemy. We make our plans but the Lord directs our steps (Proverbs 16:9), so we must seek Him for grace to carry out the plans. Notice David's understanding of grace in the rest of Psalm 18 and see that we must be dependent on and united with Him.

> You armed me with strength for battle; you made my adversaries bow at my feet. You made my enemies turn their backs in flight, and I destroyed my foes" (vs. 39, 40). Jesus said, "Without Me you can do nothing (John 15:5).

Friend, in order to overcome drunkenness in our lives we must have a grace-empowered battle plan. One man I know plans his victory strategy for the entire next day before he goes to bed at night, and then prays to accomplish his plan. He knows that things don't always go according to schedule so He asks God for grace to deal with the unexpected. He is wise, and is enjoying much lasting victory.

Our desire is that this teaching would inspire you to stop treating your enemy as your friend; begin to take the offensive in the war, use healthy aggression toward eradicating the bondage to alcohol or drugs, and be spiritually violent in the destruction and annihilation of it. It can be done, by the grace of God!

Please read through the following Scriptures and provide your comments on how they apply to the teaching today of using offensive, aggressive violence in this battle. We give you a "starter thought" before each passage.

Deuteronomy 7:1-6: Be merciless when it comes to all sin.

> When the LORD your God brings you into the land you are entering to possess and drives out before you many nations-the Hittites, Girgashites, Amorites, Canaanites, Perizzites, Hivites and Jebusites, seven nations larger and stronger than you- and when the LORD your God has delivered them over to you and you have defeated them, then you must destroy them totally. Make no treaty with them, and show them no mercy. Do not intermarry with them. Do not give your daughters to their sons or take their daughters for your sons, for they will turn your sons away from following me to serve other gods, and the LORD's anger will burn against you and will quickly destroy you. This is what you are to do to them: Break down their altars, smash their sacred stones, cut down their Asherah poles and burn their idols in the fire. For you are a people holy to the LORD your God. The LORD your God has chosen you out of all the peoples on the face of the earth to be his people, his treasured possession (Deuteronomy 7:1-6, emphasis ours).

Questions

Question 1. Please record your thoughts about the passage here:

Exodus 32:19, 20: No matter what it may be worth, destroy it.

> When Moses approached the camp and saw the calf and the dancing, his anger burned and he threw the tablets out of his hands, breaking them to pieces at the foot of the mountain. And he took the calf they had made and burned it in the fire; then he ground it to powder, scattered it on the water and made the Israelites drink it (Exodus 32:19-20).

Question 2. Record your thoughts about the above passage here:

Deuteronomy 7:17, 21-22: The Lord will drive them out little by little. You may say to yourselves:

> These nations are stronger than we are. How can we drive them out?" Do not be terrified by them, for the LORD your God, who is among you, is a great and awesome God. The LORD your God will drive out those nations before you, little by little. You will not be allowed to eliminate them all at once, or the wild animals will multiply around you (Deuteronomy 7:17, 21-22).

Question 3. Record your thoughts on the above passage here:

Questions

Judges 8:4: We can be weary, yet pursuing.

> Gideon and his three hundred men, exhausted yet keeping up the pursuit, came to the Jordan and crossed it (Judges 8:4).

Question 4. Record your thoughts on the above passage here:

Ephesians 5:11-13: Expose them!

> Have nothing to do with the fruitless deeds of darkness, but rather expose them. For it is shameful even to mention what the disobedient do in secret. But everything exposed by the light becomes visible, for it is light that makes everything visible. This is why it is said: "Wake up, O sleeper, rise from the dead, and Christ will shine on you" (Ephesians 5:11-13).

Question 5. Record your thoughts on the above passage here:

So Friend, we can see that there must be an offensive, aggressive, violent battle plan in order to eradicate our enemy. Do you have such a battle plan? What have you learned from the Scriptures today?

Question 6. If you have not developed a battle plan in the past, will you now? Write your thoughts here:

Scripture to Consider

He has delivered us from such a deadly peril, and he will deliver us. On him we have set our hope that he will continue to deliver us (2 Corinthians 1:10).

Did you feast on God's Word in the last 24 hours?

     Yes   No

If so, how did you feast? In other words, circle the ways you enjoyed God today. Reading? Prayer? Worship? Fellowship? Witnessing?

Were you free from drug and alcohol abuse since you did the last lesson?

     Yes   No

Did you spend personal time with the Lord since you did the last lesson?

     Yes   No

If you answered "no" to any of the above questions, describe what led to your fall.

If you answered "yes" to the above questions, you may use this area for additional comments.

DAY 46 - FOCUS!

Read the following passage of Scripture to see how God judged the israelites with venomous snakes:

> They traveled from Mount Hor along the route to the Red Sea, to go around Edom. But the people grew impatient on the way; they spoke against God and against Moses, and said, "Why have you brought us up out of Egypt to die in the desert? There is no bread! There is no water! And we detest this miserable food!" Then the LORD sent venomous snakes among them; they bit the people and many Israelites died. The people came to Moses and said, "We sinned when we spoke against the LORD and against you. Pray that the LORD will take the snakes away from us." So Moses prayed for the people. The LORD said to Moses, "Make a snake and put it up on a pole; anyone who is bitten can look at it and live." So Moses made a bronze snake and put it up on a pole. Then when anyone was bitten by a snake and looked at the bronze snake, he lived (Numbers 21:4-10).

In order to be cured of the snakebites, the truth to memorize is this: ***The cure for sin is to focus on Jesus Christ!***

Questions

Please review the passage above and answer the following questions:

Question 1. The people above were complaining against God. What did He do to them to make them stop?

Question 2. When the people died from snakebite, what did God tell Moses to do to fix the problem?

Question 3. What were the people to do with the bronze snake upon the pole? Please write out the "Truth to memorize" from above:

Questions

Question 4. What happened as the people looked at the snake on the pole?

OK, so I'm not getting it here . . . people get bit by snakes, Moses puts up a pole with a snake on it, people look at the snake and they're cured. So, what does that have to do with me, my drunkenness, sin, drug addiction, overcoming, etc. and them?

Let's examine this story a little closer. Think of it like this:

The serpent of sin has bitten you and me, Friend! It's a deadly bite, the venom of sin is running through our veins, and we will die from the fatal wound. But God erected a cross-like pole, and on that pole He hung a Savior, and if we look at the Savior we will live. We will be cured from the snakebite of sin, and we will not perish, but have everlasting life!

But wait a minute! Is this the correct way to interpret and understand this story? How can a snake represent Jesus Christ? Actually, it is not that the snake represents Christ, but rather that it points forward to our sin that was nailed to the cross with Christ.

> "Just as Moses lifted up the snake in the desert, so the Son of Man must be lifted up, that everyone who believes in him may have eternal life" (John 3:14).

Observe: The people who were bitten by snakes were simply to look! That is what would cure them. Jesus Christ was lifted up on a cross, where He died for our sins. LOOK! Do you see Him there? He is being wounded in His hands for the wrong we've done with our hands. His feet are pierced because of the wrong places our feet have taken us. He is wearing a crown of thorns because of the wrong thoughts we've cherished, His heart is being gashed open because of the wrong loves we've had. LOOK! There He is! Do you see Him there on the cross? He's our cure! Look, believe and live!

Questions

There are many "cures" being offered on the market today. But if we examine most of them, we will see several consistent themes: the "cure" is to examine the snakebite. Focus on your pain, your past and your parents. Dear friends, these other "cures" are not of much value in helping us overcome bondage to heroin or alcohol. The cure for the snake-bitten Israelites was simple, yet profound: LOOK! The cure for habitual drunkenness, or impurity of any kind, is to have the focus of our lives be on Jesus Christ.

Question 5. Why do you think God chose a serpent to be uplifted on the pole? What did the serpent represent? What are your thoughts?

A snake is used in Scripture as a symbol of evil. Satan embodied a serpent when he tempted Adam and Eve.

Notice 2 Corinthians 5:21: "God made him who had no sin to be sin for us, so that in him we might become the righteousness of God."

"God made Him . . . to be sin for us." On the cross, Jesus Christ took our sins upon Himself. This passage, 2 Corinthians 5:21 refers back to the Mosaic Law (Leviticus 4-5) where the priest laid his hands on the animal that was to be the sin offering, symbolically placing the sins of the people on the animal so the sacrifice would atone for those sins. Jesus Christ bore our sins in His own body on the tree of the cross, and by looking at Him, our Sin-Bearer, we will discover that drunkenness loses its appeal, and we are cured.

Guilt and bondage to sin go hand in hand. In the physical realm, when a criminal is declared guilty by the judge, incarceration soon follows. But if we look on the cross of Jesus Christ we see our sin being paid for and our guilt being removed. Freedom from guilt and freedom from the power of sin go hand in hand. Look on that cross and see guilt and sin, from that which has "bitten us" being crucified with Christ! Look at the cross and be healed!

Question 6. Write out how the following three verses go with the teaching we've seen in this lesson:

Look to Me, all the ends of the earth, and be saved! (Isaiah 45:22)

Let us fix our eyes on Jesus, who for the joy set before Him, endured the cross (Hebrews 12:2).

For we have no power to face this vast army that is attacking us. We do not know what to do, but our eyes are upon you (2 Chronicles 20:12).

Question 7. Write your thoughts on the three verses here:

Friend, one of the verses you commented on above is 2 Chronicles 20:12. This verse contains everything we need to know to defeat the "vast army" of drunken images that attack us. There are three specific steps listed in that verse. Note them with me:

1. They admitted their powerlessness. They said, "For we have no power."

2. They admitted their ignorance. They said, "We do not know what to do." In order to truly defeat our enemy, we must admit that we are without resources to fight it. We have neither the power to fight nor the knowledge of how to win.

3. They focused on God. Having admitted their own lack of power and ability, knowledge and resources, they did not stop there. They looked to God for help, and "focused" on Him as their Resource. If you read the rest of this story in 2 Chronicles 20, you will see that God totally defeats the "vast army." Here is the key, "But our eyes are upon you." Focus!

My eyes are ever on the LORD, for only he will release my feet from the snare (Psalm 25:15).

Note: Notice the connection between focusing on the Lord and escaping from the trap!

When your children sinned against him, he gave them over to the penalty of their sin. But if you will look to God and plead with the Almighty, even now he will rouse himself on your behalf and restore you to your rightful place (Job 8:4-6).

The gracious hand of our God is on everyone who looks to him, but his great anger is against all who forsake him (Ezra 8:22-23).

During the fourth watch of the night Jesus went out to them, walking on the lake. When the disciples saw him walking on the lake, they were terrified. "It's a ghost," they said, and cried out in fear. But Jesus immediately said to them: "Take courage! It is I. Don't be afraid."

"Lord, if it's you," Peter replied, "tell me to come to you on the water."

"Come," he said.

Then Peter got down out of the boat, walked on the water and came toward Jesus. But when he saw the wind, he was afraid and, beginning to

Questions

sink, cried out, "Lord, save me!" Immediately Jesus reached out his hand and caught him. "You of little faith," he said, "why did you doubt?" (Matthew 14:25-31).

As long as he was looking at Jesus he walked on water, but when he "saw the winds and the waves" he began to sink. Please note how this passage applies to our teaching today, and draw comparisons between this story and our own victory over drunkenness and drugs:

- Now, let us note what "looking at Jesus" means in each of the eight passages of Scripture above, so we can begin to apply this teaching to our lives today:

- In Numbers 21 above, looking at the serpent meant that they were in need of a cure for their snakebite. In just this way, we look to Jesus Christ to eradicate sin from our lives.

- In Isaiah 45:22 above, we are instructed to look to Jesus for salvation.

- In Hebrews 12:2, the context of the passage calls us to focus on Christ as a preventative to weariness and discouragement, and to give us strength to finish the race.

- In 2 Chronicles 20:12, we are instructed to look to Jesus to defeat the vast army of sin, and to give us victory over the world, the flesh and the devil.

- In Psalm 25:15, we are instructed to focus on Jesus in order to be released from the trap of sin.

- In Job 8:4-6 we are instructed to look to Jesus to restore us.

- In Ezra 8:22-23 we are invited to look to Jesus to receive grace.

- In Matthew 14:25-31 above, we are shown that looking to Jesus enables us to live supernaturally, walking on the water of our sin.

So to summarize these passages, we are to look to Jesus to save us, to eradicate sin in our lives, to strengthen us for the race, to defeat all our enemies, to release us from the trap of sin, to restore us and give us grace, and to enable us to be victorious. See why focusing on Christ is so important?

Question 8. For the final question of the day, please write out what it would look like practically to have your life "focused" on Jesus Christ. Be specific. What will you do differently because of this teaching?

Oh how I wish I could sit down with you and explain to you the joy in my heart as my life is now focused on Jesus

Christ. Those years involved in drunkenness and drug use feel like a total waste. I know that it was my choice that led me down that path, but the darkness of all those years is like a huge void that I will never get back. If you are staring at your life and your past as a "void" as well, let me give you this encouragement: the time that we have ahead will be sweeter, by God's grace, than the blackness and bitterness of the past. Yes, my past was terrible and I was blinded and robbed of joy and purpose. But now God has opened the eyes of this blind man, and granted me the ability to turn from my idolatry and to focus on the living God. And focusing on Him brings all other areas of my life into perspective too. I can see how to be a good husband, and father, how to bless my employer by doing a good job, how to interact with others so as to bless them, how to build up the body of Christ instead of tear it down, and many others. Focusing on Jesus Christ has brought amazing clarity and focus in all other areas of my life. Amen to God's grace and His ability to refocus us!

Scripture to Consider

If then you were raised with Christ, seek those things which are above, where Christ is, sitting at the right hand of God. Set your mind on things above, not on things on the earth.
For you died, and your life is hidden with Christ in God (Colossians 3:1-3).

Did you feast on God's Word in the last 24 hours?

     Yes   No

If so, how did you feast? In other words, circle the ways you enjoyed God today. Reading? Prayer? Worship? Fellowship? Witnessing?

Were you free from drug and alcohol abuse since you did the last lesson?

     Yes   No

Did you spend personal time with the Lord since you did the last lesson?

     Yes   No

If you answered "no" to any of the above questions, describe what led to your fall.

If you answered "yes" to the above questions, you may use this area for additional comments.

DAY 47 - ROMANS 6

Today we're going to do something a little bit different. We will do a Bible study, where you'll be doing the teaching simply by answering questions. This will be fun! We are **about to drink from the living water!**

> What shall we say, then? Shall we go on sinning so that grace may increase? By no means! We died to sin; how can we live in it any longer? (Romans 6:1, 2)

Questions

Question 1. What is the central truth taught in the above verse, Friend? Write your answer here:

Question 2. If we are indeed "dead to sin," when did we die to it? (Romans 6:3 gives the answer.) Write your thoughts here:

> Or don't you know that all of us who were baptized into Christ Jesus were baptized into his death? We were therefore buried with him through baptism into death in order that, just as Christ was raised from the dead through the glory of the father, we too may live a new life (Romans 6:3-4).

Question 3. There is a reason why we died to sin, why we were buried with Christ and why we have risen from the dead with him. That reason is stated at the bottom of verse 4. That we too may _____ __ _____ ____.

Question 4. What application does this have for us who were previously into various types of substances?

> If we have been united with him like this in his death, we will certainly also be united with him in his resurrection (Romans 6:5).

Question 5. This verse gives us hope! But it is a hope that is conditional (if we have . . .) according to this verse, upon what should we base our assurance of eternal life?

Questions

Friend, right about here some people are quick to point out that we are to trust in the righteousness of Christ alone for salvation, not in our own overcoming of sin (or lack thereof). But the one who is righteous by the imputation of Christ's righteousness will have imparted righteousness working daily in his or her life. It can be no other way as the Holy Spirit that is sent to dwell in us will not allow ongoing sin in our life without rebuke and chastisement. Here is the important matter. He who is righteous by imputation is saved. BUT if he is not striving with imparted righteousness, he HAS NO assurance of his imputed righteousness. Assurance of imputed righteousness can only come through imparted righteousness. One (imputed) is actual birth and the other (imparted) is actual proof. We will have both **imputed** righteousness and **imparted** righteousness. Let us examine these two thoughts for a second:

Imputed righteousness is that which Christ gives me as a free gift (Romans 5:12-18). It is an immediate gift to me, happening at once, and is not progressive. It is done to me, or imputed. That is, His righteousness is credited to my account, similar to someone depositing money into my bank account (Romans 4:23-25).

Imparted righteousness is that righteousness that is progressively changing my heart and life by the power of the Holy Spirit (Philippians 2:13). Whereas imputed righteousness is an instant and immediate gift, imparted righteousness is a progressive and eternal gift. My heart continually becomes more broken before the Lord. My self-will is continually crushed, my rebellion is progressively broken, and my pride is being overcome, all by God's grace. I am openly and overtly changed to detest the sin I once loved and to love the Savior to whom I was once an enemy.

Those who are in bondage to sin but profess salvation often cling to imputed righteousness, saying, "we must not look to ourselves for any assurance of salvation, but only to Christ." This is dangerous, for there are those who live in lust like unbelievers, but who are presuming that Christ has given them imputed righteousness. They do not understand that imputed and imparted righteousness always go together. As we are reading Scripture it takes careful discernment to know whether a particular passage is referring to imputed righteousness or imparted righteousness.

> For we know that our old self was crucified with him so that the body of sin might be done away with, that we should no longer be slaves to sin -- because anyone who has died has been freed from sin (Romans 6:6-7).

Question 6. What was crucified with Christ? And what was the purpose for our crucifixion in him?

Question 7. What hope is Paul expressing here?

> Now if we died with Christ, we believe that we will also live with Him. (Romans 6:8).

Question 8. According to the above verses, if we continue in slavery to drunkenness, or any other sin, should we have assurance of eternal life in Christ?

Question 9. Do you have the hope of living with Jesus Christ throughout eternity? If you do, upon what is your hope based?

> For we know that since Christ was raised from the dead, he cannot die again; death no longer has mastery over him. The death he died, he died to sin once for all; but the life he lives, he lives to God. In the same way, count yourselves dead to sin but alive to God in Christ Jesus (Romans 6:10, 11).

Question 10. Verse 10 says that death no longer has mastery over Christ. Since we are united with Christ, what does this mean for us?

Question 11. What does it mean to count ourselves dead to sin but alive to God in Christ Jesus?

Question 12. Can a dead person sin? How will this teaching help us in times of temptation?

> Therefore do not let sin reign in your mortal body so that you obey its evil desires (Romans 6:12).

Question 13. The above verse contains imagery. We are not to let sin reign in our bodies. How is sin pictured?

Question 14. How does Colossians 1:13 compare with our study today? "For He has rescued us from the dominion of darkness and brought us into the kingdom of the Son He loves, in whom we have redemption, the forgiveness of sins." Please write your thoughts here:

Do not offer the parts of your body to sin, as instruments of wickedness, but rather offer yourselves to God, as those who have been brought from death to life; and offer the parts of your body to him as instruments of righteousness (Romans 6:13).

Question 15. The above verse states that our body's "parts" are to be offered to the Lord. Describe how you can offer each "part" to the Lord. Your head, heart, hands, etc.

For sin shall not be your master, because you are not under law, but under grace (Romans 6:14).

Question 16. How is being "under grace" different than being "under law?" What does it mean to be "under grace" and how are we free from sin's mastery by being under grace?

Question 17. Please record how you are progressing in the grace of God. What is going on in your life today, this week, and this month?

Scripture to Consider

I put this in human terms because you are weak in your natural selves. Just as you used to offer the parts of your body in slavery to impurity and to ever-increasing wickedness, so now offer them in slavery to righteousness leading to holiness. When you were slaves to sin, you were free from the control of righteousness. What benefit did you reap at that time from the things you are now ashamed of? Those things result in death! But now that you have been set free from sin and have become slaves to God, the benefit you reap leads to holiness, and the result is eternal life. For the wages of sin is death, but the gift of God is eternal life in Christ Jesus our Lord (Romans 6:19-23).

Did you feast on God's Word in the last 24 hours?

      Yes   No

If so, how did you feast? In other words, circle the ways you enjoyed God today. Reading? Prayer? Worship? Fellowship? Witnessing?

Were you free from drug and alcohol abuse since you did the last lesson?

      Yes   No

Did you spend personal time with the Lord since you did the last lesson?

      Yes   No

If you answered "no" to any of the above questions, describe what led to your fall.

If you answered "yes" to the above questions, you may use this area for additional comments.

DAY 48 - DARK NIGHT OF THE SOUL (ROMANS 7)

Notice how Paul describes this experience.

> I do not understand what I do. For what I want to do I do not do, but what I hate I do (Romans 7:15).

Friend, have you ever fought drugs so hard, and lost so much that you felt that there would be no way to gain the victory? Have you felt like the Apostle Paul—that you are sold as a slave to sin?

Believe it or not, this is a common experience in the lives of Christians. As we will see later in this chapter, Paul struggled with sin to the point of despair (Romans 7:24). Have you? Are you currently falling so often that you feel like you are a slave to sin? Many people by this time in the course are walking in habitual victory over substance abuse, but some continue to fall. Of course, if you have followed the earlier lessons about "radical amputation" there is no opportunity for you to fall, and yet some still struggle and fall often.

I went through this dark night of the soul, where sin seemed to have dominion over me, and where I felt that I was to be sold as a slave to sin. Does that mean I was not a Christian? It could. Or it could also have meant that I was being tried in the furnace and that I was going through a desert experience; a dark night of the soul. We must be careful about being too quick to judge those who fall often, and then repent.

> We know that the law is spiritual; but I am unspiritual, sold as a slave to sin (Romans 7:14).

The dark night can lead to overwhelming despair. It can be so dark in sin that you see no way out. All your friends tell you to read your Bible and pray, and you hear some people talk about overcoming sin as if it were a small thing for them. And you wonder if God has forsaken you for good, because their experience is not yours.

Friend, if this is you, take heart. God is at work even still. For God must break a man before He remakes him (Hosea 6:1-3); He must "hand all men over to sin" so that He can have mercy on them (Romans 11:32). This does not make God the author of our sin; rather it shows that He works through the sin to bring forth a good outcome.

Is your night dark? Are you frustrated, disappointed, discouraged or near suicidal? If so, you are right there with the Apostle Paul. I've been there too. I thank God that Paul did not stay in Romans 7, but moved on to Romans 8, which is what we will study tomorrow.

So please have hope, that if your darkness is thick, and you are feeling yourself to be sold as a slave to sin, and in the prison of sin and can't get out, that God's grace will make a way for you, as He has me.

Again, it is possible that you are entirely beyond this Romans 7 experience by this time in the course. If you are walking in victory please never forget your struggle. It will help you deal in grace with your brothers and sisters who are falling.

Paul's horrible struggle with sin ended in praise of Jesus Christ. "But thanks be to God, through Jesus Christ our Lord." Here is where we need to run when the night is dark. If you are feeling the power of sin, run to Jesus. Give thanks to God for giving you His Son.

Questions

Question 1. Have you had this experience? Describe it here:

> And if I do what I do not want to do, I agree that the law is good. As it is, it is no longer I myself who do it, but it is sin living in me" (Romans 7:16, 17). Now if I do what I do not want to do, it is no longer I who do it, but it is sin living in me that does it (Romans 7:20).

Here is one of the greatest teachings we can learn, and that is the teaching of "identity." Paul's identity, as a Christian, was in his "new man" not his old sinful self. When he sinned he said, "it is no longer I myself who do it" because he knew that his old man was crucified with Christ, as we saw in yesterday's lesson. Christians are those who are redeemed, who are new creations in Christ, whose inner man is created in true holiness and righteousness. But Christians still have flesh, which is the residue of the old nature or the old man. Christians are indeed new creations, but they live in fallen flesh and so still sin.

Question 2. This is honesty time. How do you see yourself right now? Do you see your identity as a sinner, or as a saint who sins sometimes? Write your thoughts here:

Questions

I know that nothing good lives in me, that is, in my flesh. For I have the desire to do what is good, but I cannot carry it out (Romans 7:18).

Paul, as a Christian, had the desire to do good, but he lacked the power to carry it out. This describes me, just a few years ago. I desired to do good and be free from alcohol and drugs, but did not have the power to accomplish it.

Question 3. Has this been your experience as well? Describe what it was like:

For what I do is not the good I want to do; no, the evil I do not want to do-this I keep on doing (Romans 7:19).

Paul did not want to sin. Everything within him opposed it, and yet he "kept on" sinning. Friends, this is a horribly dark night to experience. You want to do what is right, you want to cease habitual sin, but somehow you just can't. You don't have the power. Oh, the pain of this is so fresh in my memory. I think back on the years spent sinning against my family, friends, and of course, God, which I did not want to do. Yet I did it anyway, and kept on doing it.

Question 4. Have you been mastered by sin as Paul describes here? Share your thoughts:

So I find this law at work: When I want to do good, evil is right there with me (Romans 7:21)

Are you tracking with Paul here as I am, Friend? I recall longing to be free from drunkenness, committing to not set foot in a particular bar, resolving all day long to stay free from it. But in all my desires to do good, evil was right there with me. Oh what a dark night of the soul this is. If you are going through this right now, please know that the dark of night precedes the light of day. Morning is coming, and with it grace and mercy to enable you to be free from this plaguing sin.

Question 5. What are your thoughts on Romans 7:21?

For in my inner being I delight in God's law; 23 but I see another law at work in the members of my body, waging war against the law of my mind and making me a prisoner of the law of sin at work within my members (Romans 7:22-23).

Oh, how the long, dark night drags on sometimes. I remember one particular night when I asked God to take all the pain away. I had not really prayed for years and I felt as if there was only one end left—death. I really thought God was done with me. I was becoming a broken man as I felt God had left me to die in my sins. Paul describes himself above as a "slave" and a "prisoner."

Question 6. Have you felt this war going on inside you?

What a wretched man I am! Who will rescue me from this body of death? (Romans 7:24).

Now, please read the following quote by **Matthew Henry**:

"Who shall deliver me?" says he (v. 24), as one at a loss for help. At length he finds an all-sufficient friend, even Jesus Christ. When we are under the sense of the remaining power of sin and corruption, we shall see reason to bless God through Christ, (for, as he is the mediator of all our prayers, so he deserves all our praises). It is Christ who stands between us and the wrath due to us for our sin. If it were not for Christ, this iniquity that dwells in us would certainly be our ruin. He is our advocate with the Father, and through him God pities, and spares, and pardons, and lays not our iniquities to our charge. It is Christ that has purchased deliverance for us in due time. Christ's death will put an end to all these complaints, and waft us to an eternity which we shall spend without sin or sigh. Blessed be God that giveth us this victory through our Lord Jesus Christ!

His great comfort lay in Jesus Christ (v. 25): "I thank God, through Jesus Christ our Lord." In the midst of his complaints he breaks out into praises. It is a special remedy against fears and sorrows to be much in praise: many a poor drooping soul hath found it so. And, in all our praises, this should be the burden of the son, "Blessed be God for Jesus Christ."

Questions

Question 7. Please provide your comments on the above quote here:

Read the following quote by **John Bunyan** from his classic book *Pilgrim's Progress,*

> Then Christian fell down at his feet as dead, crying, Woe is me, for I am undone! At the sight of which Evangelist caught him by the right hand, saying, "All manner of sin and blasphemies shall be forgiven unto men." Matthew 12:31. "Be not faithless, but believing." John 20:27. Then did Christian again a little revive, and stood up trembling, as at first, before Evangelist. (From Pilgrim's Progress)
>
> This also shall not be, any more than that. It is the glory of God that he multiplies to pardon, that he spares, and forgives, to more than seventy times seven times."

Question 8. Where are you in your spiritual life right now? Is your night pitch black? Do you see some rays of dawn approaching? Or are you walking in the light of day and enjoying it? Please record your thoughts here:

Scripture to Consider

For though a righteous man falls seven times, he rises again, but the wicked are brought down by calamity (Proverbs 24:16).

Then Peter came to him and asked, "Lord, how often should I forgive someone who sins against me? Seven times?" "No!" Jesus replied, "seventy times seven!" (Matthew 18:21-22).

Did you feast on God's Word in the last 24 hours?

Yes   No

If so, how did you feast? In other words, circle the ways you enjoyed God today. Reading? Prayer? Worship? Fellowship? Witnessing?

Were you free from drug and alcohol abuse since you did the last lesson?

Yes   No

Did you spend personal time with the Lord since you did the last lesson?

Yes   No

If you answered "no" to any of the above questions, describe what led to your fall.

If you answered "yes" to the above questions, you may use this area for additional comments.

DAY 49 - NO CONDEMNATION! (ROMANS 8)

Oh dear friends, the dark night of the soul is temporary! The intense struggle against sin does not last forever! If we are in Christ we will be victorious! Let us see this truth from Romans 8:

> Therefore, there is now no condemnation for those who are in Christ Jesus, (Romans 8:1)

Friend, how wonderful it is to know that this shining sentence declaring no condemnation follows Romans 7 where the intense war with sin is pictured. What do those who battle sin and lose often dread the most? Condemnation! And here Paul declares under the inspiration of the Holy Spirit that there is no condemnation for those who are in Christ Jesus.

Questions

Question 1. Can you sense the joy in the placement of this particular verse? Write your thoughts here:

> …because through Christ Jesus the law of the Spirit of life set me free from the law of sin and death (Romans 8:2).

Talk about "setting captives free!" Paul is a released captive. He has been set free from the law of sin and death. Not only is he not condemned, he is not enslaved either. Freedom has come, through the Spirit of life. The Holy Spirit came to Paul and set him free from habitual sin, and enabled him to triumph over the law of sin and death. Friend, with God life always triumphs over death. We have no record of Jesus attending anyone's funeral without raising them to life.

Question 2. Where are you currently? Are you under "the law of sin and death" or are you a freed captive, where life and victory are triumphing? Write your answer here:

> For what the law was powerless to do in that it was weakened by the sinful nature, God did by sending his own Son in the likeness of sinful man to be a sin offering. And so he condemned sin in sinful man (Romans 8:3).

Let's understand this one well! The law was powerless. It could command me to cease drinking alcohol, but it could not enable me to do so. It was powerless to change my heart, give me new desires, or release me from the trap of the devil in drunkenness. But what the law could not do, God did! And how did He do it?

Questions

Question 3. God did what the law could not do; free us from sin's power. How did God do this?

Oh Friend, the death of Jesus Christ has everything to do with our being free from drugs! Don't miss the connection here between Jesus becoming our sin offering, and us becoming free from sin. Jesus took our sin upon Himself; therefore we are neither condemned nor enslaved! He breaks the power of canceled sin, He sets the captives free.

> …in order that the righteous requirements of the law might be fully met in us, who do not live according to the flesh but according to the Spirit (Romans 8:4).

Again, we see that Jesus' death has done something magnificent. It not only frees us from sin's penalty and sin's power, but it fulfills the law in us. You see, the law said, "Do this or die." The law requiring death for sin was fulfilled when Jesus died. He died in order that the righteous requirements of the law might be fully met in us! And now, we who are in Christ are counted as law-keepers.

Question 4. Verse 4 above describes we who are in Christ as living a certain way. What way is it?

> [5] Those who live according to the flesh have their minds set on what the flesh desires; but those who live in accordance with the Spirit have their minds set on what the Spirit desires. [6] The mind of sinful man is death, but the mind controlled by the Spirit is life and peace; [7] he sinful mind is hostile to God. It does not submit to God's law, nor can it do so. [8] Those controlled by the sinful nature cannot please God (Romans 8:5-8).

Questions

Question 5. Please write out everything verses 5-8 above say about those who live according to the flesh. I'll write the first one:

1. They have their minds set on the fleshly desires

2.

3.

4.

Question 6. What do verses 5-8 above say about those who live according to the Spirit? Write your answer here:

1.

2.

3.

4.

> You, however, are controlled not by the flesh but by the Spirit, if the Spirit of God lives in you. And if anyone does not have the Spirit of Christ, he does not belong to Christ (Romans 8:9).

The above verse makes it clear that if God's spirit is living in us He will control us. While I was drinking alcohol my flesh controlled me. That is what characterized me. But God's Spirit is now living in me and controlling me.

Question 7. Overall, would you say you are controlled by the Spirit of God or by your flesh?

> [10]But if Christ is in you, your body is dead because of sin, yet your spirit is alive because of righteousness. [11]And if the Spirit of him who raised Jesus from the dead is living in you, he who raised Christ from the dead will also give life to your mortal bodies through his Spirit, who lives in you (Romans 8:10-11).

According to verse 10 above, Christians are characterized by "dead flesh." Their bodies are dead because of sin. In other words, they are not characterized by giving in to the flesh and sinning, but by being controlled by the Spirit of God.

Now, see how interesting it is that Paul here connects our "dead flesh" with our assurance of eternal life. Our bodies are dead because of sin, but will live forever through the Spirit of Christ who lives in us. Those who know that their flesh is crucified also know that they will live forever with Christ.

> [12]Therefore, brothers, we have an obligation-but it is not to the flesh, to live according to it.[13]For if you live according to the flesh, you will die; but if by the Spirit you put to death the misdeeds of the body, you will live, [14]because those who are led by the Spirit of God are sons of God (Romans 8:12-14).

This chapter started out with "no condemnation" (v. 1) and ends with "no separation" (vs. 35-39), but right in the middle we are told that we have "no obligation" to live according to the flesh. Catch this truth, friend. When our flesh cries out to be satisfied, we have no obligation to gratify it.

Question 8. If we do live to gratify our flesh, according to verse 13 above what will happen?

Question 9. What are we to do with the misdeeds of the body?

Paul started off this discourse by sharing his freedom from sin with us, and here he instructs us to put to death the misdeeds of the body. Freedom from habitual sin includes the crucifying of our flesh. Paul said "I die daily" and he was referring to putting to death his flesh daily. This shows that our flesh is to be crucified, not gratified.

Question 10. Is God giving you grace to crucify your flesh? Or are you gratifying it?

Friend, let me share with you that there is much discomfort and pain involved in crucifying our flesh. For us, denying ourselves drugs or alcohol when we are burning with desire is most uncomfortable and even painful. I remember the ache and the sweating in the face of desire. It sure seemed that it was more than any human being could ever endure. It hurt worse than any injury I could imagine.

Questions

Please know that the pain is indeed worth the gain. Our bodies adjust, our habits change, and soon we aren't even thinking of drugs any longer. And please don't let the false notion that alcohol somehow prevents cardiac disease creep in as a temptation to sin. God did not make our bodies, and then require us to sin in order to stay healthy.

The words of the following hymn by **Charles Wesley** summarize today's teaching in a passionate way:

And Can It Be

And can it be that I should gain an interest in the Savior's blood?

Died He for me, who caused His pain? For me, who Him to death pursued?

He left His Father's throne above, so free, so infinite His grace!

Emptied Himself of all but love, and bled for Adam's helpless race.

No condemnation now I dread; I am my Lord's and He is mine:

Alive in Him, my living Head, and clothed in righteousness divine.

Refrain: Amazing love! How can it be that Thou, my God, shouldst die for me?"

Question 11. Please summarize your thoughts about today's teaching as best as you can:

Question 12. How are things going in your life right now?

Scripture to Consider

But now he has reconciled you by Christ's physical body through death to present you holy in his sight, without blemish and free from accusation- if you continue in your faith, established and firm, not moved from the hope held out in the gospel. This is the gospel that you heard and that has been proclaimed to every creature under heaven, and of which I, Paul, have become a servant (Colossians 1:22-23).

But I will bring the people of Israel back to their own pasture. They will eat on Mount Carmel and in Bashan. They will eat and be full on the hills of Ephraim and Gilead. The LORD says, "At that time people will try to find Israel's guilt, but there will be no guilt. People will try to find Judah's sins, but no sins will be found, because I will leave a few people alive from Israel and Judah, and I will forgive their sins" (Jeremiah 50:19-20)

Did you feast on God's Word in the last 24 hours?

     Yes   No

If so, how did you feast? In other words, circle the ways you enjoyed God today. Reading? Prayer? Worship? Fellowship? Witnessing?

Were you free from drug and alcohol abuse since you did the last lesson?

     Yes   No

Did you spend personal time with the Lord since you did the last lesson?

     Yes   No

If you answered "no" to any of the above questions, describe what led to your fall.

If you answered "yes" to the above questions, you may use this area for additional comments.

DAY 50 - DRUNKENNESS CAN'T HOLD WATER

Friend, today we are going to examine two things:

1. What God is like

2. What alcohol is like

Please read the following scripture in preparation for today's study. You may want to memorize this verse, as there will be several questions on it today.

> My people have committed two sins: they have forsaken me, the spring of living water, and have dug their own cisterns, broken cisterns that cannot hold water (Jeremiah 2:13.)

Then the angel showed me the river of the water of life, as clear as crystal, flowing from the throne of God and of the Lamb down the middle of the great street of the city. On each side of the river stood the tree of life, bearing twelve crops of fruit, yielding its fruit every month. And the leaves of the tree are for the healing of the nations. No longer will there be any curse (Revelation 22:1-3).

Question 4. Write your thoughts on Revelation 22:1-3 here:

Questions

Question 1. In the above verse, how does God describe himself?

Question 2. What do you believe that living water can provide?

My people have committed two sins: They have forsaken me, the spring of living water, and have dug their own cisterns, broken cisterns that cannot hold water (Jeremiah 2:13).

Question 5. Write your thoughts on Jeremiah 2:13 here:

Note: God describes himself as the spring of living water. He alone is the source of life, refreshment, joy, and nourishment for us. He is ever fresh and new, like a spring, and to drink of God is to receive life and be satisfied!

Please read and comment on the following Scriptures:

> There is a river whose streams make glad the city of God, the holy place where the Most High dwells (Psalm 46:4).

Question 3. Write your thoughts on Psalm 46:4 here:

Course Member André writes:
"The first sin we have committed is that we have rejected God and the satisfying water that He provides. We have laid down our beautiful, holy cisterns, and picked up dirty, broken cisterns that cannot hold water, leaving us thirsty. The only way to find satisfaction again is to repent, to go back to our true cisterns and start drinking of the living water again."

Questions

Question 6. According to Jeremiah 2:13 above, when people forsake God, they turn to something else. According to the above verse, Friend, to what do they turn?

Question 7. On Day 1 of this course, we learned two important truths:

    1. Alcohol/drugs will not ultimately satisfy

    2. Only Jesus can satisfy.

How does Jeremiah 2:13 teach these two truths? Please write your answer here:

Question 8. Please read this quote from the famous preacher, **Charles Spurgeon**, and record your comments about it:

> "Men are in a restless pursuit after satisfaction in earthly things. They will exhaust themselves in the deceitful delights of sin, and, finding them all to be vanity and emptiness, they will become very perplexed and disappointed. But they will still continue their fruitless search.
>
> Though wearied, they still stagger forward under the influence of spiritual madness, and though there is no result to be reached except that of everlasting disappointment, yet they press forward. They have no forethought for their eternal state; the present hour absorbs them. They turn to another and another of earth's broken cisterns, hoping to find water where not a drop was ever discovered yet."

From Jeremiah 2:13, please complete these sentences:

Question 9. God is like...

Question 10. Alcohol is like...

Question 11. How does Ephesians 4:19 apply to what we are studying? "Having lost all sensitivity, they have given themselves over to sensuality so as to indulge in every kind of impurity, with a continual lust for more." Write your answer here:

Course Member Chris writes, "I've had many experiences with beer bottles. Most of them regrettable. But from time to time I'd pick up a bottle of beer that looked like a perfectly good bottle only to have the bottom fall out. Of course most of the bottles were not faulty as far as the glass, but every one of them were broken, a cesspool of a cistern that always promised to give me happiness, fun, friends, unstressed times, and hundreds of other lies that ultimately led to it stealing my hope, my identity, very nearly destroying everything that I held dear and boy, did it try to kill me. Broken cisterns, just like all those beer bottles are after only one thing: to kill, steal, and destroy.

The living waters that Christ offers are exactly the opposite. The deeper I move into them, the more I drink from them, the more I trust that they are not after my destruction, that I will not drown. I find I know, once again, who I am in Christ. I find security. I find life. I find purpose. He is not a broken bottle or a leaky cistern. There are no faults in Him in any way and the bottom never falls out."

Questions

Question 12. Please comment on the following quote:

"For what is the sum and substance of these simple words? It is this: Christ is that Fountain of living water, which God has graciously provided for thirsting souls. From Him, as out of the rock smitten by Moses, there flows an abundant stream for all who travel through the wilderness of this world. In Him, as our Redeemer and Substitute, crucified for our sins and raised again for our justification, there is an endless supply of all that men can need: pardon, absolution, mercy, grace, peace, rest, relief, comfort and hope" (**J. C. Ryle**).

Sometimes it is difficult reading the Puritan writers because of their style. But we can hardly find writing that matches theirs for practical godliness. This is **Matthew Henry's** commentary on Jeremiah 2:13. I believe you will profit from reading this:

"There is in Him an all-sufficiency of grace and strength; all our springs are in Him and our streams from him; to forsake Him is, in effect, to deny this. He has been to us a bountiful benefactor, a fountain of living waters, overflowing, ever flowing, in the gifts of his favor; to forsake Him is to refuse to acknowledge His kindness and to withhold that tribute of love and praise which His kindness calls for.

Those who forsake Him cheat themselves, they forsook their own mercies, but it was for lying vanities. They took a great deal of pains to hew themselves out cisterns, to dig pits or pools in the earth or rock which they would carry water to, or which should receive the rain; but they proved broken cisterns, false at the bottom, so that they could hold no water. When they came to quench their thirst there they found nothing but mud and mire, and the filthy sediments of a standing lake. Such idols were to their worshippers, and such a change did those experience who turned from God to them.

If we make an idol of any creature-wealth, or pleasure, or honor, if we place our happiness in it, and promise ourselves the comfort and satisfaction in it which are to be had in God only, if we make it our joy and love, our hope and confidence, we shall find it a cistern, which we take a great deal of pains to hew out and fill, and at the best it will hold but a little water, and that dead and flat, and soon corrupting and becoming nauseous. No, it is a broken cistern, which cracks and cleaves in hot weather, so that the water is lost when we have most need of it. Let us therefore with purpose of heart cleave to the Lord only, for where else shall we go? He has the words of eternal life."

Scripture to Consider

For with You is the fountain of life... (Psalm 36:9).

A despairing man should have the devotion of his friends, even though he forsakes the fear of the Almighty. But my brothers are as undependable as intermittent streams, as the streams that overflow when darkened by thawing ice and swollen with melting snow, but that cease to flow in the dry season, and in the heat vanish from their channels. Caravans turn aside from their routes; they go up into the wasteland and perish. The caravans of Tema look for water, the traveling merchants of Sheba look in hope. They are distressed, because they had been confident; they arrive there, only to be disappointed. Now you too have proved to be of no help; you see something dreadful and are afraid" (Job 6:14-21).

As a deer thirsts for streams of water, so I thirst for you, God. I thirst for the living God. When can I go to meet with him? (Psalm 42:1-2)

Did you feast on God's Word in the last 24 hours?

       Yes   No

If so, how did you feast? In other words, circle the ways you enjoyed God today. Reading? Prayer? Worship? Fellowship? Witnessing?

Were you free from drug and alcohol abuse since you did the last lesson?

       Yes   No

Did you spend personal time with the Lord since you did the last lesson?

       Yes   No

If you answered "no" to any of the above questions, describe what led to your fall.

If you answered "yes" to the above questions, you may use this area for additional comments.

DAY 51 - SUCH WERE SOME OF YOU

One of the greatest benefits of being a Christian is that God makes us different people than we used to be. As God rescues us from impurity and makes us slaves of righteousness, we become totally different people. This truth is so good to know, because I used to be a drunkard and enslaved to cocaine; but I am no more. Some of you may have had an extreme addiction to alcohol, you may have been hooked on heroin, you may have been in jail, or have lost your family; you may have permanently damaged your body through the horrible physical toll of some type of substance abuse. The truth of Scripture is, that no matter what you were, that is not what you are, if you're in Christ.

This truth is important because who we see ourselves to be is how we act, Friend. I am no longer a drunkard so I do not act like one. I am not addicted to anything impure, so I do not stare at alcoholic beverages with lust in my heart, nor do I even glance a second time at magazines with advertisements in them. I am not who I used to be, nor do I act like I used to act. You see?

Today we will see this truth in Scripture, and then we will read a phenomenal testimony of how the grace of God has changed a friend of ours into a totally new person.

Please read the following passage and answer the questions below:

> [9]Do you not know that the wicked will not inherit the kingdom of God? Do not be deceived: Neither the sexually immoral nor idolaters nor adulterers nor male prostitutes nor homosexual offenders [10]nor thieves nor the greedy nor drunkards nor slanderers nor swindlers will inherit the kingdom of God. [11]And that is what some of you were. But you were washed, you were sanctified, you were justified in the name of the Lord Jesus Christ and by the Spirit of our God" (1 Corinthians 6:9-11).

Questions

Question 1. What kind of people made up the church at Corinth during Paul's day?

Question 2. In verses 9-10 above, Paul mentions the kinds of people who will not inherit the kingdom of God. Why do you think he warns against being deceived about this (verse 9)? Write your thoughts here:

Questions

Question 3. Were the people to whom Paul was writing still practicing these sins? Before you answer, carefully review verse 11.

Question 4. What verses tell us these people were no longer the same?

Question 5. According to the above passage, what changed them? How were they changed?

The New Testament church has inspired both exciting and disastrous experiments down through history. Hoping to create the perfect New Testament community, some have tried to design groups where all the gifts are expressed, worship is spontaneous and fellowship is deep. But they forget the common element of all New Testament churches—problems!

In chapters one through four of 1st Corinthians, Paul dealt with divisions in the church. Now he focuses on serious moral problems in Corinth. Incest and drunkenness (chapter 5) during communion are hardly what we hope to find in church. But we must remember that growing churches are not always filled with well-scrubbed Christians, but rather with a motley collection of sinners being saved.

Paul warns against being deceived because we're so easily deceived about this. After all, salvation is by grace, not by works, and Jesus came to save sinners. What does it matter, we think, if sinners keep on sinning? But such thinking overlooks the fact that a new life in Christ results in a new lifestyle (verse 11). Genuine salvation is to actually be saved from ongoing, habitual sin.

The sins listed referred to a continuous lifestyle or practice and not to a one-time involvement. Paul's list is similar to the works of the flesh in Galatians 5:19-21 (See also Ephesians 5:5.) In both cases a persisting in fleshly living is implied.

Likewise, Paul's mention of both male prostitutes and homosexual offenders does not mean that a person with homosexual tendencies, who is living chastely, is excluded from the kingdom. The two words Paul uses here, malakoi (men or boys who allow themselves to be misused homosexually) and arsenokoitai (a male homosexual, pederast, sodomite) both have an active meaning.

The teaching today is that Christians are no longer who they used to be. Please state how the following passages confirm this truth:

> I have been crucified with Christ and I no longer live, but Christ lives in me. The life I live in the body, I live by faith in the Son of God, who loved me and gave himself for me (Galatians 2:20).

Question 6. Please state how this passage confirms that Christians are no longer who they used to be.

> ³For you died, and your life is now hidden with Christ in God. ⁴When Christ, who is your life, appears, then you also will appear with him in glory (Colossians 3:3, 4).

Question 7. Please state how this passage confirms that Christians are no longer who they used to be.

Now let me share with you some writings that will confirm this truth, and have you comment on them:

> The previous character of those who seem to have been converted was various. I could name many who have been turned from the paths of open sin and profligacy, and have found pardon and purity in the blood of the Lamb, and by the Sprit of our God; so that we can say to them, as Paul said to the Corinthians, "Such were some of you; but you were washed, but you are sanctified, but you are justified." I often think, when conversing with some of these, that the change they have undergone might be enough to convince an atheist that there is a God, or an infidel that there is a Savior." **Memoirs of McCheyne**

Question 8. Please write your comments here:

He puts them in mind what a change the gospel and grace of God had made in them: Such were some of you (verse 11), such notorious sinners as he had been reckoning up. The Greek word is tauta—such things were some of you, very monsters rather than men. Note some that are eminently good after their conversion have been as remarkably wicked before. How glorious a change does grace make! It changes the vilest of men into saints and children of God. Such were some of you, but you are not what you were. You are washed, you are sanctified, you are justified in the name of Christ, and by the Spirit of our God.

Note the wickedness of men before conversion is no bar to their regeneration and reconciliation to God. The blood of Christ, and the washing of regeneration, can purge away all guilt and defilement. Note, none are cleansed from the guilt of sin, and reconciled to God through Christ, but those who are also sanctified by His Spirit. All who are made righteous in the sight of God are made holy by the grace of God. **Matthew Henry Commentary**

Question 9. Please comment on the above quote by Matthew Henry here:

Friend, let me show you how this teaching is applied practically. We do what is according to our nature. If we are sinners who are trying to be good we will inevitably fall. But if we are saints, who occasionally sin, then our nature is such that we hate sin, and our habitual pattern of life will be to walk in righteousness. See it?

Questions

Friend, if we are in Christ, we are not who or what we were. The story is told of Augustine who passed a familiar prostitute without turning a second glance at her. She turned and said, "Augustine, it is I." To which he replied, "Yes, but it is not I." He knew the truth that he was not who he used to be. Do you? One of our course members always signs his posts to the discussion group, "Not I, Not Ever!"

Question 10. How are you doing today? Please record your progress here:

Scripture to Consider

[13]For you have heard of my previous way of life in Judaism, how intensely I persecuted the church of God and tried to destroy it. [14]I was advancing in Judaism beyond many Jews of my own age and was extremely zealous for the traditions of my fathers. [15]But when God, who set me apart from birth and called me by his grace, was pleased [16]to reveal his Son in me so that I might preach him among the Gentiles, I did not consult any man, [17]nor did I go up to Jerusalem to see those who were apostles before I was, but I went immediately into Arabia and later returned to Damascus.

[18]Then after three years, I went up to Jerusalem to get acquainted with Peter and stayed with him fifteen days. [19]I saw none of the other apostles-only James, the Lord's brother. [20]I assure you before God that what I am writing you is no lie. [21]Later I went to Syria and Cilicia. [22]I was personally unknown to the churches of Judea that are in Christ. [23]They only heard the report: "The man who formerly persecuted us is now preaching the faith he once tried to destroy." [24]And they praised God because of me (Galatians 1:13-24).

Did you feast on God's Word in the last 24 hours?

     Yes   No

If so, how did you feast? In other words, circle the ways you enjoyed God today. Reading? Prayer? Worship? Fellowship? Witnessing?

Were you free from drug and alcohol abuse since you did the last lesson?

     Yes   No

Did you spend personal time with the Lord since you did the last lesson?

     Yes   No

If you answered "no" to any of the above questions, describe what led to your fall.

If you answered "yes" to the above questions, you may use this area for additional comments.

DAY 52 - WALKING IN THE SPIRIT

So I say, live by the Spirit, and you will not gratify the desires of the flesh (Galatians 5:16).

Scripture gives us a way to live that is honoring to the Lord, Friend. That way involves a continual drinking of the Living Water, continuous and unbroken fellowship with Christ, and a refusal to gratify the desires of the flesh. This type of a life is extremely rewarding, as Scripture says, "Happy is he whose God is the Lord" (Psalm 144:15).

Most of us would acknowledge this truth, and yet we find that within us there are competing desires and inner conflict. "For the flesh desires what is contrary to the Spirit, and the Spirit what is contrary to the flesh. They are in conflict with each other, so that you do not do what you want" (Galatians 5:17).

So, are we to live the rest of our lives with this inner struggle going on all the time? Should we just give up and say that we will always have these intense temptations, these fiery darts from the enemy, and at times we will have victory over them and at other times we will give in to them? Many people do just that. They are tired of fighting, tired of resolving to stop only to fall again, tired of the vicious cycle. But friend, this does not have to continue. Scripture makes a declarative statement: "So I say, live by the Spirit and you will not gratify the desires of the sinful nature." We may still have the desires, but we are enabled to live above them as we live by the Spirit.

So, what does it mean to live by the Spirit? Please read this quote from **Matthew Henry** and be ready to answer the question below:

"Note, the best antidote against the poison of sin is to walk in the Spirit, to be much conversing with spiritual things, to mind the things of the soul, which is the spiritual part of man, more than those of the body, which is his carnal part, to commit ourselves to the guidance of the word, wherein the Holy Spirit makes known the will of God concerning us, and in the way of our duty to act in a dependence on his aids and influences. And, as this would be the best means of preserving them from fulfilling the lusts of the flesh, so it would be a good evidence that they were Christians indeed; for, says the apostle 'if you would be led by the Spirit, you are not under law.' As if he had said, 'You must expect a struggle between flesh and spirit as long as you are in the world, that the flesh will be lusting against the spirit as well as the spirit against the flesh; but if, in the prevailing bent and tenor of your lives, you be led by the Spirit, if you act under the guidance and government of the Holy Spirit and of that spiritual nature and disposition he has wrought in you, if you make the word of God your rule and the grace of God your principle, it will hence appear that you are not under the law, not under the condemning..." (Comments on Galatians 5:16-18).

Questions

Question 1. Please write down everything you can find from the quote above that would define what living by the Spirit means:

Question 2. Obviously we have come to a crucial portion of Scripture for overcoming slavery to alcohol or oxycontin when we read, "So I say, live by the Spirit, and you will not gratify the desires of the flesh." Please explain, in your own words, what you think it means to "live by the Spirit." Write your answer here:

Please read the passage we are studying in context, and answer the questions below:

> [16]So I say, live by the Spirit, and you will not gratify the desires of the flesh. [17]For the flesh desires what is contrary to the Spirit, and the Spirit what is contrary to the flesh. They are in conflict with each other, so that you do not do what you want. [18]But if you are led by the Spirit, you are not under law.
>
> [19]The acts of the flesh are obvious: sexual immorality, impurity and debauchery; [20]idolatry and witchcraft; hatred, discord, jealousy, fits of rage, selfish ambition, dissensions, factions [21]and envy; drunkenness, orgies, and the like. I warn you, as I did before, that those who live like this will not inherit the kingdom of God.
>
> [22]the fruit of the Spirit is love, joy, peace, patience, kindness, goodness, faithfulness, [23]gentleness and self-control. Against such things there is no law. [24]Those who belong to Christ Jesus have crucified the sinful nature with its passions and desires. [25]live by the Spirit, let us keep in step with the Spirit. [26]Let us not become conceited, provoking and envying each other" (Galatians 5:16-26).

Questions

Question 3. Please list the acts of the flesh found in verse 19:

Notice that "drunkenness" is stated by name here. Drunkenness is listed as part of the acts of the flesh, and if our lives are characterized by these acts, we are not living by the Spirit.

Note: There is a real possibility of being deceived when involved in acts like this. So Paul warns in verse 21 "I warn you, as I did before, that those who live like this will not inherit the kingdom of God." Oh how we need to heed the warning. Friends, please understand Paul's words, and don't try to explain them away. He is issuing a warning to those who live in the acts of the flesh, that they will not inherit the kingdom of God. In other words, hell is the destination of all who live by these acts, regardless of how much knowledge they have, how articulate they are, or what position they have in the church. This is serious. Do not be deceived.

Question 4. Friend, according to verse 24 above, what evidence must be in our lives to show that we belong to Christ?

Question 5. What does the above passage teach about our relationship to the Spirit? What are we to do in relationship to Him?

Question 6. Please list the fruit of the Spirit from verse 22 above:

Question 7. In the context of this passage, what does it mean to be led by the Spirit?

Question 8. What does it mean to "keep in step with the Spirit?"

Note: The Christian life can be described as a walk with God. Just as "Enoch walked with God, and was no more" so we are to be in a daily relationship with Him. And it is this daily relationship, or this walking with God, that keeps us away from sin. Compare Psalm 56:13: "because you have saved me from death. You have kept me from being defeated. So I will walk with God in light among the living. (NCV)

The Christian life begins with a step of faith for salvation. Then it continues step by step toward spiritual maturity as we develop a growing closeness to God.

It is a painful business to get through into the stride of God, it means getting your 'second wind' spiritually. In learning to walk with God there is always the difficulty of getting into His stride; but when we have got into it, the only characteristic that manifests itself is the life of God. The individual man is lost sight of in his personal union with God, and the stride and the power of God alone are manifested.

It is difficult to get into stride with God, because when we start walking with Him we find He has outstripped us before we have taken three steps. He has different ways of doing things, and we have to be trained and disciplined into His ways.

Question 9. How does 1 John 1:7 add perspective on the above teaching? "If we walk in the light, as He is in the light, we have fellowship with one another and the blood of Jesus, His Son, purifies us from all sin." Write your answer here:

Questions

Question 10. Paul talks above about the battle between the flesh and the Spirit. The two are at war. And then he states, "so that you do not do what you want." Does this refer to believers or unbelievers?

John Calvin adds some clarity here: "So that you do not do what you want. This refers, unquestionably, to the regenerate (believers). Carnal men have no battle with depraved lusts, no proper desire to attain to the righteousness of God. Paul is addressing believers. The things that you want must mean, not our natural inclinations, but the holy affections which God bestows upon us by grace.

Paul therefore declares, that believers, so long as they are in this life, whatever may be the earnestness of their endeavors, do not obtain such a measure of success as to serve God in a perfect manner. The highest result does not correspond to their wishes and desires" (**John Calvin**, commentary on Galatians 5).

Note: Because of the war in the soul of every believer (the flesh against the Spirit, the Spirit against the flesh) we are unable to perfectly do what we would like to do. We desire to seek God wholeheartedly but the flesh wars against that desire. We desire ongoing intimacy and unbroken fellowship with Jesus Christ, but the flesh vehemently resists this. We want to show others only a sweet aroma of Christ, letting our gentleness be evident to all; we want to be gracious at all times, completely humble, submitting to one another always and forgiving each other as we have been forgiven. The flesh resists and fights against all of this so that we cannot perfectly and at all times do what we want to do. Should we then despair and give up?

The above passage states that there is a way to keep from fulfilling the lusts of the flesh. It is to live by the Spirit. It is to be led by the Spirit. It is to walk with the Spirit. So, our "fight" is not so much with drunkenness, or not being greedy, selfish or divisive, it is with maintaining our walk with the Lord. For if we live by the Spirit, are led by the Spirit, and walk with the Spirit, the promise of Scripture is that we will not gratify our flesh. We will not get drunk. We will not be sexually immoral...etc. There is our answer!

Dear friend, I have been learning, over the past several years what it means to walk with God. It is an experience to be sure, and it is not like anything we can learn in school. It is exercising the spiritual disciplines of being in the Word daily, of being in prayer continually, of recognizing the leading and prompting of God in our daily activities. This is all foreign to us. But I tell you that I would not trade it. I love walking in and living by the Spirit of God (though my flesh hates it) and I don't ever want to return to the acts of the flesh. My wife, also, is thankful that I am walking in the Spirit, as she and I are much closer than when I was living in sin. I hope you are finding the same thing.

Question 11. How are you doing right now? Are you learning to live by the Spirit? Share any prayer requests with us that you have.

Scripture to Consider

He has shown you, O man, what is good; and what does the LORD require of you but to do justly, to love mercy, and to walk humbly with your God? (Micah 6:8).

Did you feast on God's Word in the last 24 hours?

    Yes   No

If so, how did you feast? In other words, circle the ways you enjoyed God today. Reading? Prayer? Worship? Fellowship? Witnessing?

Were you free from drug and alcohol abuse since you did the last lesson?

    Yes   No

Did you spend personal time with the Lord since you did the last lesson?

    Yes   No

If you answered "no" to any of the above questions, describe what led to your fall.

If you answered "yes" to the above questions, you may use this area for additional comments.

DAY 53 - FREEDOM THROUGH FELLOWSHIP

The final weekend before Christmas is not the time to visit a shopping mall. If you are fortunate enough to find a parking spot, the press of people inside makes shopping almost impossible. One mother I heard was giving final instructions to her young son before plunging into the crowd: "Stay close to me and hold my hand all the time. We won't get separated if we hold on to each other."

As Jesus prepared his disciples to face life without his visible presence, he impressed on them the importance of staying close to him spiritually. He said, "Remain in Me." If you have ever longed to understand the secret of spiritual growth, you will find it in Jesus' words to us in John 15.

Here is a truth to memorize:

Truly stopping habits of drunkenness and drug use requires ongoing intimacy with God.

Or, stated another way, **enjoying true intimacy with Jesus Christ breaks the attraction of false intimacy that alcohol and drugs offer**. This is the reason why all psychologically based programs to "change behavior" will not produce genuine and lasting freedom. Enjoying Jesus Christ Himself must replace the love of the drug.

Please read the following Scripture:

> [4]Remain in me and I will remain in you. No branch can bear fruit by itself; it must remain in the vine. Neither can you bear fruit unless you remain in me. [5]I am the vine; you are the branches. If a man remains in me and I in him, he will bear much fruit; apart from me you can do nothing. [6]If anyone does not remain in me, he is like a branch that is thrown away and withers; such branches are picked up, thrown into the fire and burned. [7]If you remain in me and my words remain in you, ask whatever you wish, and it will be given you. [8]This is to my Father's glory, that you bear much fruit, showing yourselves to be my disciples.
>
> [9]As the Father has loved me, so have I loved you. Now remain in my love. [10]If you obey my commands; you will remain in my love, just as I have obeyed my Father's commands and remain in his love. [11]I have told you this so that my joy may be in you and that your joy may be complete" (John 15:4-11).

Spend a little time thinking through the above passage to the delight of your soul. When you're ready, please answer these questions.

Question 2. What is the significance of calling His disciples "branches?"

Note: See here the necessity of actually being a "branch." Nobody shares in the life of Christ unless there is an actual faith relationship with Christ.

Question 3. Please select how many times the word "remain" is used in the verses above:

Question 4. Instead of commanding us to bear fruit, why is Jesus' only command to "Remain in Me" (v. 4)?

Now, let us summarize: Remain in the love of Jesus and your joy will be complete. And if your joy in Jesus is complete, Friend, you will not have to look for it anywhere else. Your slavery to sin is broken when your love and joy are complete.

Question 5. What do you think it means to remain in Christ?

Questions

Question 1. Jesus' instructions to his disciples in this passage revolve around three symbols - the vine, the gardener, and the branches. What is Jesus communicating by calling Himself the Vine?

Question 6. The fruit produced by the remaining branch is often viewed as a reference to new converts. But branches produce grapes, not other branches. What other possible meanings are there for fruit?

Question 7. Read Galatians 5:22-23: "But the fruit of the Spirit is love, joy, peace, patience, kindness, goodness, faithfulness, gentleness and self-control." How do these verses fit into what we are studying?

Note: We can do "nothing" on our own, certainly not overcome drunkenness, sexual impurity . . . etc. But if we remain in Jesus He will produce fruit through us, and one particular fruit of being in Him is "self-control." So, we do not focus as much on overcoming drugs as we do on abiding, or dwelling in Jesus Christ. This is the "secret" to growing in Christ, to leaving alcohol and the abuse of prescription meds behind, to experiencing genuine love and real joy!

Please read the following story:

⁵⁴Then seizing him, they led him away and took him into the house of the high priest. Peter followed at a distance. ⁵⁵But when they had kindled a fire in the middle of the courtyard and had sat down together, Peter sat down with them. ⁵⁶A servant girl saw him seated there in the firelight. She looked closely at him and said, "This man was with him."

⁵⁷But he denied it. "Woman, I don't know him," he said.

⁵⁸A little later someone else saw him and said, "You also are one of them."

"Man, I am not!" Peter replied.

⁵⁹About an hour later another asserted, "Certainly this fellow was with him, for he is a Galilean."

⁶⁰Peter replied, "Man, I don't know what you're talking about!" Just as he was speaking, the rooster crowed. ⁶¹The Lord turned and looked straight at Peter. Then Peter remembered the word the Lord had spoken to him: "Before the rooster crows today, you will disown me three times." ⁶²And he went outside and wept bitterly (Luke 22:54-62).

We find in the above story that Peter denied Christ, began cursing, and stated that he did not know Jesus. And he fell three times in a row, one right after the other. Why? What happened?

Question 8. Please write out the second sentence of verse 54 above:

"And Peter followed at a distance." Friend, this is a warning for us: anytime we begin distancing ourselves from Christ we will fall. We must remain intimate with Him, enjoying fellowship with our Savior moment by moment. This is the key to ongoing victory and fruitfulness.

Next, please read the following quote from **Robert Murray McCheyne**, and write your thoughts on it below:

"Not all that seem to be branches are branches of the true Vine. Many branches fall off the trees when the high winds begin to blow-all that are rotten branches. So in times of temptation, or trial, or persecution, many false professors drop away. Many that seemed to be believers went back, and walked no more with Jesus. They followed Jesus, they prayed with Him, they praised Him; but they went back, and walked no more with Him. So it is still. Many among us doubtless seem to be converted; they begin well and promise fair, who will fall off when winter comes. Some have fallen off, I fear, already; some more may be expected to follow. These will not be blessed in dying. Oh, of all deathbeds may I be kept from beholding the deathbed of the false professor! I have seen it before now, and I trust I may never see it again. They are not blessed after death. The rotten branches will burn more fiercely in the flames.

"Oh, think what torment it will be, to think that you spent your life in pretending to be a Christian, and lost your opportunity of becoming one indeed! Your hell will be all the deeper, blacker, hotter, that you knew so much of Christ, and were so near Him, and found Him not."

Question 9. Write your thoughts on the above quotation here:

Questions

Question 10. How does 1 John 2:27 compare with what we are studying today? "As for you, the anointing you received from him remains in you, and you do not need anyone to teach you. But as his anointing teaches you about all things and as that anointing is real, not counterfeit—just as it has taught you, remain in him."

Question 11. And finally, please provide your thoughts on this quote from **Charles Spurgeon**:

"We are plainly taught in the Word of God that as many as have believed are one with Christ: they are married to him, there is a conjugal union based upon mutual affection. The union is closer still, for there is a vital union between Christ and his saints. They are in him as the branches are in the vine; they are members of the body of which he is the head. They are one with Jesus in such a true and real sense that with him they died, with him they have been buried, with him they are raised; with him they are raised up together and made to sit together in heavenly places. There is an indissoluble union between Christ and all his people: I in them and they in me.

"Thus the union may be described: 'Christ is in his people the hope of glory, and they are dead and their life is hid with Christ in God.' This is a union of the most wonderful kind, which figures may faintly set forth, but which it is impossible for language completely to explain.

"Oneness to Jesus is one of the fat things full of marrow. For if it be so, indeed, that we are one with Christ, then because he lives we must live also; because he was justified by his resurrection, we also are justified in him; because he is rewarded and forever sits down at his Father's right hand, we also have obtained the inheritance in him and by faith grasp it now and enjoy its earnest."

Question 12. Philippians 4:13 says, "I can do all things through Christ, who gives me strength." Can you break free from an addiction to alcohol and all drugs through Jesus Christ?

Scripture to Consider

My prayer is not for them alone. I pray also for those who will believe in me through their message, that all of them may be one, Father, just as you are in me and I am in you. May they also be in us so that the world may believe that you have sent me. I have given them the glory that you gave me, that they may be one as we are one: I in them and you in me. May they be brought to complete unity to let the world know that you sent me and have loved them even as you have loved me (John 17:20-23).

Did you feast on God's Word in the last 24 hours?

      Yes   No

If so, how did you feast? In other words, circle the ways you enjoyed God today. Reading? Prayer? Worship? Fellowship? Witnessing?

Were you free from drug and alcohol abuse since you did the last lesson?

      Yes   No

Did you spend personal time with the Lord since you did the last lesson?

      Yes   No

If you answered "no" to any of the above questions, describe what led to your fall.

If you answered "yes" to the above questions, you may use this area for additional comments.

DAY 54 - LIVE FOR PLEASURE!

Friend, did you know that it is biblical to live for pleasure? In fact, as we will see later on, it is commanded of us to live for pleasure. We are to be, as John Piper puts it, "Christian Hedonists." This was a totally new concept to me. Some people in the Christian world are not happy until they are miserable, and that is the way I was for years. But we are not doomed to this type of an existence, and today's teaching has the power to change your entire world. I know, it did mine.

I also have to share this. Sometime when you are bored, do a search for "Alcoholism" on the Internet, look for some "experts" who deal with this kind of thing, and begin reading the solutions they provide. I just did this yesterday, and I truly am thankful that I did not get sucked in to the teaching that is out there today.

Most of it is a joyless to-do list of things to change your behavior. When hit with temptation, visualize a policeman running up to you with a big red stop sign and handcuffs. Then begin to picture an emotionally charged moment, the death of a parent or the birth of a child, so as to have an equally emotional pull as the temptation. Or place a rubber band on your wrist and every time you are tempted simply snap the rubber band hard on your wrist. That way you will associate pain with temptation and want to stop the temptation.

Oh Friend, how sad, how lifeless, how ineffective are the cures of the world. What about the heart? Jesus said lust is a heart problem (Matthew 15:18) and no amount of snapping my wrist or thinking of a policeman will change my heart. What can so motivate my heart with love and joy that I can't possibly think of going back to cocaine or alcohol? Oh friend, we have a Savior who has come to us in passion! He has come not only to suffer and die to remove the penalty of our sins, but to live in our hearts and ravish us with love. Oh how He does delight the soul and stir the affections. Oh how pleasurable it is to live in love with Him. A cop with a red stop sign and handcuffs, or a Savior who ravishes the heart. Hmm . . . let me think. The key is that we are to be people who live for pleasure in God!

> "It is a bad world, an incredibly bad world. But I have discovered in the midst of it a quiet and holy people who have learned a great secret. They have found a joy that is a thousand times better than any pleasure of our sinful life. They are despised and persecuted, but they care not. They are masters of their souls. They have overcome the world. These people are the Christians—and I am one of them." **Saint Cyprian** (200-258).

Dear friend, this is our calling: finding a joy that is a thousand times better than any pleasure of our sinful life. Sometimes I cannot believe that I spent 17 long years following the "pleasures of sin" in drunkenness when there was Someone "a thousand times better" waiting for me. And it is the ongoing experience of Jesus Christ that keeps me from having any desire to go back. I can't get enough of this Man. This God-Man who longs to pour His life in to me, and to fill me to all the fullness of God. Today we will examine the sheer pleasure available in God.

Oh friend, open your heart to this God, for you will live in pleasure for the rest of your life, and then throughout all eternity if you do.

> Live while you live, the Epicure would say,
> And seize the pleasures of the present day;
> Live while you live, the sacred preacher cries,
> And give to God each moment as it flies;
> Lord, in my view let both united be;
> I live in pleasure when I live to thee.
> **Philip Doddridge** (1702-1751)

Questions

Please study through the following passages and provide your comments on them:

> You have made known to me the path of life; you will fill me with joy in your presence, with eternal pleasures at your right hand (Psalm 16:11).

Question 1. According to this verse, what is at the right hand of God?

> The Son is the radiance of God's glory and the exact representation of his being, sustaining all things by his powerful word. After he had provided purification for sins, he sat down at the right hand of the Majesty in heaven (Hebrews 1:3).

Question 2. According to this verse, who is at the right hand of God?

Note: The above verses tell us that there are eternal pleasures at the right hand of God, and that Jesus Christ is at the right hand of God. Do you see it? The message is clear: In Jesus Christ is eternal pleasure! Sin's pleasures are only "for a season" but with Jesus Christ the pleasure never ends!

> A fool finds pleasure in evil conduct, but a man of understanding delights in wisdom (Proverbs 10:23).

Question 3. What kind of a person finds pleasure in the abuse of alcohol, drugs, or other evil conduct?

> Pleasure is our greatest evil or our greatest good. (**Alexander Pope**, 1688-1744).

Question 4. According to Proverbs 10:23 above, how does a man of understanding approach wisdom?

To whom can I speak and give warning? Who will listen to me? Their ears are closed so they cannot hear. The word of the LORD is offensive to them; they find no pleasure in it (Jeremiah 6:10).

Question 5. According to Jeremiah 6:10 above, what is the attitude of these people toward the Word of God?

Question 6. If the unrighteous are characterized as people who find no pleasure in the Word of God, how are we who love God to approach Scripture?

Hannah prayed and said: "My heart rejoices in the LORD; in the LORD my horn is lifted high. My mouth boasts over my enemies, for I delight in your deliverance" (1 Samuel 2:1).

Question 7. This verse is the record of Hannah praying to the Lord. What is her attitude toward the Lord and His deliverance?

"There is no pleasure comparable to not being captivated by any external thing whatever" (**Thomas Wilson**, 1663-1735).

Delight yourself in the LORD and he will give you the desires of your heart (Psalm 37:4).

Question 8. According to Psalm 37:4 above, what are we to do with the Lord?

Question 9. According to the above verse (Psalm 37:4), what is the reward for delighting in the Lord?

Praise the LORD. Blessed is the man who fears the LORD, who finds great delight in his commands (Psalm 112:1).

Question 10. In what does the man who fears the Lord delight?

Come, all you who are thirsty, come to the waters; and you who have no money, come, buy and eat! Come, buy wine and milk without money and without cost. Why spend money on what is not bread, and your labor on what does not satisfy? Listen, listen to me, and eat what is good, and your soul will delight in the richest of fare. Give ear and come to me; hear me, that your soul may live. I will make an everlasting covenant with you, my faithful love promised to David" (Isaiah 55:1-4).

Question 11. These verses make it clear that there is a "delight of soul" awaiting all who will eat what is good. Are you eating what is good (God's Word)? Are you learning to delight in the Lord now, Friend? Please write your answer here:

I delight greatly in the LORD; my soul rejoices in my God. For he has clothed me with garments of salvation and arrayed me in a robe of righteousness, as a bridegroom adorns his head like a priest, and as a bride adorns herself with her jewels (Isaiah 61:10).

Question 12. In whom or what is the author finding pleasure?

Question 13. Why is he rejoicing?

Note: Remember Adam and Eve, who after their sin were naked and ashamed. God came along and clothed them with a sacrifice. God provides all of His children with the garments of salvation; that is, with the sacrifice of Jesus Christ. This brings us pleasure and causes us to rejoice.

"To stand by the shadows of a friendly tree with the wind tugging at your coattail and the heavens hailing your heart, to gaze and glory and to give oneself again to God, what more could a man ask? Oh the fullness, pleasure, sheer excitement of knowing God on earth." (**Jim Elliot** in *The Journals of Jim Elliot*, Christianity Today, Vol. 31, no. 12.)

"When we look at the Song of Songs, we see the joy we're supposed to find in Jesus Christ. That's the model we have to go by - not one of drudgery, but pleasure, joy and anticipation." (**Mary Ann Mayo**, Marriage Partnership, Vol. 7, no. 3.)

Questions

"Nothing will supply the needs, and satisfy the desires of a soul, but water out of this rock (Jesus Christ), this fountain opened. The pleasures of sense are puddle-water; spiritual delights are rock-water, so pure, so clear, so refreshing—rivers of pleasure" (**Matthew Henry**).

Now, please read through the following passage and give your thoughts below. This passage is a prescription for how to find delight in God:

> 21Submit to God and be at peace with him; in this way prosperity will come to you. 22Accept instruction from his mouth and lay up his words in your heart. 23If you return to the Almighty, you will be restored: If you remove wickedness far from your tent 24and assign your nuggets to the dust, your gold of Ophir to the rocks in the ravines, 25then the Almighty will be your gold, the choicest silver for you. 26Surely then you will find delight in the Almighty and will lift up your face to God" (Job 22:21-26).

There are four requirements in this passage that must be met in order to delight in God. What are they? I'll write the first one:

Question 14. Verse 21: Accept instruction

Question 15. Verse 22:

Question 16. Verse 23:

Question 17. Verses 23, 24:

Question 18. What does it mean when it says, "Then the Almighty will be your gold, the choicest silver for you?"

Question 19. In your own words, according to the passage above, what needs to be done in order to truly delight in God?

Friend, I hope you know there is exquisite joy and pleasure to be found in Jesus Christ. This has to be experienced to be understood, as words fall far short of being able to explain. Oh how sad to trade the temporary "pleasures of sin" for an eternity of pleasure with Christ. With Him is fullness of joy,

overflowing pleasure, ongoing delight. Won't you commit right now to seeking your pleasure in Jesus Christ? Once we taste of the joy that is found in Him we won't want to go back to the pleasures of drunkenness.

Question 20. Please record how you are doing today:

Scripture to Consider

The LORD takes pleasure in His people; He will beautify the humble with salvation. Let the saints be joyful in glory; Let them sing aloud on their beds (Psalm 149:4-5).

Did you feast on God's Word in the last 24 hours?

> Yes   No

If so, how did you feast? In other words, circle the ways you enjoyed God today. Reading? Prayer? Worship? Fellowship? Witnessing?

Were you free from drug and alcohol abuse since you did the last lesson?

> Yes   No

Did you spend personal time with the Lord since you did the last lesson?

> Yes   No

If you answered "no" to any of the above questions, describe what led to your fall.

If you answered "yes" to the above questions, you may use this area for additional comments.

DAY 55 - DO EVERYTHING TO STAND

Therefore put on the full armor of God, so that when the day of evil comes, you may be able to stand your ground, after you have done everything to stand (Ephesians 6:13).

Friend, by this time in the New Wine course, most people are enjoying consistent freedom from drunkenness and all forms of drugs. However, on occasion we encounter some who have come this far who are continuing to stumble. Over the course of time, we have discovered that all who continue to be defeated have at least two things in common:

- They have not done all they can to rid their lives of the source of the substance.

- They are not following the advice of godly mentors who can see what needs to be done to extract them from the grip of sin.

Let us examine these two things in some depth.

First, if we leave ourselves access to alcohol somewhere, we are sure to fall. Please provide your comments on the following verses.

Questions

Question 1. What are your thoughts on Romans 13:14: "But put ye on the Lord Jesus Christ, and make no provision for the flesh, to fulfill the lusts thereof."

Note: By leaving ourselves any access to alcohol we are making provision for the flesh, and in a weak moment we will fall. We simply must remove all access.

Question 2. What are your thoughts on Matthew 5:29-30: "If your right eye causes you to sin, gouge it out and throw it away. It is better for you to lose one part of your body than for your whole body to be thrown into hell. And if your right hand causes you to sin, cut it off and throw it away. It is better for you to lose one part of your body than for your whole body to go into hell."

Questions

Question 3. What are your thoughts on Joshua 7:13: "Go, consecrate the people. Tell them, 'Consecrate yourselves in preparation for tomorrow; for this is what the LORD, the God of Israel, says: That which is devoted is among you, O Israel. You cannot stand against your enemies until you remove it."

Today we want to talk very practically about the subject of "doing everything to stand." Let us review Ephesians 6:13 again: "Therefore put on the full armor of God, so that when the day of evil comes, you may be able to stand your ground, after you have done everything to stand" (Ephesians 6:13). When it comes to fighting drugs, Ephesians 6:13 tells us we not only need to be wearing armor but we must also "do all we can to stand." Since this course began, we have watched many people take this verse to heart, and do all they can to stand. Here are some things that our course members have shared with us that they have done to win the war:

- Changed careers to get away from "bar life"

- Refused to eat in restaurants where alcohol is served

- Refused to take cash or credit cards with them when having to drive by an old favorite bar

- Spend all night in prayer, begging God for grace to overcome

- Drive different (and longer) routes to work and back to avoid areas of temptation

- Refuse to go out of town except with spouse

- Asked local store owners not to sell alcohol to them

- Started going to church

- Started working with an accountability partner

- Began counseling with pastor

Questions

- Smashed all bottles in the home

- Not gone to grocery stores alone so that they could not buy alcohol

- Stopped counseling with worldly counselors

- Refused to drive out of town where temptation has been strong

- Cut off relationships that promoted sin

- Confessed to spouse, asked for their assistance

- Moved out of current residence where alcohol was in use

- Moved to a different city

- Called spouse in the middle of the night from hotel to ensure avoidance of sin

- Called us every time he had to go somewhere tempting, and called when finished

- Confessed openly to their church family and asked for prayer and assistance

Question 4. Please list here everything you have done to stand:

Friend, by now we all should recognize that being free from alcohol is an act of God and by His grace: "For it is by grace you have been saved, through faith—and this not from yourselves, it is the gift of God not by works, so that no one can boast" (Ephesians 2:8-9). "For the grace of God that brings salvation has appeared to all men. It teaches us to say 'No' to ungodliness and worldly passions, and to live self-controlled, upright and godly lives in this present age" (Titus 2:11-12). Had it not been for God's grace we would still be serving sin, self and Satan. Sin is so powerful, and our wills so enslaved to it by nature, that we could not, on our own, extricate ourselves from its grip.

And yet there is nothing contradictory to the above truth in stating that we must "do all we can do to stand." In fact, the two work together. We do all we can do because of the grace God has given us. "I worked harder than all of them, yet not I, but the grace of God that was with me" (1 Corinthians 15:10). "For we are God's workmanship, created in Christ Jesus to do good works, which God prepared in advance for us to do" (Ephesians 2:10).

Question 5. How does Philippians 2:12, 13 compare with what we are studying today? "Therefore, my dear friends, as you have always obeyed-not only in my presence, but now much more in my absence, continue to work out your salvation with fear and trembling, for it is God who works in you to will and to act according to his good purpose."

Friend, we indeed must "do all we can do" to stand. We must "work harder than all the rest" by God's grace. We must work out our salvation that God is working in us, for if we don't, we will continue to fall. And continuing to fall weakens us every time. Those who continue to fall may find themselves back in the death-grip of drunkenness and impurity again. This is serious business.

So, the passage we are studying today says that we must put on the full armor of God, and that after we "do all we can do" to stand, that we do indeed stand by grace. By grace we do not fall into sin. If we do not do all we can do to stand, we should not be surprised when we fall.

Question 6. During your reading of the above material, has God brought to mind anything else that you could do to stand?

Some will continue to believe that they can go places and continue lifestyles that are around alcohol and those that drink. This is a prescription for destruction. Some are taught or believe that they will someday be able to drink socially. This is another lie as one drink can send us lower than we were before coming to New Wine. Some have even turned to other measures, such as other drugs, thinking that the addiction process will be different or that they can "handle" anything other than their drug of choice. This only provides another avenue for the enemy to further enslave them. If any of these things fits you, then please take this to heart. We cannot flirt with the enemy by being around alcohol and drinking. We will never be able to drink socially. We cannot turn to drugs as another option, including those that are supposedly "non-addictive." In other words, declare war on lust, make a battle plan to defeat it, and beg God for grace to carry it through to completion.

Friend, the story of Achan (which we studied on Day 19) teaches us there must be a total eradication of not only the cause of sin, but of everything associated with that sin. When we are dealing with alcohol, we must declare all-out war on evil desires leading to drunkenness, and do all we can do to cease this insidious habit.

174

Questions

Here are some things I have personally done to break the power of sin, by God's grace:

- Smashed the bottles in my home
- Changed careers
- Called a godly friend when severely tempted
- Read Scripture
- Changed the routes I drove home to avoid temptation
- Sang Songs
- Maintained accountability with my pastor

Maybe these seem too radical; but not to a dying man who needs to be free from sin to live. We need to "do all we can do" until the habit of refusing drugs is deeply ingrained into our very being. Once the habit is developed, we can slowly begin to go back to a less war-oriented lifestyle, always being watchful that we are not sucked back into the trap from which we barely escaped.

This day in the course was developed out of seeing heartbreaking falls from some course members as they are well along in this course. Each and every time someone falls to drunkenness it is evident that they have not done all they can do to rid their lives of the sin, and to stand in grace.

Oh Friend, purity in Christ and freedom from sin are worth the battle. As we give up drunkenness we gain far more than we lose. We gain mastery over ourselves, enjoyment of the presence of God, freedom from enslaving habits, power in witnessing, etc. It is worth it. It is worth "doing all we can do" to stand by grace.

Question 7. Please make an honest assessment of where you are spiritually. Are you truly becoming free from habits that would master you? And specifically, have you done all you can do to stand?

Scripture to Consider

Jesus looked at them and said, "With man this is impossible, but not with God; all things are possible with God" (Mark 10:27).

Did you feast on God's Word in the last 24 hours?

     Yes   No

If so, how did you feast? In other words, circle the ways you enjoyed God today. Reading? Prayer? Worship? Fellowship? Witnessing?

Were you free from drug and alcohol abuse since you did the last lesson?

     Yes   No

Did you spend personal time with the Lord since you did the last lesson?

     Yes   No

If you answered "no" to any of the above questions, describe what led to your fall.

If you answered "yes" to the above questions, you may use this area for additional comments.

DAY 56 - DON'T LOOK BACK!

There is much worldly teaching in the area of alcohol addiction recovery that attempts to take us back to the past. If you do a search on the Internet for "addiction" you will find much teaching about returning to your past, digging up repressed memories, reliving past hurts . . . etc. as an aid in escaping your current trap. Here is one example from a book advertisement: "Buried memories of sexual abuse can have a devastating impact on relationships, work and health. Uses case histories to stress the importance of recovering these memories as a crucial step in healing and explains various therapeutic processes used in memory retrieval."

We as Christians do not treat abuse, family history, or any other situation in the past lightly. We do not pass it off as insignificant, nor tell people to "just get over it." The compassion that a Christian has in dealing with the past must exceed that of the unbelieving world, for Christ in us has compassion for the hurting. And it is helpful for us to know a person's background in order to show that compassion as we interact with them.

However, the Bible nowhere instructs us to return to our past to understand how to get out of sins in the present. In fact, quite the opposite, we are instructed "Brothers, I do not consider myself yet to have taken hold of it. But one thing I do: Forgetting what is behind and straining toward what is ahead, I press on toward the goal to win the prize for which God has called me heavenward in Christ Jesus" (Philippians 3:13, 14).

Questions

Question 1. In Philippians 3:13, 14 above, what did Paul say he did with his past?

We live in a world of "therapy," so this teaching may come as quite a shock to some. They have been taught that the past is the key to the present, and that reliving the pain of the past will remove the pain in the present. This is not biblical truth, but rather man's theories. Personally, alcohol was never used in my home and I grew up with loving, Christian parents. We work with many here that grew up in the same type of situation I did, but are just as thoroughly addicted as others who did not.

Question 2. Where are you currently with understanding the past and the present? If you believe the past is key to the present, please state where you learned it. Write your thoughts here:

Questions

Christians are not focused backward and downward, but rather forward and upward. If we are in a burning building, we aren't so much interested in how the fire started; we want to get out!

Please read the following story and provide your comments below.

> So Joseph went after his brothers and found them near Dothan. But they saw him in the distance, and before he reached them, they plotted to kill him. "Here comes that dreamer!" they said to each other. "Come now, let's kill him and throw him into one of these cisterns and say that a ferocious animal devoured him. Then we'll see what comes of his dreams."
>
> When Reuben heard this, he tried to rescue him from their hands. "Let's not take his life," he said. "Don't shed any blood. Throw him into this cistern here in the desert, but don't lay a hand on him." Reuben said this to rescue him from them and take him back to his father.
>
> So when Joseph came to his brothers, they stripped him of his robe—the richly ornamented robe he was wearing—and they took him and threw him into the cistern. Now the cistern was empty; there was no water in it.
>
> As they sat down to eat their meal, they looked up and saw a caravan of Ishmaelites coming from Gilead. Their camels were loaded with spices, balm and myrrh, and they were on their way to take them down to Egypt. Judah said to his brothers, "What will we gain if we kill our brother and cover up his blood? Come, let's sell him to the Ishmaelites and not lay our hands on him; after all, he is our brother, our own flesh and blood." His brothers agreed. So when the Midianite merchants came by, his brothers pulled Joseph up out of the cistern and sold him for twenty shekels of silver to the Ishmaelites, who took him to Egypt" (Genesis 37:17-27).

Questions

Joseph's brothers plotted his death, cruelly mistreated him by throwing him into a pit and leaving him for half-dead. Then they sold him into the hands of slave traders where he became a slave in a foreign land, and was eventually lied about and thrown in jail. These were horrible injustices done to one who was innocent of any crime. Can you imagine the temptation toward bitterness that Joseph must have had? He could have felt terribly angry in his heart towards his brothers, and even toward God.

Question 3. Friend, please take a moment to write down any injustices that were done to you in your past. We are not asking for a book here, but rather simple statements of any mistreatment you have endured.

If we follow the story of Joseph in the remaining chapters of Genesis we read of how he became exalted to the position of Prime Minister of all Egypt, and how he was second in command of the entire nation, second only to Pharaoh himself. And because of a famine, his brothers had to travel to Egypt to buy food. Through the providence of God, they had to ask Joseph for food, and when they discovered it was him—their brother—whom they had mistreated so badly—they were scared to death. Would Joseph now get even with them? Would he have them killed? Oh no, for because Joseph walked with His God, he was not bitter or angry, nor did he seek revenge. Notice his answer to his brothers as they came trembling before him:

> But Joseph said to them, "Don't be afraid. Am I in the place of God? You intended to harm me, but God intended it for good to accomplish what is now being done, the saving of many lives. So then, don't be afraid. I will provide for you and your children." And he reassured them and spoke kindly to them (Genesis 50:19-21).

How did Joseph deal with the abuse of his past? He recognized God was in control of all things, and that God had a purpose in everything that happened to him. Oh friend, if you have been abused, here is real and lasting help. Know that God was in control even during the bad times, and acknowledge that He had a purpose in it. Joseph said that "God intended it for good..." and you can say the same thing. No, this does not make God the author of sin, but it does say that God is working out His plan at all times (please see Daniel 4:35, Ephesians 1:11 and Job 42:2).

Next, notice what Joseph named one of his children, and the reason why he named him the way he did. Before the years of famine came, two sons were born to Joseph by Asenath daughter of Potiphera, priest of On. Joseph named his firstborn Manasseh and said, "It is because God has made me forget all my trouble and all my father's household" (Genesis 41:50-51). Manasseh sounds like Hebrew word for "forget" and Joseph named his son based on the work of God in his life. God enabled him to forget all his trouble. The psychologist and psychiatrist can't do this, only God can enable us to know that He is in control of all things, and make us forget all our troubles. Praise Him!

Question 4. How does the name of Joseph's son correspond with the teaching we are studying today?

Again, as stated earlier, we are not teaching people to simply "forget about the past." No, we are teaching that God is in control, and that God has a purpose and a plan for all things, and that He is able to bring good out of bad. I have talked with many who were abused or grew up with parents who were addicted to alcohol. Those that are looking forward and upward look at the sovereign nature and work of God and take comfort in His control over all things. I am sure they will never forget the past, but they have gone beyond living in the past, and they look to the future with joy in God's purpose for their lives.

Nowhere is this thought of God using sin for His own purposes more clearly shown than in the cross of Jesus Christ. It was the Jews who demanded His death, though He had done nothing wrong. And it was the Romans who crucified Him, though there were no legitimate charges. And both were sinning as they did so. But ultimately it was God Who gave His Son, and He used the sin of the people involved to bring about the salvation of all who will believe. Notice how these two thoughts, of men doing the sinning, but of God being in control, are woven together in this passage:

> "This man was handed over to you by God's set purpose and foreknowledge; and you, with the help of wicked men, put him to death by nailing him to the cross" (Acts 2:23).

Finally, not only are we taught to "go back" if we have been abused, but if we are the abuser we will be tempted to remain in the past as well. Guilt is like the undertow that can drag us back out into the sea of sin again. Likewise, consequences of our sin can last a lifetime in some cases, and can be very discouraging at times. And the devil is called "the accuser of the brethren" and he works in that capacity very well.

Many of us have been an abuser as alcohol can bring out a horrible rage in many who would otherwise never strike or hurt another. I can never go back and 'fix' everything I tore down during 17 long years of drunken addiction. I hurt many people who did not deserve what I did to them. The responsibility falls squarely on my shoulders and I have tried to mend as many hurts as possible. Some are beyond my ability to fix. Many of you have lost families and relationships because of your actions that will never be repaired. There is no bridge that can be burned or no words we can say that are beyond the forgiveness of God. There are consequences that we must face, but we face them with the forgiving and powerful healing presence of God by our side. If you need any help in this area please share it with your mentor so he / she can help you with this. Many of us have faced this and I know how difficult it can seem.

Questions

But the Christian has the unique ability to run to Jesus when plagued with guilt, discouraged by consequences, or accused by the enemy. We can pour out our hearts to our Father and ask for help in time of need. Christians have the ability to turn to Scripture in these times:

• If we are feeling guilty we can read Hebrews 9.

• If we are sad about the lasting consequences we can read Revelation 21:3-4.

• If we are being accused by the evil one, we can read Colossians 1:22-23.

Question 5. Of the three things listed above (guilt, consequences, the devil), which one bothers you the most? Write your answer here:

So Friend, whether abuser or abused, we do not focus on the past to help us. We go to Christ, for He is sufficient for every problem. We have worked with those who were horribly abused in childhood and have seen them restored to wholeness, and we have worked with those who have abused and caused much pain, and have seen them restored as well. But the method is by listening to the stories of abuse, having compassion on the ones involved, and then seeking to gently point to Christ as the answer.

Question 6. How are you doing now? What are your thoughts on today's lesson?

Scripture to Consider

"For I know the plans that I have for you," declares the Lord, "plans for welfare and not for calamity to give you a future and a hope. Then you will call upon Me and come and pray to Me, and I will listen to you" (Jeremiah 29:11-12).

Did you feast on God's Word in the last 24 hours?

Yes   No

If so, how did you feast? In other words, circle the ways you enjoyed God today. Reading? Prayer? Worship? Fellowship? Witnessing?

Were you free from drug and alcohol abuse since you did the last lesson?

Yes   No

Did you spend personal time with the Lord since you did the last lesson?

Yes   No

If you answered "no" to any of the above questions, describe what led to your fall.

If you answered "yes" to the above questions, you may use this area for additional comments.

DAY 57 - CUT HIS HEAD OFF

Friend, there is a giant in the land, and he is wreaking havoc among God's people. He is more powerful than all of God's army, by themselves, and he is out to kill and destroy us. His hatred is against God Himself, and there is not a man (or woman) among us who can stand against him. His name is Satan! He is filthy and vile, armed with cruel hate, and he rides forth taking captive numerous slaves for his kingdom. He is never satisfied, always wanting to have more pawns to serve him, and he sets his sights specifically on the church of Jesus Christ. He despises us!

What are we to do? Is there a David among us? One who can't stand to hear the mockings of the giant, and who knows that the battle belongs to the Lord? Who will take him on? Who has an arsenal of five stones of grace with which to knock the giant down, and can use the Sword of the Spirit, which is the Word of God, to take his head off? And who wants to take the offensive, vindicate the Name of God, and bring victory for the people of God? I hope you are saying, "ME!" because in this day and age the church of Jesus Christ needs a David: one who takes no confidence in the armor of kings, or in his own ability, but one who relies on the sovereign grace of God and the power of the gospel to defeat sin's giant.

Are you the one who wants a piece of the giant? Are you sick and tired of seeing the devil gain more and more captives for his kingdom? Do you want to do something about it? You can!

Please read the following passage and answer the questions following:

> [41]Meanwhile, the Philistine, with his shield bearer in front of him, kept coming closer to David. [42]He looked David over and saw that he was only a boy, ruddy and handsome, and he despised him. [43]He said to David, "Am I a dog that you come at me with sticks?" And the Philistine cursed David by his gods. [44]"Come here," he said, "and I'll give your flesh to the birds of the air and the beasts of the field!"
>
> [45]David said to the Philistine, "You come against me with sword and spear and javelin, but I come against you in the name of the LORD Almighty, the God of the armies of Israel, whom you have defied. [46]This day the LORD will hand you over to me, and I'll strike you down and cut off your head. Today I will give the carcasses of the Philistine army to the birds of the air and the beasts of the earth, and the whole world will know that there is a God in Israel. [47]All those gathered here will know that it is not by sword or spear that the LORD saves; for the battle is the LORD's, and he will give all of you into our hands."
>
> [48]As the Philistine moved closer to attack him, David ran quickly toward the battle line to meet him. [49]Reaching into his bag and taking out a stone, he slung it and struck the Philistine on the forehead. The stone sank into his forehead, and he fell facedown on the ground.
>
> [50]So David triumphed over the Philistine with a sling and a stone; without a sword in his hand he struck down the Philistine and killed him. [51]David ran and stood over him. He took hold of the Philistine's sword and drew it from the scabbard. After he killed him, he cut off his head with the sword.
>
> When the Philistines saw that their hero was dead, they turned and ran. [52]Then the men of Israel and Judah surged forward with a shout and pursued the Philistines to the entrance of Gath and to the gates of Ekron. Their dead were strewn along the Shaaraim road to Gath and Ekron. [53]When the Israelites returned from chasing the Philistines, they plundered their camp. [54]David took the Philistine's head and brought it to Jerusalem, and he put the Philistine's weapons in his own tent (1 Samuel 17:41-54).

Questions

Question 1. Verse 44 above speaks of the intent of the Philistine toward David, and it is also the intent of the devil toward us. What is that intent?

Friend, make no mistake: this is a fight to the death! Goliath wanted to kill and destroy not only David but also the entire Israelite army. This is the intention of Satan against us. Either we will triumph over this giant or we will die by his hands.

Question 2. According to verse 45 above, Goliath came against David with "sword, and spear and javelin." What did David use to come against Goliath?

Question 3. Consider 2 Corinthians 10:3-4 and write your thoughts: "For though we live in the world, we do not wage war as the world does. The weapons we fight with are not the weapons of the world."

Note: If we want to do battle with the devil by rescuing others from drunkenness, we better make sure that 1, we are free ourselves, and 2, God is fighting for us.

Question 4. What are your thoughts on verse 48 above? Apply it to yourself and your life right now. Write your thoughts here:

Questions

Friend, as soldiers in the Lord's army, we need to have an eagerness to kill the enemy, through the power of God. There must be a "running quickly" toward the battle line to meet him. The Bible says that the gates of hell will not prevail against us (Matthew 16:18), which implies that we take the offensive and storm the fortified city of the devil. And we can fully expect to have success since the gates of hell will not be able to keep us out.

Let me share with you that this type of eagerness to take on the enemy comes from experiencing many previous victories over the power of the devil. In this same chapter we are studying today, David recalls previous victory and uses it as present conviction of the power of God to destroy the giant. He says, ³⁴"Your servant has been keeping his father's sheep. When a lion or a bear came and carried off a sheep from the flock, ³⁵I went after it, struck it and rescued the sheep from its mouth. When it turned on me, I seized it by its hair, struck it and killed it. ³⁶Your servant has killed both the lion and the bear; this uncircumcised Philistine will be like one of them, because he has defied the armies of the living God" (1 Samuel 17:34-36).

If you have been experiencing several victories over sin then you may be ready to take on the giant.

Question 5. From verse 51 above, what did David use to kill the giant?

Verse 51 tells us that David used Goliath's own weapon to kill the giant, and by so doing he freed all Israel from their fear of the giant. This is an amazing foreshadow of the work of Jesus Christ as He took death, the devils own weapon, and used it to destroy the devil. Notice how Hebrews 2:14 compares: "...He too shared in their humanity so that by His death he might destroy him who holds the power of death—that is, the devil—and free those who all their lives were held in slavery by their fear of death." Do you see it? Jesus took the devil's own weapon, death, and used it to destroy the devil!

> **Pastor Joe writes:** "Just living and hoping the attacks of Satan will go away will never give us victory. I have found that I must be on the offensive in every area of spiritual life and warfare. Most of my life I have just tried to dodge Satan's bullets. Now I seek not only to stay undefeated by his power, but to defeat him in the name of the Lord Jesus and for His glory."

Question 6. According to verse 55 above, what did David do to the giant?

According to verse 55 above, David not only killed the giant but he also cut off his head. Isn't this a bit much? Overkill, so to speak? Here is an important lesson for us: when dealing with our sins we need to take such drastic action against them that we prevent them from ever rearing their ugly heads in our lives again. Do not merely kill the giant, but cut his head off!

Question 7. What did the Israelite army do when they discovered that Goliath was dead?

Friend, your own pursuit of purity—of defeating the giant in your life—will have an effect on others, to encourage them toward victory also. As the months of victory over the power of the devil roll on, you soon discover that God's power is stronger and you have killed the enemy. But helping others to enjoy victory is like cutting the enemy's head off.

You are nearing the end of this 60-Day course, and if you are free from alcohol and drugs, then that is a great victory. But now it is time for you to start thinking and praying about God giving you a ministry to help others out of the fire from which He rescued you. Don't merely relish your own victory over the giant, but cut his head off and inspire numerous others to pursue victory also, as David did.

But be cautious! Please do not become involved in ministry if you are still drinking. The reason for this is that your soul is still in deception. You are intoxicating yourself at the devil's bar and you will not be able to truly help others to freedom. Knowledge is not enough. Power in the life is essential. "Who can bring what is pure from the impure? No one!" (Job 14:4).

Some people have asked how long they need to be pure before they begin a ministry. We don't know. God will make it known at the time, but you simply need to know in your heart that you are completely and fully done with drugs and alcohol, for good, and have an eagerness to help others out of the trap also.

There are so many ministries we could become involved in to help those enslaved to alcohol and we cannot list them all here. Here are some examples. With some thought I am sure you can add to this list.

- Be a mentor with us to assist others to purity.

- Build your own website ministry.

- Start an email list specifically for reaching people trapped in drunkenness.

- Share your freedom with the pastor of your church and ask for his help in starting a ministry at your church. You can use our curriculum if you would like, and we have other tools available for you to use as well.

Questions

- Begin a Bible study in your home for drunkards, addicts . . . etc. Advertise it in churches, on the Internet, in newspapers . . . etc. The way the cancer of drunkenness is spreading, you may have a huge group show up.

- Open a chat room with discussions about overcoming alcohol.

- Share your testimony with your church and see what God does with it.

- Write out your testimony and post it all over the Internet, while inviting people to email you.

- Begin a prison ministry to help inmates find freedom from alcohol.

- Write periodicals for Christian sites such as Crosswalk.com and others, about the way to be free from substances.

- Begin a newsletter to circulate through churches and on the Internet.

Question 8. Are you ready to begin taking the offensive in the battle with the giant, to help your fellow brothers and sisters to victory?

Question 9. What ministries can you think of that would fit your style, and how can you go about initiating them? Write your answer here.

Scripture to Consider

Brethren, even if anyone is caught in any trespass, you who are spiritual, restore such a one in a spirit of gentleness; each one looking to yourself, so that you too will not be tempted (Galatians 6:1).

Did you feast on God's Word in the last 24 hours?

    Yes   No

If so, how did you feast? In other words, circle the ways you enjoyed God today. Reading? Prayer? Worship? Fellowship? Witnessing?

Were you free from drug and alcohol abuse since you did the last lesson?

    Yes   No

Did you spend personal time with the Lord since you did the last lesson?

    Yes   No

If you answered "no" to any of the above questions, describe what led to your fall.

If you answered "yes" to the above questions, you may use this area for additional comments.

DAY 58 - FINAL REVIEW

This lesson material is a review of the material covered in the 60-day course. Feel free to look back over the days of the course to answer the questions. Primarily, we are interested in how the scriptural truths and testimonies have affected your heart and changed your life. We are approaching the end of the 60 lessons, and the question we have is "Are you actually becoming free from all forms of substance abuse?" Please keep this question in mind as you answer the following questions.

Questions

Question 1. Early in the New Wine course, we taught through John chapter 4, the story of the woman at the well. We remember that Jesus taught her that the "well" from which she had been drinking would leave her thirsty, and that He had water to give to her that would eternally quench her thirst. Please summarize the teaching of this chapter, state what you have learned from it, and how you have personally applied it in your life.

Question 2. One of the most important teachings in the course is on the subject of repentance. We showed from Scripture how repentance is a gift of God (2 Timothy 2:21-26), and that genuine repentance includes both godly sorrow and turning from sin to God. Please think through this issue of repentance, and write out your understanding of it, noting specifically whether or not you have repented of the sin of drunkenness and/or misuse of drugs.

Questions

Question 3. Radical Amputation! This truth is prevalent throughout the course. Basically, this truth teaches us that we must do whatever it takes to rid our lives of any access to drugs and alcohol. Please state here what you specifically have "cut off" and "plucked out" and whether or not there is anything left with which to indulge your flesh in a moment of weakness.

Question 4. In this course, we taught the necessity of accountability. What role has accountability played in your escaping from the trap of drug use and coming to freedom in Jesus Christ? Have any accountability partners meant something important to you, and helped you in any way? Feel free to mention them here as you describe their importance in your coming to freedom.

Questions

Question 5. In lesson 31, we discussed the majesty, greatness, power and grace of God. This is one of the more important teachings in the course, for to see and savor the supremacy of Christ is to see substances become weak and powerless. Whereas, those who view Christ as small and powerless find that drugs are big and powerful. Are you learning to treasure the supremacy of Jesus Christ in all things? How has your view of Christ changed since coming into freedom?

Question 6. Toward the latter part of the course, we encouraged you to "walk in the Spirit." We described this "walking in the Spirit" as immersing ourselves in God's Word and prayer, worshiping the Lord always, walking with Him in constant fellowship, etc. Do you remember what the Bible says that the result of walking in the Spirit is (Galatians 5:16)? Please describe how you "walk in the Spirit," and if you are, indeed, experiencing the biblical result of this "walking."

Of course, there is also the need to confess all sin (it is helpful to confess to your pastor and/or elder, and especially your spouse) and have the understanding that God set you free for HIS glory and HIS name's sake, and that you are sharing your testimony of freedom with those whom God would bring across your path. But the above six truths are the main teachings of this course, so please take a moment and review the questions above and your responses. If we ensure that these truths are implemented in our lives, we may realistically expect to remain free from sin's trap for the rest of our lives, and to honor God in doing so. To summarize, we can quench our thirst in Jesus Christ if we repent of sin and turn to Him, removing that which trips us up, being accountable to others, discovering the greatness and majesty of our Lord Jesus Christ, and continually walking in the Spirit.

Scripture to Consider

. . . that he who began a good work in you will carry it on to completion until the day of Christ Jesus (Philippians 1:6).

Did you feast on God's Word in the last 24 hours?

Yes   No

If so, how did you feast? In other words, circle the ways you enjoyed God today. Reading? Prayer? Worship? Fellowship? Witnessing?

Were you free from drug and alcohol abuse since you did the last lesson?

Yes   No

Did you spend personal time with the Lord since you did the last lesson?

Yes   No

If you answered "no" to any of the above questions, describe what led to your fall.

If you answered "yes" to the above questions, you may use this area for additional comments.

DAY 59 - YOUR TESTIMONY

Today, Friend, we want to give you a place to share your testimony. Feel free to share however the Lord leads you, but keep in mind that the most effective testimonies are brief (usually one page in length), and should include three aspects. Job 33 tells us the formula for sharing a testimony: "Then he comes to men and says, I sinned, and perverted what was right, but I did not get what I deserved. He redeemed my soul from going down to the pit, and I will live to enjoy the light" (Job 33:27-28). Notice the three aspects to this testimony: "I sinned . . . God redeemed . . . I will live." A biblical testimony touches on:

- "My sin" and what areas I was involved in, and what that brought about in my life (though be cautious about sharing any details so as to not stir up sin in others).

- Redemption. This explains how I was bought out of the slave market of sin. How did God reach me, give me repentance and bring me into the Light. What means did He use?

- How I am living to enjoy the Light (Christ).

Please try to include those three aspects in your testimony. Take your time, and may your story of God's grace honor the Lord. (If you find that you do not yet have a testimony of true freedom from drunkenness and drugs, please consider working through this course again slowly.)

Testimony

Write your testimony here:

Questions

That's it! Enjoy telling your story, and pray that God would make it useful to others who need hope that it is possible to be free from these sins, by the grace of God!

Since the beginning of the Setting Captives Free ministry, we have placed great importance on sharing our testimonies. We do this for the purpose of encouraging others to find hope and freedom in Jesus Christ. This does, indeed, seem to be the pattern of Scripture, as we note in many places. One such place is 1 Timothy 1:13-14:

> Even though I was once a blasphemer and a persecutor and a violent man, I was shown mercy because I acted in ignorance and unbelief. The grace of our Lord was poured out on me abundantly, along with the faith and love that are in Christ Jesus." (NIV)

And the reason God poured out His grace on Paul is stated in verse 16:

> But for that very reason I was shown mercy so that in me, the worst of sinners, Christ Jesus might display his unlimited patience *as an example for those who would believe on him* and receive eternal life. 1 Timothy 1:16 (NIV, emphasis mine)

Paul received the grace of a changed life "as an example for those who would believe . . . "

The reason for Paul's changed life is to glorify God by providing hope to others, that they too might believe on Jesus and receive mercy and a changed life through the gospel.

We who have found freedom from drinking, drugs, or smoking are literally saved from death, both spiritual and physical, as the smoke, chemicals and drugs leave our bodies and we become clear thinking and healthier.

People who are in bondage need to hear how your life has been changed since God granted you repentance and forgiveness and you walked free from bondage to alcohol, drugs, pills or smoking. Many will be greatly encouraged to seek freedom in Christ through our studies here at Setting Captives Free if they could read and hear many testimonies from people like you. This is a wonderful opportunity to make a real difference in many lives in the years to come.

We encourage you to share your testimony and invite others to come and find freedom in Jesus Christ. Will you "be an example" of God's grace and patience, and of the new life that comes through Jesus Christ?

Scripture to Consider

For it is by grace you have been saved, through the faith—and this is not from yourselves, it is the gift of God—not by works, so that no one can boast. For we are God's handiwork, created in Christ Jesus to do good works, which God prepared in advance for us to do (Ephesians 2:8-10).

Did you feast on God's Word in the last 24 hours?

     Yes   No

If so, how did you feast? In other words, circle the ways you enjoyed God today. Reading? Prayer? Worship? Fellowship? Witnessing?

Were you free from drug and alcohol abuse since you did the last lesson?

     Yes   No

Did you spend personal time with the Lord since you did the last lesson?

     Yes   No

If you answered "no" to any of the above questions, describe what led to your fall.

If you answered "yes" to the above questions, you may use this area for additional comments.

DAY 60 - FEEDBACK

Dear Friend,

Today is the final day of the New Wine course, and we would like to solicit your input and receive feedback from you regarding your experience here. Please answer the questions below. If possible will you make a copy of this questionnaire and send it to:

Mike Cleveland
PO Box 1527
Medina, OH 44258

Questions

Question 1. Overall, what was the best part of the course?

Question 2. On a scale of 1 to 10, how helpful was this course to you in overcoming drunkenness or drugs? 1 being of little help, 10 being of great help:

Question 3. Friend, please describe what changes have taken place in your heart and life since starting this course:

Question 4. Have you started any kind of a ministry of your own to help others break free from substance abuse?

Question 5. If you answered "Yes" to the above question, please describe your ministry, and state whether or not you would like Setting Captives Free to link to you, or assist you in any other way. If you desire this, contact us at www.settingcaptivesfree.com and describe what you are doing.

Question 6. Was there any specific thing that bothered you about the course as you went through it?

Question 7. How could we improve the course? What are your suggestions?

Question 8. Have you told anyone else about this course, and if so, have they reacted to you?

Questions

Question 9. Here is a place for your final comments. Write anything you would like to convey to us.

Scripture to Consider

If we claim to have fellowship with him and yet walk in the darkness, we lie and do not live out the truth. But if we walk in the light, as He is in the light, we have fellowship with one another, and the blood of Jesus, His Son, purifies us from all sin (1 John 1:6-7).

Did you feast on God's Word in the last 24 hours?

     Yes   No

If so, how did you feast? In other words, circle the ways you enjoyed God today. Reading? Prayer? Worship? Fellowship? Witnessing?

Were you free from drug and alcohol abuse since you did the last lesson?

     Yes   No

Did you spend personal time with the Lord since you did the last lesson?

     Yes   No

If you answered "no" to any of the above questions, describe what led to your fall.

If you answered "yes" to the above questions, you may use this area for additional comments.

We hope this SCF 60-Day **New Wine** course has blessed your life!

Notes

Notes

More Books by Mike Cleveland

www.focuspublishing.com

The Way of Purity: Enjoy Lasting Freedom in Christ

The Lord's Table: A Biblical Approach to Weight Loss

Men of Honor: Men's Group Study

95 Theses for Pure Reformation